FOUNDATIONS OF THE LAW

An Interdisciplinary and Jurisprudential Primer

Bailey Kuklin
Professor of Law
Brooklyn Law School

and

Jeffrey W. Stempel
Professor of Law
Brooklyn Law School

WEST GROUP

Bancroft-Whitney • Clark Boardman Callaghan
Lawyers Cooperative Publishing • WESTLAW® • West Publishing

For Customer Assistance Call 1-800-328-4880

Copyright © 1994   WEST PUBLISHING CO.
                   610 Opperman Drive
                   P.O. Box 64526
                   St. Paul, MN 55164-0526

ISBN 0-314-03720-9

 TEXT IS PRINTED ON 10% POST
CONSUMER RECYCLED PAPER

To

Susan

To

Ann, Ryan, Shanen, and Reed

FOUNDATIONS OF THE LAW

An Interdisciplinary and Jurisprudential Primer

Bailey Kuklin
Professor of Law
Brooklyn Law School

and

Jeffrey W. Stempel
Professor of Law
Brooklyn Law School

TABLE OF CONTENTS

INTRODUCTION

THE IMPORTANCE OF
THE OFTEN OVERLOOKED

Recently, a prestigious law school's alumni magazine devoted its cover story to the interdisciplinary courses offered at the law school and the interdisciplinary scholarship of its faculty. A preface to the article remarked, almost matter-of-factly, that "[l]aw no longer can be studied or practiced as if it were a discipline referenced only by its own norms. The fact is that law is a derivative discipline, one which draws on other disciplines to explain how rules have developed and should develop. The law is not received dogma, and it cannot be taught as such."[1]

This view, once considered heretical, now prevails among legal scholars. Today, our thinking about both law and its practice has become expansive and multidisciplinary. One professor has stated, in words perhaps too disparaging, that "law is a scavenger" which "grows by feeding on ideas from outside" without "inventing new [ideas] of its own."[2] A prominent federal judge and former professor has spoken of the "decline of law as an autonomous discipline"[3] while another scholar has spoken more euphemistically of "law turning outward."[4]

Whatever one's favorite term or phrase, there is no denying that within the past generation, the legal establishment has recognized that law is not an island unto itself. Law reflects the impact of other disciplines, social forces, and historical events. This phenomenon is not confined to the academy. Practicing lawyers frequently make use of nonlegal learning and data in arguing cases, as do political actors who shape the law. So do judges who interpret the law and apply it to specific factual contexts.

---

[1] *The Spirit of the Renaissance*, NYU LAW SCHOOL MAGAZINE 45, 45-46 (Spring 1993).

[2] E. Donald Elliot, *The Evolutionary Tradition in Jurisprudence*, 85 COLUM. L. REV. 38 (1985).

[3] Hon. Richard A. Posner, *The Decline of Law as an Autonomous Discipline 1962-1987*, 100 HARV. L. REV. 761 (1987).

[4] Martha A. Minow, *Law Turning Outward*, 73 TELOS 79 (1987).

1

Consequently, learning law and about law has become a more complex and difficult, but ultimately more enriching experience. Students of the law, whether in college, graduate programs, or law school, must be familiar with and appreciate these external perspectives if they are to fully understand the law. More than half a century ago, the noted legal scholar Karl Llewellyn compared the process of learning the law to encountering a "bramble bush." He portrayed the experience as stinging because of its complexity, novelty, and seeming indeterminacy. According to Llewellyn, however, the determined student who continues wading through the thicket eventually achieves the insight of understanding.[5] Today, Llewellyn's metaphorical bramble bush is both internally thornier because of law's increasing volume (more statutes, cases, and theories to learn) and much larger because of law's increasing recognition of the importance of the teachings of other disciplines.[6]

Law's underpinnings, like many foundations or backgrounds, can be easily overlooked because we usually stand upon them or because we are straining to see something more specific on the horizon. This book seeks to provide to those studying law a roadmap or blueprint of its foundations in order to facilitate understanding of what has been built upon them. Despite the many excellent legal coursebooks, we have yet to see an introductory book that adequately addresses the often unstated foundational or background aspects of the law, particularly the multidisciplinary factors affecting it. In attempting to fill that gap with this book, we have sought to be relatively brief but comprehensively informative, with separate "free-standing" chapters that can be read alone for background on a particular perspective. Unlike some books, this one covers most of the related fields rather than focusing on only one discipline, movement, or period. Unlike other books that stitch together an edited collection of the writings of others, we have endeavored to provide a coordinated overview. However, each chapter is designed to function as a self-contained reading. This book, useful to a broad range of courses, is organized into six chapters:

---

[5] *See* KARL N. LLEWELLYN, THE BRAMBLE BUSH iv, 110, 122 (3d ed. 1960) (1st ed. 1930) ("There was a man in our town and he was wondrous wise: he jumped into a BRAMBLE BUSH and scratched out both his eyes -- and when he saw that he was blind, with all his might and main he jumped into another one and scratched them in again.").

[6] *See generally* Peter H. Schuck, *Legal Complexity: Some Causes, Consequences, and Cures*, 42 DUKE L.J. 1 (1992) (defining law today as complex because its rules are numerous and encompassing, technical, administered by many legitimate institutions, and because outcomes are often indeterminant).

• Chapter One addresses the underlying moral or ethical theory undergirding the legal system, including notions of justice and goodness.

• Chapter Two provides an introduction, summary, and assessment of the economic analysis of law, including a description of the contemporary law and economics movement.

• Chapter Three is a primer on political theory, showing how implicit political beliefs and theories of governance have shaped views of law and legal institutions.

• Chapter Four describes American political structures, particularly federal-state relations and separation of powers, notions that affect the analysis of numerous legal issues, especially questions of constitutional law.

• Chapter Five focuses on dispute resolution theory, especially the adversary system and alternatives as well as the relative strengths and weaknesses of courts as compared to other methods of dispute resolution.

• Chapter Six summarizes modern legal history and the evolution of legal education and jurisprudential movements of note, including today's important schools of legal thought, as well as insights from other fields that have affected these movements.

We hope readers enjoy our brief tour of the law's foundations. Questions or comments about the book can be sent to either of us at Brooklyn Law School, 250 Joralemon Street, Brooklyn, New York 11201.

CHAPTER ONE

ETHICAL THEORY AND THE LAW

- **Introduction**
    - **Intrinsic Value**
    - **The Good**
    - **Justice**
    - **Teleology and Utilitarianism**
    - **Deontology and Kantianism**
- **Utilitarianism**
    - **Universal Utilitarianism**
    - **Egoistic Utilitarianism**
    - **Act Utilitarianism**
    - **Rule Utilitarianism**
- **Kantianism**
    - **Categorical Imperative**
    - **Hypothetical Imperative**
- **Hybrid Theories**
- **"All Things Considered"**
- **Justice**
    - **Corrective Justice**
    - **Distributive Justice**
- **"Is-Ought" or "Fact-Value"**
- **Metaethics and Noncognitivism**
- **Ethical Relativism**
- **Social Learning and Cognitive Development Theories**
- **Feminist Moral Theory**
- **Communitarianism**
- **Ethics and the Legal Process**
- **References for Further Reading**

Ethics or morals relate to normative issues. A normative precept is simply a standard of behavior. In light of this broad applicability, many normative statements are not moral ones (*e.g.*, "you should keep your bat steady to improve your hitting" or "symmetrical designs are more beautiful"). Western normative moral theory stems from questions posed by Socrates in Athens in the fifth century B.C. A fundamental one is: What is it that is of **intrinsic value**, that is worthwhile in itself? Is it a state of mind, a feeling, a behavior, etc.? Is there a unique characteristic of things having intrinsic value, or are there a variety of features? The principle alternatives turn on two central questions: What is **the Good**? What is **Justice**? These questions are far from identical since they are directed at different concerns. The Good relates to states of being -- what kind of persons or society should we be? Justice relates to actions -- what are our duties, rights, or obligations; what is it that we ought or ought not to do? Obviously, the answers are not unrelated.

Because, as a matter of fact, it turns out that doing the right thing will sometimes diminish goodness, and conversely, increasing goodness will sometimes require doing the wrong thing, the nature of the relationship between goodness and justice is crucial. This has led to the main disagreement between the two major modern schools of moral theory: **teleology** or, in its best known form, **utilitarianism**, and **deontology** or, in its best known form, **Kantianism**. Teleological ethics declares that goodness dominates justice, that the just act is that which is required to increase the Good. Deontological ethics declares that justice dominates goodness, that the just act, one's duty, is to be done even if it decreases the Good.

Utilitarianism. The utilitarian, like other teleologists, considers that which is of intrinsic value, the Good, to relate to a state of being. While utilitarianism has roots among the ancient Greeks, Jeremy Bentham, an eighteenth century Englishman, is the modern father. He declared that the Good is happiness. This theory of the Good is categorized as hedonistic utilitarianism since happiness is a sensuous satisfaction. Other hedonistic utilitarian conceptions of the Good have been expressed in terms of pleasure or the avoidance of pain. Ideal utilitarians espouse nonhedonistic qualities as those which have intrinsic worth, such as virtue, friendship, love, solidarity, knowledge, or aesthetic contemplation. Hedonistic utilitarians tend to adopt monistic theories of the Good (*i.e.*, that there is one basic quality with intrinsic value), while ideal utilitarians are often pluralistic (*i.e.*, that there is more than one). The most common conception of the Good among current utilitarians is preference satisfaction. It is good when an individual's own preference is satisfied. This version diverges from hedonistic ones because preference satisfactions may not be hedonistic, as when one prefers something that gives pleasure to no one.

Utilitarianism generally is aggregative and consequentialist (*i.e.*, acts are judged by their effects). In seeking the state of affairs in which goodness is maximized, **universal utilitarianism** typically aims for the greatest good for the greatest number. A state of affairs is better, under this version, when aggregated goodness (often expressed in terms of utility) is increased, even when some individuals suffer losses in order to facilitate greater gains by others. Under **egoistic utilitarianism**, on the other hand, a person strives to increase her own good, irrespective of effects on others. Most theorists reject egoism or its apparent implication that the interests of others are to be disregarded. Among other reasons, some have argued that self-interest aligns with benevolence in the long run. Under both versions of utilitarianism, in determining the proper action under the circumstances, the actor looks to the probable consequences of the options, doing a cost-benefit analysis of sorts to choose the option which maximizes utility. In some sense, the ends justify the means. A just act increases utility.

Many criticisms have been leveled against utilitarianism, or versions of it. One is that it is unrealistic to demand a cost-benefit analysis of every action. The very process of the analysis will often cost more in time and effort than the potential gains warrant, especially for routine matters. For example, in deciding whether to jay walk or cross the street against a red light, a detailed analysis each time of the tradeoffs seems overly demanding. In response to this criticism, some theorists have rejected **act utilitarianism**, or the version of it which requires a calculation for each act, in favor of **rule utilitarianism**, which adopts general rules based on cost-benefit analyses of common situations. Under this latter approach, individual acts must be evaluated only when the particular situation is not routine (*e.g.*, whether to cheat on one's lover), or when the circumstances take the case away from the core of the stock situation (*e.g.*, for the adopted general rule that "white" lies are proper when they avoid gratuitously hurting others, whether to tell one in order to avoid a social invitation from an insistent, unpleasant boor).

Among the complications the utilitarian must confront are those called boundary problems. These involve the question of whose satisfactions are to count and whether all satisfactions are to count equally. For instance, the utility of foreigners would seem to have the same intrinsic value as that of neighbors. Some utilitarians who take this observation seriously have advanced a world-wide egalitarianism. Ignoring for the moment the redistributive claims within the immediate community, under this egalitarian view a person in a prosperous nation should send money to the less fortunate nations until the person's last dollar brings more satisfaction at home. Everyone world-wide would end up with a low but presumably sufficient standard of living. This has been countered somewhat by the observation that radical egalitarianism has high administrative costs (*i.e.*, the strict taxing and policing systems would be very expensive and invasive of privacy) and would hinder utility by eliminating both the positive incentive effects of wealth accumulation (*i.e.*, people would not bother to work as hard if the earnings go elsewhere) and also the concentrated sources of capital required for industrial development (*i.e.*, the money needed to establish a factory comes from people with wealth to spare). Animals, for that matter, also feel pain that is undeniably real, which argues for kinder treatment of animals and even vegetarianism. As far as the types of satisfactions that should count, malicious satisfaction hardly seems like the Good, but rather more like the Bad. On the positive side, some commentators have insisted that certain satisfactions (*e.g.*, the "higher pleasures") have greater intrinsic value than others. How are these various satisfactions to be judged?

In aggregating total utility, some people may be required to suffer in order to increase society's net satisfaction, as, so it seems, in a regime of slavery in which the resulting happiness of the masters greatly outweighs the unhappiness of the contented slaves. In this sense, utilitarianism closely aligns with the economic policy favoring "wealth maximization," whereby the wealth of some persons may be sacrificed to increase overall wealth. In extreme cases, such as slavery, the intuitively objectionable conclusion that people can be grossly used as an expedient for the overall benefit of society may be averted sometimes by rejecting total utility as the standard for utilitarian measures and adopting instead the standard that the average utility of the populace is to be maximized. Averaging is more sensitive to the distribution of utility among individuals. But still, it is conceivable that benign slavery can be justified by utilitarians.

Finally, there is the problem of interpersonal utility comparisons: when tradeoffs in utility are required, how can one actually determine whether, and by how much, the losses of some persons are offset by the gains of others? There may even be "utility monsters" or "pleasure freaks" who obtain unusually great satisfaction from social resources, thereby having a utilitarian claim to disproportionate amounts. On the other hand, it seems that generally the more resources one has, the less one obtains satisfaction from an incremental increase, as suggested by the intuitive proposition that the millionaire values her last dollar less than she did when she was a pauper ("the declining marginal utility of wealth"). These observations support a utilitarian case for the substantial redistribution of wealth, such as taking money from the rich or the ascetic and giving it to the poor or the hedonistic.

Under utilitarianism, the ends (*e.g.*, happiness) may justify the means. A strict utilitarian, therefore, may treat as unimportant or unjustified an array of well-recognized moral and legal rights and duties as well as claims to personal liberty. For example, along with the slavery hypothetical, a judge or prosecutor may properly convict a person known by them alone to be innocent of a notorious crime if the benefits derived from increased deterrence and community security and appeasement outweigh the pain of the defendant, her family and supporters. Similarly justifiable, though less controversial, are extreme penalties unrelated to the guilty defendant's blameworthiness, "to make an example for others." While utilitarians have rehabilitated their theories by various strategies and empirical assumptions, including the denial that the probable consequences under these and other problematic hypotheticals would actually increase utility, or the rejection of them as too extreme to be relevant to the daily concerns of moralists, they remain as formidable problems that have driven away many erstwhile subscribers.

Kantianism. Immanuel Kant, an eighteenth century Prussian, is the leading figure among deontologists. He declared that the only thing that is of intrinsic value without qualification is a "good will," or, basically, a worthy character. An individual's character is good when she is conscientious, willing to do her duty for the sake of duty alone and not for other reasons such as generosity, sympathy, or benevolence. While a good will is fundamental to Kant, his writings emphasize duty. In explicating duty, Kant espoused a universalizability principle, the first form of his famous **categorical imperative**: one should act pursuant to a maxim that could be willed or chosen as a universal law. A categorical imperative is a moral rule or law that is to be observed in all events, whereas a **hypothetical imperative** is a non-moral normative judgment, a rule or "counsel" of prudence that is to be observed only as a means to further a purpose of the actor, such as the rule that in order to write better, she should keep a dictionary by her side. While right actions could be determined case by case (as in act utilitarianism), and some deontologists have adopted this approach of "situation ethics," Kant argued that in doing one's duty by acting according to universal rules without special exceptions, the actor existentially embodies or exhibits her essence, her humanness, her authenticity.

Even though the first form of the categorical imperative, by rejecting special exceptions for the actor, seems similar to the Golden Rule ("Do unto others as you would have them do unto you"), Kant specifically rejected this analogy. He defended the universalizability principle on the basis of consistency. For example, a person cannot subscribe to the maxim that promises must be kept, but the rule does not apply personally. To do so would involve a contradiction of the "will," or rational choice, for the result would be self-defeating. The institution of promise-keeping cannot be realized if people are free to except themselves from the maxim. The problem with making oneself an exception to the maxim, according to Kant, is not that it will occasion bad consequences, though it may well indeed, but that it creates an inconsistency. On the one hand, one wills the maxim that promises are to be kept, or truth-telling is to be inviolable. On the other hand, to will that oneself is an exception to the maxims will prevent these very practices from coming into fruition because others will also except themselves. While, according to some Kantians, concern for the consequences is germane to the decision of what maxims are to be adopted, Kant approached the question more formally: the problem with excepting oneself from an otherwise universalized maxim is that, since others will similarly do so, to will both ways is inconsistent, self-contradictory.

The second form of Kant's categorical imperative is that all persons, as rational beings with autonomy of the will, are to be treated as ends in themselves, and not as a means only to another's ends. All humans, as ethical beings, are to be respected. A key word in this formula is "only." In having the faucet fixed, one does not use the plumber as a means only to one's own ends, because the plumber has chosen this vocation and has consented to the employment; it then is her duty to fix the faucet. Slavery, obviously, does not satisfy the second form of the categorical imperative. Between these extremes are the problematic practices of personal exploitation and advantage-taking.

While Kant stated other forms of the categorical imperative and developed his position at length, the two forms above go to the heart of his moral philosophy and establish the essential outline. There is much that is obscure in Kant's writings, but the basic ideas ring true, as is also true for utilitarianism. The label "Kantian" today covers a substantial range of philosophical thought that, with respect to moral theory, adopts Kant's emphasis on the centrality of just acts rather than good consequences. In current parlance, one must "do the right thing." Problems, however, have been raised against Kant's version of deontology and other versions, a few of which follow.

Which maxims are to be universalized? Kant argued, for one, that there is the duty to help others. Even a rich person would rationally will this as a universal maxim, he contended, because she realizes that the human condition is such that she might sometime need "love and sympathy" from others. Under the interpretation of some objectors, the rich person may instead feel sufficiently secure in her position that she would fail to realize that all persons might need assistance, and in fact never need it herself. If this is the case, she may not rationally will the maxim of helping others, or might never be in a needy position where she would will to except herself from the maxim of not helping others. Because it would not be inconsistent or contradictory for this person not to will the maxim of helping others, therefore the maxim to help others applies to no one. A moral scheme that does not include the duty to help others is then said to be defective.

Kant spoke of maxims as absolutes. As two instances: one is always (1) to keep promises and (2) to tell the truth. Suppose one has promised to meet a friend at eight o'clock. While rushing to be on time, the promisor sees a person drowning. The promisor knows that she could rescue this person with ease, but this would cause a delay that would prevent her from meeting her friend on time. Kant, it seems, would have the promisor pass by the drowning person. Promises must be kept! Similarly, this next hypothetical was submitted to Kant. Suppose that while entertaining a neighbor at home, there is a knock at the door. When the host opens the door, a vicious looking stranger with a gun demands that the host tell him where the neighbor is so that he can kill her. Kant insisted that the host tell the truth, otherwise she would be responsible for whatever happens. Truth-telling is unqualified. A third hypothetical will further demonstrate the tug of utilitarian reasoning on Kantian absolutism. Suppose a world-wide fatal epidemic is slowly killing everyone on earth except one person who has a natural immunity. If this person would donate her brain, an antidote could be developed which would save everyone else. She respectfully declines to contribute. A utilitarian would respond, "off with her head." A strict Kantian would say, "since she cannot be used as a means only to our ends, the world population must perish." Most people demur to these three Kantian judgments. When this far down the slippery slope, the universalized maxims of promise-keeping and truth-telling, and the categorical imperative to respect the autonomy of others, have gone too far.

One way to escape the first two dilemmas above is to universalize maxims that are less general in reach. Instead of "always keep promises" or "always tell the truth," adopt maxims such as "keep promises [tell the truth] except when lives can otherwise be saved." On further thought, since Kant espoused the maxim that one is to help others in need, this seems inconsistent with his position on the first two hypotheticals. The drowning person and "fingered" neighbor were hardly helped by the promise-keeper and truth-teller. The impression from Kant's writings notwithstanding, absolute maxims may conflict. Somehow they must be reconciled. In theory one could do this by universalizing maxims, as above, with appropriate "except when" clauses (which are themselves derived from maxims, *e.g.*, "help others in need"), each subordinate clause reducing the reach of the principal clause to allow the qualified maxim to account for situations in which conflicts may arise. Because there are many moral maxims, a full statement of each one which takes into account the numerous types of possible conflicts with all the others would be most unwieldy and, as a practical matter, exceedingly difficult or impossible to work out.

The practice of reducing the generality of maxims can be abused. The reach of the universalized principle may be unduly narrowed if this is found to be convenient to the agent. For example, the agent may will as a universal maxim that everyone is to give ten percent of their income to charity except when the person is W feet tall, weighs X pounds, and was born in Y village on the date of Z. Not surprisingly, the W, X, Y and Z fit the particular agent to a tee. The generality of this maxim effectively excepts only the willing agent. There has been an end run around the universalization principle.

These are examples of the practical and theoretical problems raised against Kant's moral theory. Some of the universalized maxims run counter to our deepest intuitions and the failure to dictate other maxims is intuitively seen as a moral shortcoming. Kantians have dealt with these difficulties with varying degrees of success. In any event, much that is valid and crucial flows from Kantian reasoning. Most moral philosophers today consider themselves essentially Kantian.

Hybrid Theories. Examples of the weaknesses in utilitarianism and Kantianism reveal why neither one is generally accepted in unalloyed form. Attempts to hybridize the two include the following constructs. The first approach, centered on utilitarianism, has already been mentioned: rule utilitarianism. General rules are adopted which usually promote the Good. In a sense, these are (nearly) universalized maxims derived from a type of cost-benefit analysis. Because there is a conflict of interest when a person evaluates contemplated conduct in which she has a personal stake, one can even argue that an individual should not have the discretion to forsake the general rules when unanticipated circumstances occur. Another approach is to embrace one of the two basic theories except in cases where this would lead to a moral catastrophe, as in the utilitarian hypothetical of contented slavery and the Kantian one of the world-wide fatal epidemic. A third approach is to consider both the utilitarian and Kantian mandates for particular acts and, when they conflict, to incorporate their relative thrust in the final determination of what to do. The difficulty, of course, is in measuring the forces of the utilitarian pull and the Kantian push. Unfortunately, all three of these hybrid approaches have limitations, including the use of interested, personal judgment to apply nebulous standards.

"All Things Considered."   Although the last few decades have seen remarkable refinement in moral reasoning, no single theory, pure or hybrid, enjoys a broad consensus of unqualified approval. Critics have faulted them all. A common formality among philosophers, the gentle ones anyway, is to praise the work of another writer as a prelude to undermining the writer's moral construct.   The quicksand beneath the theories is that their foundations are built on propositions supported by questionable proofs, or that must be taken as self-evident or "in the nature of things." While the theorist may claim that the foundation of her theory is grounded on the bedrock of objective reason or self-evidence, most current philosophers reject all versions of these contentions. Among the challenged maxims are: the Good is happiness or preference satisfaction; seek the greatest good for the greatest number; moral maxims are to be universalized; people are to be treated as ends in themselves, and not as a means only to another's ends. Once a proposition is denied the certainty of logic or self-evidence, it must stand on weaker grounds. Indeed, it still may be true, but then it must resist doubters with depleted defenses, which has not been done with much success, as evidenced by the lack of agreement about the particular propositions that are said to be beyond question. (Examples are provided in the discussion below of the distinction between fact and value.) Again, though much progress in moral reasoning is occurring, the end is not in sight.

The inability to formulate a rock solid moral system has induced many philosophers to adopt a "good reasons" or "all things considered" approach to the problems of ethics. When analyzing and resolving a complex issue, it is important to account for all reasonable values that may be at stake. One may go even further and incorporate non-normative factors as well, such as history and positive economics (assuming these are non-normative). Under one approach, all relevant factors must be weighted by determining the comparative importance of each factor, and weighed by measuring the extent to which each one comes into play. This may be very difficult. For example, one may find that a proposed solution to a quandary may deny some individuals due process of law while providing others with freedom from offensive hate speech. The decisionmaker must determine the relative weight or value of due process and freedom from hate speech when they conflict in full force, and then weigh the degree to which due process would be denied, or the hate speech would be offensive under the particular circumstances. This is a matter of judgment for which no formulas are available. It is no wonder that "political correctness" and "hate speech" issues seem so intractable.

Justice.   While Kant provided the modern analytical framework for questions of justice, the inquiry into the nature of justice goes much further back in time. As mentioned before, Socrates brought the focus on justice (and goodness) to the Western moral consciousness. Socrates' student, Plato, passed the baton of inquisitiveness to his student, Aristotle, whose writings on justice still command exceptional respect. Aristotle advanced the basic precept of justice to treat like cases alike and different cases differently. The difficulty occurs in judging whether the particular cases are alike or different. This turns partially on the accepted theory of justice. In his NICHOMACHEAN ETHICS, Aristotle developed notions of justice. **Corrective justice**, in Aristotle's translated words, "supplies a corrective principle in private transactions," both voluntary (*e.g.*, contract) and involuntary (*e.g.*, negligence). Sometimes called or associated with rectificatory, commutative or compensatory justice, among other labels, it generally declares that when one person injures or harms another through blameworthy conduct, the first should compensate the second. According to Aristotle, corrective justice requires one not only to make reparations for injuries from, say, negligence, but also to avoid harming another, for example, by knowingly inducing her to enter an ill-advised contract, though she has no legal remedy. **Distributive justice** "is exercised in the distribution of [public valuables such as] honor, wealth, and the other divisible assets of the community." Each is to obtain in proportion to her merit. Today, distributive justice is thought to reach questions regarding the effects of legal rules and statutes, regardless of whether they turn on merit, as well as criminal matters. (Aristotle considered criminal matters as private rather than public affairs, and thus subject to the principles of corrective justice instead of distributive justice.) For example, if a court adopts the rule that all smoke pollution is enjoinable as a nuisance, the distributive consequence is that wealth is effectively transferred from factory owners to neighboring homeowners, as easily seen in the scenario in which the factory must pay to install smokestack scrubbers and the neighboring property values increase. The penal form of distributive justice depends on demerit rather than merit. Under one view of the **lex talionis** standard of reciprocity ("an eye for an eye"), the criminal is to suffer as much as she causes suffering. Arguably, a more civilized standard would reduce the penalty by declaring that she must suffer in reduced proportion to the caused suffering.

As dimly seen in the discussions of the Greek philosophers, and as specified by Kant's universalization principle, maxims of justice take the following form: To each according to X, from each according to Y. This is a principle of formal or abstract justice. To apply the formal principle by means of a specific maxim of justice, and thereby advance a material or concrete formulation of justice, one must fill in the X or the Y, or both. For example, Karl Marx's conception of justice is: To each according to need, from each according to ability. When referring to distributive justice, the X is often called "desert," though this term is inordinately stretched in some instances. There are many modern conceptions of desert. Among them are virtue (merit), effort (labor), contribution to society, agreement with others, "the same thing" (equality), need(s), rank, and society's rules (legal entitlement).

These conceptions of desert fall into two categories. Some are liberty-oriented, such as virtue, effort, contribution to society, and agreement with others, while others are equality-oriented, such as "the same thing," need, rank and society's rules. Those that are liberty-oriented find desert in what one does; those that are equality-oriented aim at parity within specified classifications. Most modern theories of distributive justice incorporate a number of these conceptions, thereby balancing and blending liberty and equality. This is no mean trick, for liberty and equality are often at odds. For example, the more one broadens the liberty of people to associate with whom they wish (and hence allow discrimination against others), the more one narrows the right of all citizens to be treated equally when associating with others.

The conceptions of justice vary widely in giving material content to the Y side of the formal equation. For torts, one version of the Aristotelian notion of corrective justice declares Y to be (nonmoral) fault: from each according to fault. "Fault" may even be rigidly interpreted to simply mean that one causes an injury to another by force or fraud. This corresponds to a standard of strict liability. If she hits him, she is liable, irrespective of intention or negligence. Another interpretation of the Y in Aristotle's corrective justice is: from each according to (moral) blameworthiness. Insofar as one is blameworthy, one must make private reparations to the harmed person. If the monetized blameworthiness is less or, perhaps, more than the harm, the victim is either left short of the status quo ante or, as when recovering punitive damages, ends up ahead.

Leaving aside other versions of corrective justice, another general, material conception of the Y is known as "deep pocket" or horizontal equity: from each according to wealth. For example, a court's decision in a close case may be influenced by the fact that one of the parties is considerably wealthier than the other. One of the main justifications of this is based on the declining marginal utility of wealth. (For further discussion, see Chapter Two on law and economics.) Since the wealthy generally feel the loss of their last dollar less than do the poor -- the richer one is, the less one values each dollar -- "deep pocket" boils down to something like: from each according to felt impact. "Deep pocket" is also justified by the argument that the wealthy get more from society than do the poor. On this grounding, the formula amounts to: from each according to benefits from society. The contemporary theory of progressive taxation, often put in terms of horizontal equity, is akin to "deep pocket": from each according to economic circumstance. People in similar tax brackets should pay similar taxes. In each of these formulations, a conception of equality is realized because parity is maintained within the specified classifications.

Although the full formula of justice specifies the givers and the receivers, under the law the quantifications of the two sides of the formula may not be equal. First, an example of where they are equal by definition. Under one interpretation of the strict liability standard of corrective justice "from each according to (nonmoral) fault, to each according to consequent injury," the defendant pays directly to the plaintiff compensation for her injury, and nothing more or less. But under the culpability-based standard of corrective justice "from each according to moral blameworthiness, to each according to consequent injury," the amounts on the two sides of the formula are likely to diverge, as mentioned above. For example, a defendant driver, distracted by a leaping deer, takes her eyes off the road for a mere instant, but in doing so she runs a school bus coming around a bend over a cliff. Though her moral blameworthiness is slight, her liability under our legal system is enormous. For a contrary example, consider the vicious scam operator who, in a "get-rich" scheme, does her best to defraud thousands of desperate people of their last dimes by selling them gold mines in Alaska she believes to be worthless. As it turns out, there is oil under the land. Though her moral blameworthiness is great, her legal liability is zero. Similarly, criminal attempts are penalized less than successful crimes even though the actors' blameworthiness seems identical. That blameworthiness may differ from legal liability has given commentators much to ponder.

In sum, the legal standards of blameworthiness and personal harm diverge. The law could be adjusted to take into account the differences. For example, a state could adopt a tort scheme in which an injurer pays to the government an amount proportional to her blameworthiness and the injured party receives from the government an amount which compensates for her injuries. A culpability-based standard of corrective justice would be satisfied. The standard of corrective justice reflected in the tort doctrine of negligence fits neither a strict liability nor a rigorous culpability-based version. It is: from each according to whether through fault she injures another, to each according to consequent injury. First, the liability is not strict since material fault (negligence) is required. Second, notice that it is "from each according to *whether* through fault she injures another," not "from each according to fault." Negligence does not give rise to liability unless harm ensues (*e.g.*, a grossly negligent driver, though blameworthy, is not liable to another person unless she injures her). But once one is at fault, one is liable for the consequent injury irrespective of whether the injury is disproportionally greater or less than the degree of fault. While the legal notion of fault is not identical to the moral notion of blame-worthiness, there is a fair degree of overlap. Insofar as they overlap, the negligence doctrine is a threshold version of a pure culpability-based stan-dard of corrective justice. When one is sufficiently blameworthy to be considered negligent, then one must pay for the entire, proximately caused injury.

"Is-Ought" or "Fact-Value." Moral controversies exist partially because moral propositions cannot be based on fact alone. As made clear by David Hume, an eighteenth century British philosopher, though doubters have not been entirely silenced, there is an unbridgeable chasm between "is" and "ought," fact and value. A syllogism that reaches a normative conclusion (*e.g.*, "therefore, a person should do Y"), must have a normative premise ("if X is the case, then a person should do Y"). To put this idea in a different way, one cannot conclude that something ought to be the case (has normative value) just because it is the case (is empirically correct). This is true even of a normative rule as well-settled as "one should not commit murder." To the question "Why should one not commit murder?", a person cannot properly answer fully with assertions such as: "Because that is the rule," or "Because everyone knows that one should not commit murder." These factual pronouncements, though they may be true, are inadequate. In the past there have been normative rules, even ones nearly everyone in the particular state accepted, that were immoral, for example, rules governing slavery. Fact alone does not determine value. Sooner or later the competent defender of the rule against murder must resort to a basic moral premise, such as: "Because murder curtails the victim's happiness and inflicts pain on others, happiness is good and pain is bad, and one ought not to do an act with consequences that decrease goodness or increase badness," or, "Because the victim is a reasoning being worthy of respect who ought not to be used by the murderer simply for her own purposes." The first of these responses is of teleological (utilitarian) orientation and the second is deontological (Kantian). The "Ought" or "Good," explicit or implicit, make the propositions normative.

While these normative responses go beyond the purely factual and prescribe behavior by means of value judgments, notice that they do include factual assertions, including: "murder curtails happiness and inflicts pain," and "the victim is a reasoning being." These factual aspects are critical to the normative propositions. If, for example, death was definitely found to lead to a blissful state surpassing life, or humans were not subject to pain, or the victim was not a reasoning being (*e.g.*, in a brain-dead, perpetual coma), then the propositions would be undermined, though not necessarily beyond reformation.

On the other hand, the accuracy of these factual aspects alone does not fully justify the normative propositions. First, one might challenge the basic prescriptive aspects, such as: "happiness is good and pain is bad." and "a reasoning being [is] worthy of respect." For example, one could argue that the teleological mandate is flawed because happiness-seeking is decadent and pain builds character, or because some people obtain happiness from odious conduct. Against the deontological maxim, one could argue that there are some disgusting humans who are clearly not worthy of the slightest respect, or that using a person as a means only to one's own ends is permissible when the actor's gains are great and the other person's losses are trivial. Second, the feasibility of the prescriptive aspects is also challengeable. One might insist, for example, that because one can never be confident of the ultimate consequences of a significant act, since the unpredictable usually commences somewhere in its rippling effects, the utilitarian mandate to increase goodness and decrease badness is unworkable as a practical matter. The plausibility of articulating a full panoply of consistent, coherent Kantian rights may also be doubted.

Factualness aside, mere assertion cannot alone justify normative propositions. Kant's view notwithstanding, it seems that ultimate normative truisms can be neither proved nor disproved, they can only be maintained. At some point the argument typically depends on a given, a self-evident proposition, "the nature of things," or, since these groundings are not firm, effectively a "leap of faith." When the debate ends without logical conclusiveness, either the debaters believe that, for example, utility should be maximized or people should never be flagrantly used, or they do not. Rationality is not enough. Next question.

Metaethics and Noncognitivism. The inconclusiveness of moral positions has induced some moral philosophers to reject altogether the pursuit of normative theories and instead concentrate on metaethics, the analysis of moral concepts and the types of arguments that justify moral stances. They analyze the forms rather than propound the contents. Others have gone in a different direction. Some, for example the "noncognitivists" contend that moral propositions cannot be validly justified and instead are simply expressions of emotion (*e.g.*, "murder -- hiss"), or, less extremely, that while they can be reasoned about, they are essentially expressions of the speaker's attitude or attempts to evoke the attitude in the listener (*e.g.*, "I favor the proscription of murder because it will have X results"), or, least extremely, that they are endorsements, prescriptions, evaluations, etc. (*e.g.*, "murder is socially unacceptable and, since moral judgments imply the judger's willingness to universalize them, should be generally proscribed").

Ethical Relativism. The rejection of conclusive moral standards may lead to ethical relativism of various types, which basically is the belief that conflicting moral propositions may be equally valid. For example, what might be right in this society may be wrong in another society. A telling, though not definitive, response to this view is that for the important ethical issues it has not been shown that rational persons, having agreed on the relevant facts and the proper point of view (*e.g.*, utilitarianism or Kantianism), will draw irreconcilable conclusions when conscientiously examining the particular issue. In positive terms, a moral proposition can be justified by the general agreement that would be reached ideally by clear-headed, rational, fully informed persons who examine the specific circumstances from the moral point of view.

Social Learning and Cognitive Development Theories. Because logic alone cannot support a moral consensus, instead a common intuition regarding underlying values is necessary, one should address the source of this commonality. Two theories, with variations, currently predominate. The social learning theorists contend that moral knowledge is taught to each individual. Society's values are instilled as one grows in understanding and learns from environmental influences. The cognitive development theorists claim that environment is not enough. As a person matures, she naturally evolves through stages of moral cognition in a manner largely programmed genetically.

There are as many as five or six invariant, sequential, hierarchical stages of development according to Lawrence Kohlberg, a leading cognitive development theorist, which an individual goes through as she comes to realize the deficiencies of the prior stages of moral awareness. In the earliest stages, an individual internalizes moral rules which are simply egoistic responses to personal needs, such as threats of punishment and promises of rewards. In the middle stages, the individual conceives of fairness as based on social convention. In the highest, most integrated and discriminating stages, the individual arrives at a sense of objective fairness based on equality and reciprocity about which all rational persons can agree. Those who reach the highest stages come to realize that proper moral behavior entails generally Kantian principles of universalized rules which recognize the equal worth of all persons. Few people achieve the highest stage.

While producing his theory of cognitive development, Kohlberg tested people by posing moral dilemmas. Their answers revealed the natural progression through stages of moral consciousness, and once this progression was understood, indicated the degree of moral maturity of the individual respondent. The flavor of this project is revealed by the famous hypothetical, "Heinz's dilemma." Suppose that a person's spouse is dying of a fatal condition that can be cured only by an expensive medicine which he cannot afford or otherwise obtain legally. Would it be right to steal the medicine from a druggist? In the highest stage of moral development the respondents perceived that it would not be right to steal the medicine. Kohlberg found that, as Kantian universalists recognizing the necessity of reason and the law, they grasp the importance of following the rules against theft, though they may steal the medicine nonetheless and face the legal consequences, hopefully mitigated.

The prevailing dispute among theorists reflects the old nature-nurture controversy. Social learning theorists emphasize the role of nurture in the formation of moral character, while cognitive development theorists emphasize nature. As in the other spheres of the nature-nurture controversy, the general conclusion is that both nature and nurture are important factors, the debate being over their mechanisms and relative sway.

Feminist Moral Theory. Based on hypothetical moral quandaries such as Heinz's dilemma, Kohlberg and other cognitive development theorists concluded that males reach the highest stages of moral development more frequently than do females. Furthermore, females are more eager to avoid dilemmas, as above, by seeking to borrow money for the medicine or obtain it at a reduced price or on credit by reasoning with the druggist. Stealing the drug would be wrong, they typically agree, but a common reason for this view is that the theft may have bad consequences. Imprisonment would deprive the ill spouse of needed support or, for that matter, the medicine may not even effect a cure.

One of the persons working on this project with Kohlberg was Carol Gilligan. At some point she asked why the reactions to moral dilemmas seen more often among females than males were considered to reflect a lower stage of development. Trying to avoid moral conflict, or resolving it by compromise, hardly seems to be an indication of moral immaturity. Nor is the mediation of the conflict by means of communication and interpersonal connection, rather than impersonal law and logic. In her famous book, IN A DIFFERENT VOICE: PSYCHOLOGICAL THEORY AND WOMEN'S DEVELOPMENT (1982), she argues that females are not less likely than males to reach the highest stages of moral development, whatever that may be. Rather, females, who identify closely with the family caregivers and nurturers, are more likely to speak "in a different voice" that emphasizes the importance of relations and interdependence among persons, and the need to communicate. Rights, which are objective and devoid of historical constraints, may properly be seen as morally less important than are responsibilities, which stem from situations of intimacy and care. When there is a moral conflict, the solution may not be simply to defer "rationally" to rights, but rather, if the dilemma cannot be avoided, to work out a compromise through discussion, if possible, in order to get along with one another and, if necessary, to act with preference to one's own and one's affiliates for whom one is more responsible than for others. In sum, both voices need expression in a mature ethics.

Gilligan's observations have become one of the linchpins of modern feminist theory, commonly embraced by the full range of feminists from the conservative to the radical. But there are objectors. Some feminists, for example, question whether this different voice is not simply that of an oppressed person. If women were not subordinated in a social and legal hierarchy established and maintained by men, they ask, what would be the true, undominated voice of women? Notice that Gilligan's objections are not a rejection of the claim that moral development goes through cognitive stages, nor is the "different voice" said to be uniquely or universally feminine. Both males and females may develop this moral consciousness in various degrees, but empirically it is more pervasive among females.

While this is controversial among feminists, notice also that the different voice can be analyzed as somewhat consistent with Kantianism and utilitarianism. First of all, there is no Kantian maxim that is abridged by avoiding moral conflict. Nor is the emphasis on compromise necessarily contrary to Kantianism, since the obtained consent of the compromising parties fully protects their private autonomy. Finally, preferring one's own and affiliates to others may be rationally universalized as a moral maxim of a less generalized form. For example, rather than adopting the maxim "help other people," one may adopt the maxim "help other people except when it significantly interferes with one's primary responsibilities to loved ones and affiliates." If everyone embraced this maxim, it would not be inconsistent with the broad aim to advance a social practice in which persons helped one another. The Kantian problems seriously begin when one tries to formulate a maxim which would allow, if it comes to this, the theft of property to save loved ones (or oneself). If everyone acted on the maxim, this would be inconsistent with the standard notion of property rights and the social system it produces. Perhaps the crises that give rise to the need to steal to save life fall within the catastrophic situations (the world-wide fatal epidemic writ small) that are ill served by Kantian universalizations. Finally, it should be evident that feminist moral theory may be consistent with utilitarianism. Following the mandates of the different voice may well create a society in which the Good is maximized. In any event, in the end, this different voice espouses a legitimate moral stance that can be justified as amply as can other moral viewpoints.

Communitarianism. An age-old moral ideology that has much in common with some aspects of feminist moral theory is communitarianism. While the reasoning which supports it follows a dissimilar track, some of the conclusions are alike. (The reasoning is outlined in Chapter Three on political philosophy.) Those within the community are to be given priority over those outside it. While historically the community meant the state (among the ancient Greeks, the city-state), some modern communitarians see many communities as having varying moral claims against the individual. The most central community is the household family unit and the most peripheral one is the world at large. As one travels outward from the family center, one encounters increasingly less intimate communities for which one has decreasingly demanding moral obligations. From household to block, neighborhood, city, county, state, region, nation, continent, hemisphere, and planet (and eventually, beyond), the spheres of community grow larger and morally demand reduced concern. The spheres are also drawn in a nonterritorial manner. The community may be based on family (with its various degrees of kinship), social organizations, profession, culture, language, religion, race, etc. But the mandate is similar: all else equal, it is more proper to support a "near" community than a "far" one.

Ethics and the Legal Process. In the legal process, ethical theory arguably enters judicial decisionmaking in the following way. In resolving a dispute, the court must determine the relevant facts and the applicable law. Once these interrelated components are found, the resolution follows in a syllogistic manner. While there may be a chain of linked syllogisms, the crucial syllogism has the rule as its major premise (step 1), the facts as the minor one (step 2), and the outcome as the conclusion (step 3). Schematically it is: 1. If X (material facts), then Y (the legal consequence); 2. X (the finding of the material facts); and 3. Y (the legal consequence). For example, suppose the rule is: "If one negligently injures another, then one is liable to that person for proximately caused damages." The facts are found to be: "The defendant negligently injured the plaintiff." The legal consequence is: "The defendant is liable to the plaintiff for proximately caused damages."

This process is quite straightforward, but one must notice that all three statements in the example are factual: "The rule is . . . . The facts are . . . . The legal consequence is . . . ." At the initial step, at least when the law is controversial or being established, the court must cope with the question of why the law *should* be that "the negligent injury of others subjects one to liability for proximately caused damages." In other words, what is the warrant or justification for adopting the major premise of the legal syllogism? The answer to this question is not purely factual. The word "should" in the question, whether implicit or explicit, indicates the need to arrive at a standard of behavior. As seen in the above discussion of the distinction between fact and value, the court's inquiry must therefore enter the normative realm.

The entry into the normative realm is severely truncated under the old, formalist approach to judicial decisionmaking whereby a rule is justified by analogizing the material facts to existing precedents. Under formalistic stare decisis, the doctrine of precedent, the holding of the most analogous, generally binding precedent should control. Not articulated by formalists, however, is that behind the determination of which precedent is most analogous often lurks a tacit normative judgment regarding which facts are considered material and which precedent is seen as closest to the case before the court.

While there are other approaches to judicial decisionmaking, under the modern, instrumental approach the judge must ground her legal rule on public policy, including moral principles. Hence, the contemporary judge must face directly the logical gap between fact and value: in order for a syllogism to have a normative proposition in its conclusion (*e.g.*, "the actor should be liable in damages [for doing X]), it must have a normative proposition in its major premise (*e.g.*, "when an action causes bad consequences, [for the sake of promoting deterrence,] the actor should be liable in damages"). (The minor premise would be: "action X causes bad consequences.")

Recall that moral argument grounded on rationality alone seemingly comes to a dead end before the normative road takes the decisionmaker to an irresistible moral conclusion. The question then arises, why bother to travel down the road if it will not go all the way? Since moral argument is not logically conclusive, why not have the court resolving a new question simply, in a long leap of faith, advance a rule as the major premise of the crucial legal syllogism without any justification, rather than go on to defend the rule in a normative discourse which itself must end in a leap of faith? In fact, this is what most judicial opinions do. Most of them include no moral reasoning, or what actually amounts to none, and summarily justify the rule with an invocation of labels such as "public policy," "fairness" or "justice," including its many offspring (*e.g.*, manifest justice, inherent justice, imminent justice, substantial justice, and natural justice). Without further explication, these terms are virtually meaningless.

To restate the point: why should we demand more of the courts by way of justification than they usually provide? The primary reason is that the process of engaging in rigorous normative discourse forces the court to examine closely the various elements of the argument and the manner in which the elements are linked. Erroneous underlying assumptions, questionable value judgments, and doubtful reasoning are less likely to endure when the court articulates the essential moral propositions and the chain of reasoning which runs from the rule down the normative road as far as possible. A leap of faith awaits at the end, but slips are fewer when the jumps are shorter.

All this said notwithstanding, we should not demand that the court produce a major tract on moral theory for each case. Among other reasons, such an exercise would not be useful. Fundamental moral principles are few in number. Once a judge drives a fundamental principle down the normative road to its end, a later repeat of the exercise is superfluous unless the judge's principles have become more refined or have changed. Secondary moral principles also need not be linked to fundamental ones each time they arise. The same can be said for primary and ancillary legal doctrines. For example, the moral underpinnings of the doctrine of precedent have not changed much over the years. On the other hand, it should be emphasized that a justification which simply refers glibly to "justice" or "public policy" is not adequate. A balance is required which is struck by weighing the centrality of the particular principle to the case and the degree of controversy surrounding it. The more central the principle, the more controversial it is, the more the court must justify it. In any event, perhaps each member of the court should be expected to articulate the full reasoning behind her adoption of a legal or moral principle on occasion. This would require her to reexamine the principle to see if it still conforms to her well-considered judgment as time goes on and her values and perceptions, and society's, evolve.

While the discussion has concentrated on the role of normative discourse in the judicial decisionmaking process, a similar role can be claimed for the legislative process. In enacting laws the legislators are supposed to keep in mind the interests of the community. These include moral concerns. In the legislative hearings, committee reports and floor debates, one should find thoughtful discussions of the normative considerations underlying the issues. But enactments are not all equally morally loaded. Some statutes, and judicial decisions for that matter, are even morally neutral. For example, whether we drive on the left or right side of the road is of no unique moral consequence; it is merely a matter of coordinating behavior for the sake of convenience and safety. Yet to the extent that a proposal does raise debatable moral issues, the legislators should be expected to address them with a consideration commensurate to their gravity.

REFERENCES FOR FURTHER READING

Quick reference:

PAUL EDWARDS (ed.), THE ENCYCLOPEDIA OF PHILOSOPHY (1967) (8 vols.).

Short introductions:

WILLIAM F. FRANKENA, ETHICS (2d ed. 1973).
D.D. RAPHAEL, MORAL PHILOSOPHY (1981).
BERNARD WILLIAMS, MORALITY: AN INTRODUCTION TO ETHICS (1972).

Further studies:

SISSELA BOK, LYING: MORAL CHOICE IN PUBLIC AND PRIVATE LIFE (1978).
RICHARD B. BRANDT, ETHICAL THEORY (1959); A THEORY OF THE GOOD AND THE RIGHT (1979).
ALAN DONAGAN, THE THEORY OF MORALITY (1977).
PHILIPPA FOOT, VIRTUES AND VICES (1978).
CHARLES FRIED, RIGHT AND WRONG (1978).
ALAN GEWIRTH, REASON AND MORALITY (1978).
CAROL GILLIGAN, IN A DIFFERENT VOICE: PSYCHOLOGICAL THEORY AND WOMEN'S DEVELOPMENT (1982).
R.M. HARE, FREEDOM AND REASON (1963).
SHELLY KAGAN, THE LIMITS OF MORALITY (1989).
DAVID LYONS, FORMS AND LIMITS OF UTILITARIANISM (1965).
A.I. MELDEN, RIGHTS AND PERSONS (1977).
Michael Moore, *Moral Reality*, 1982 WIS. L. REV. 1061.

THOMAS NAGEL, THE VIEW FROM NOWHERE (1986); MORTAL QUESTIONS
        (1979).

DEREK PARFIT, REASONS AND PERSONS (1984).

H.J. PATON, THE CATEGORICAL IMPERATIVE: A STUDY IN KANT'S MORAL
        PHILOSOPHY (1947).

JOHN RAWLS, A THEORY OF JUSTICE (1971).

DAVID RICHARDS, A THEORY OF REASONS FOR ACTION (1971).

W.D. ROSS, THE RIGHT AND THE GOOD (1930).

JOHN SABINI & MAURY SILVER, MORALITIES OF EVERYDAY LIFE (1982).

SAMUEL SCHEFFLER, THE REJECTION OF CONSEQUENTIALISM (1982).

GEORGE SHER, DESERT (1987).

HENRY SIDGWICK, THE METHODS OF ETHICS (7th ed. 1907).

PETER SINGER, PRACTICAL ETHICS (2d ed. 1993).

J.J.C. SMART & BERNARD WILLIAMS, UTILITARIANISM: FOR AND AGAINST
        (1973).

JUDITH JARVIS THOMSON, THE REALM OF RIGHTS (1990).

STEPHEN TOULMIN, AN EXAMINATION OF THE PLACE OF REASON IN
        ETHICS (1950).

BERNARD WILLIAMS, ETHICS AND THE LIMITS OF PHILOSOPHY (1985);
        MORAL LUCK (1981).

CHAPTER TWO

LAW AND ECONOMICS

- **Introduction**
- **The Basic Elements**
    - ○ **Efficiency**
    - ○ **Equity**
    - ○ **Factors of Production**
    - ○ **Command Economy (Centralized Economy)**
    - ○ **The "Invisible Hand" (Decentralized or Market Economy)**
    - ○ **Marginal Cost**
    - ○ **Economies of Scale**
    - ○ **Law of Diminishing Returns**
    - ○ **Public Goods**
    - ○ **Freeride**
    - ○ **Holdout**
- **The Conditions for the Invisible Hand**
    - ○ **Externalities**
- **The Goals of the Market Economy**
    - ○ **Pareto Optimality**
    - ○ **Pareto Superiority**
    - ○ **Kaldor-Hicks Efficiency**
    - ○ **Actual or Explicit Market**
    - ○ **Hypothetical, Shadow or Pseudo Market**
    - ○ **Moralisms**
- **The Justification of the Market Economy**
    - ○ **Utilitarianism**
    - ○ **Kantianism**
- **The Coase Theorem**
    - ○ **Property, Liability and Inalienability Rules**
- **Additional Concepts and Principles**
    - ○ **Loss Spreading**
    - ○ **Risk Attitude**
    - ○ **Moral Hazard**
    - ○ **The Declining Marginal Utility of Wealth**
        - ◦ **"Deep Pocket"**
        - ◦ **Interpersonal Utility Comparison**

27

Like every other learned discipline, the law occasionally encounters new paradigms to explain existing phenomena in a way that brings deeper understanding to the subject. During the 1920s and 1930s, it was Legal Realism (*see* the discussion in Chapter Six). Today, Legal Realism is such an integral part of our overall comprehension of the law that it can be said that we all are Realists, to some degree, whether we know it or not. The same will be said some day of the economic analysis of the law. Despite its use of jargon, grand theoretical constructs and unrealistic empirical assumptions, economic analysis is now a part of mainstream legal education, the culmination of a trend that became easily apparent during the 1970s and which, by the 1980s, had ascended beyond any credible efforts to label it a fad. This intellectual interest shown in law schools has increasingly affected the thinking of state and federal judges, who not only often hire law clerks with extensive law and economics backgrounds but also themselves may have received substantial exposure to economic analysis in law school, practice, or professional seminars. Clearly, individual instructors and law schools differ in their attraction and commitment to law and economics. Similarly, judges and cases vary in their amenability to economic analysis. Nonetheless, the well-rounded practitioner must not only be able to understand and respond to these sophisticated arguments, but also should be able to craft them on behalf of clients.

The law, obviously, did not wait until only the last few decades to recognize the usefulness of economics. The post-1970s economic analysis is occasionally referred to as the "new" law and economics. Prior to this, from the turn of the century, there was a significant amount of economic analysis found in antitrust cases (the first antitrust law was passed in 1890). This "old" Law and Economics focused on questions relevant to the factfinding necessary to adjudicate antitrust suits, such as: What is the relevant market for determining whether Acme Corp. has monopoly power? Are there reasonable economic substitutes for the product over which Acme allegedly has monopoly power? By contrast, the "new" Law and Economics is not confined to analyzing commercial issues, but views itself as a social science of human behavior which can be applied to contract, tort, property, criminal law, and every other topic. The new economics, then, is basically microeconomics (the study of specific areas of activity, such as the response of individual behavior to prices), while the old economics, classically systematized in 1936 by John Maynard Keynes, an English economist, is macroeconomics (the comprehensive study of a national economy). But for good reason the new has not vanquished the old. In advanced law school courses (*e.g.*, banking regulation, antitrust law and international law), students may find macroeconomic analysis of legal issues.

The Law and Economics movement has established a strong beachhead in law and legal education because it provides a powerful tool for assessing the costs and benefits of a given legal rule or case outcome. The microeconomic methods employed by Law and Economics scholars provide, in essence, a structured means of performing the cost-benefit analysis implicit in any reasoned discussion of legal issues. In this sense, Law and Economics has a close relationship to utilitarian ethics, which has long played an important role in the policies grounding the law. But like utilitarian philosophy, economic analysis, which may appear to be value-free, often does not speak to Kantian issues of right and wrong. Attorneys should be able to recognize these and other instances when economic analysis tends to overlook important, intangible factors in favor of emphasizing those factors that are more easily translated into dollars and cents. In the end, Law and Economics is too important to be ignored. To reemphasize the point, an attorney should be able to use its powerful tools to advance a cause, and must be able to identify its weak points in order to parry its thrust.

The Basic Elements. Every society must decide, explicitly or implicitly, how its resources and wealth are to be deployed. The matter has two aspects: **efficiency** or the allocation of resources, and **equity** or the distribution of wealth. Efficiency pertains to "the size of the pie," while equity relates to how the pie is sliced. Efficiency questions turn on the costs and benefits of the particular assignment of resources. A more efficient allocation is one that increases their net value. If one individual values a resource more than does another person, then overall personal satisfaction is increased when the first person obtains it. Economics has traditionally concentrated on this subject. Equity or distributive questions center on the effects of government action, direct or indirect, on individual wealth. On what basis should individuals be taxed? Who should receive the benefits of the government largesse? Should the relative wealth of the parties before the court, though it was irrelevant to the acts in issue, be considered in determining liability or remedies? These are questions of distributive justice, and the answers are generally thought to be political, a matter for the legislature rather than the courts.

From an economic welfare point of view, the most important resources are those that generate wealth. These are called **factors of production**. While they have been variously denominated, a common list is: land, labor, capital, and entrepreneurship. To produce goods or provide services, these four factors are required in varying amounts. There are two main ways that the factors of production may be allocated. They may be assigned from the top down via a **command economy** (**centralized economy**), as in communism, or they may be allotted from the bottom up, via **the "invisible hand"** (**decentralized** or **market economy**), as in capitalism. In a command economy the government determines what goods the people want, or should have, and accordingly allocates the factors of production to individuals and firms through a central administration by means of regulated prices. Under the invisible hand, as first articulated about two centuries ago by the Scottish philosopher and economist, Adam Smith,[7] individuals and firms with traditional property rights to their existing wealth decide what goods they want and trade for them at prices to be agreed upon through private bargains.

In effect, then, economic actors determine the way resources are to be allocated by "voting" with their dollars. As more people vote for particular goods by buying them, producers shift resources to the production of these goods in order to reap the available profits. When this capitalistic system works ideally, the government's role is limited to the protection of property rights, the enforcement of contracts, and the prevention of trades through force or fraud. The typical dynamic is that particulars such as competitive pressures and economies of scale tend to drive down the price, which in itself increases demand, thereby further driving down the price until the price bottoms out or demand is met.

---

[7] His great book is THE WEALTH OF NATIONS (1776).

The cost of producing one additional widget is referred to as the **marginal cost** of the widget. Many factors affect the marginal cost. The **economies of scale** (*i.e.*, the savings per unit, if any, that result from producing more widgets in a plant rather than fewer of them) may cause the marginal cost to decrease. For example, once a plant expands to a certain output, it may be able to employ techniques and equipment unusable or unavailable at a smaller scale, such as labor specialization. On the other hand, rather than increasing returns to scale, there may be (eventually) decreasing returns, as can arise from the difficulty of coordinating a large enterprise. Savings per unit may also result from the spreading of fixed costs over a larger output, for example, the research and development costs of the product. At some point, other considerations may drive up the marginal cost. Perhaps the demand increases to the point where the necessary materials become scarce and therefore more expensive. The **law of diminishing returns** declares that by increasing variable inputs (such as labor) relative to fixed inputs (such as a specific plant) the marginal cost will eventually increase. Realistically, how many workers can be efficiently crammed into the plant?

There are some goods that a pure market economy will not produce at an efficient level. These are **public goods**, which are distinguished because they are not consumed by use. Bubble gum, for example, is a private good which is consumed by use, and if one wishes to chew it, one must buy it. Pure public goods, such as national defense and information, can be shared by additional persons, whether or not they pay for it, without preventing others from doing so. This is also the case for goods such as police protection and highways until the system begins to become overwhelmed. Rather than pay, an individual may simply **freeride** on the expenditures of others, for example, by obtaining wanted information at a library. Consequently, freeriding will lead to the underproduction of public goods by the private market since the producer will be unable to charge all users. While freeriding can be prevented for some public goods by excluding those who do not pay (*e.g.*, highway tolls and copyright laws), government provision or subsidy of the goods is commonly required to stimulate the desired production.

There are other goods that the private market will not produce at an efficient level because of **holdout** problems. The private construction of a highway, for example, requires the agreement of all landowners along the route. If all the necessary property has been purchased except for one last lot, the owner of that lot is inclined to hold out for an exorbitant amount, in theory being able to capture virtually all the potential profit of the enterprise. For this reason endeavors of this type will not be undertaken, or, as when a developer plans to build a skyscraper on a block of smaller lots, initial land purchases will be undertaken surreptitiously by means of confidential agents. The governmental power of eminent domain can overcome holdout problems.

The Conditions for the Invisible Hand. As suggested by the discussion above, for the invisible hand to work ideally, certain criteria must be met. One version of the criteria will be presented, and then the less obvious terms will be explained. First, the criteria are:

>   (1) Information is perfect and costless regarding goods and services and all alternatives;

>   (2) The administrative costs of the exchange system are zero and all property rights are settled and stable;

>   (3) The economic actors are fully rational and they are capable of choosing appropriate means to their own chosen ends;

>   (4) Transaction costs are zero *or* there is perfect competition and zero externalities; and

>   (5) Products are undifferentiated.

Now, to explain the less obvious terms:

>   (1) These terms are fairly self-explanatory.

>   (2) The administrative costs of the exchange system are the costs of resolving disputes.

>   (3) An individual is fully rational if she has transitive preference orderings, that is, if she prefers goods A to B and B to C, then she prefers A to C. An individual is capable of choosing appropriate means to her own chosen ends if she reasonably knows how to go about getting what she wants.

>   (4) Transaction costs are the costs of making the deal (*e.g.*, coming together, bargaining, and contracting). Perfect competition exists when no buyer or seller can independently influence prices (*e.g.*, via a monopoly).

Competition is imperfect when barriers inhibit market entry or exit, as where a producer cannot freely begin or end a business, for example, because of threatened boycotts or strikes, or government regulation. **Externalities** are the "neighborhood" or "third party" effects, positive or negative, on another's well-being. As two examples, the increased property value a neighbor gains from one's newly renovated house is a positive externality, while the harm from the pollution spewing from the factory chimneys of a nonliable producer is a negative externality.

(5) Products are undifferentiated when buyers cannot distinguish among the various sellers' competitive products (they all seem the same), and sellers cannot distinguish the willingness of each buyer to buy, that is, how much above the asking price they would be willing to pay.

These five conditions for the ideal working of the invisible hand are never entirely satisfied. But this does not destroy the usefulness of the model. This standard model of economic analysis predicts with fair success the consequences of economic choices. In addition, it serves as a useful heuristic device even if it is not sufficiently accurate to definitively resolve a disputed matter.

The Goals of the Market Economy. Under the invisible hand, trades will take place according to the preferences and wealth of the individual economic actors. Wilfredo Pareto, an Italian economist, sociologist and philosopher of a century ago, pointed out that, in the end, trades will naturally cease when a condition is reached which is known as **Pareto optimality**. This occurs when resources are allocated in such a way that no one is willing to trade further. People may not be fully satisfied in this state, but no one is willing to give up what she must of what she has in order to trade for something that another person has. Notice, first, that this condition relates to the allocation of resources, not the distribution of wealth, and second, that there are an unlimited number of possible conditions of optimality. For example, it is Pareto optimal when everyone is entirely contented with what they own and have no additional wants, and it is Pareto optimal when one, self-sufficient person has everything and everyone else has nothing. In this latter case, the penniless, though wanting, have nothing for which the Midas is willing to trade.

Related to Pareto optimality are trades that give rise to **Pareto superiority**. A Pareto superior change is one that makes at least one person better off without making anyone worse off. No one has lost by the change and therefore Pareto superiority is advanced as an improvement in efficiency, but also, under individualistic and utilitarian viewpoints, as a just step. Oftentimes, however, changes preferred by some individuals would make others worse off. When the overall gains outweigh the losses, the reallocation satisfies the criterion of **Kaldor-Hicks efficiency**, so named because it stems from the writings of English economists Nicholas Kaldor and J.R. Hicks. If those who gain from the change fully compensate those who lose -- the gainers still come out ahead -- the end result is a Pareto superior move. But this is often not possible as a practical matter, as when there are myriads of winners and losers of small amounts each. But under the Kaldor-Hicks principle, actual compensation need not occur; it is sufficient under this standard of efficiency that it works in theory, even if not in practice. Notice how the Kaldor-Hicks criterion functions much like utilitarian decisionmaking: the greatest aggregative good is normatively proper.

As is implicit in the discussion above, economic analysis is applicable not only to an **actual** or **explicit market**, but also to a **hypothetical**, **shadow** or **pseudo market**, as in the context of the Kaldor-Hicks criterion where practicalities prevent actual trades. Tort cases often are analyzed on the basis of hypothetical markets. For example, in *Ploof v. Putnam*,[8] the court declared that the owner of a sailing sloop in dire straits from an approaching tempest in Lake Champlain, held a privilege of necessity which precluded a trespass action when he moored at a nonconsenter's private dock. If transaction costs had not been prohibitive, the sloop owner beforehand, as a rational person, would have negotiated with each dockowner in the Lake to obtain emergency mooring rights, perhaps agreeing to compensate the dockowners for damage, as later cases require. In Kaldor-Hicks fashion, the person in distress need not pay for the mooring rights when they are used, though requiring payment would still be efficient since in either event the avoidance of the loss to the necessitous person provides a net gain. In this example, the case for an efficient hypothetical market is easy to make. Hypothetical markets, however, may be very imprecise, their valuations merely reflecting the decisionmaker's predispositions. This is especially the case in monetizing **moralisms**, which are public goods that are beyond objective valuation (*e.g.*, some of the aesthetic and moral values supporting environmentalism). For example, is the value of preserving particular park lands with endangered species greater than the value of developing them?

---

[8] 71 A. 188 (Vt. 1908).

The Justification of the Market Economy. As is evident in Chapter One on moral theory, the goal of efficiency is easily justified on the basis of **utilitarianism** (teleology). Some economists have even equated economics with utilitarianism. When goods are traded, both parties feel better off, otherwise they would not bother with the exchange. In other words, each party, having done a cost-benefit analysis, believes the personal benefits of the trade outweigh the costs. A common way of putting this is that the goods are moved to a higher state of utility. Overall social utility or goodness increases.

The voluntary trades in the market also advance the goals of **Kantianism** (deontology). Contract, in fact, is a paradigmatic example of the just interaction. The contracting parties, each one recognizing the other as an end in herself by respecting her autonomous choice, voluntarily agree to the exchange. Justice concerns, however, become an issue when the parties are not actually fully autonomous, as where some of the conditions of the ideal market are not satisfied. For example, a consumer can hardly be declared a rational, autonomous person, certainly in a strong sense, when she has little relevant information. In such a case the utilitarian basis for the exchange may not be satisfied either, since the consumer may make a deal so bad that her utility loss is greater than the seller's utility gain. The contract doctrines of unconscionability, undue influence, duress, and others, such as restrictions on specific contract terms, stem from these concerns.

The Coase Theorem. The modern Law and Economics movement began in the early 1960s and is most commonly associated with important articles by University of Chicago economist R.H. Coase,[9] and Yale Dean Guido Calabresi.[10] In his article, Coase examined the situation in which two neighbors use their lands in incompatible ways. For example, assume a railroad passes alongside a farmer's field and the engines emit sparks which ignite grain growing within 50 feet of the tracks. To give content to the hypothetical, assume that the farmer could earn an additional $100 per year by growing grain in the fire zone, and that it would cost the railroad a pro rata $50 per year to maintain spark arrestors on the engines. Does it make any difference whether the railroad is liable for damage from the fires? The surprising answer is that it makes no difference with regard to whether the grain will be grown. In more technical terms, the Coase Theorem is that, under the ideal market, the assignment of legal entitlements in cases of

---

[9] *The Problem of Social Cost*, 3 J.L. & ECON. 1 (1960).

[10] *Some Thoughts on Risk Distribution and the Law of Torts*, 70 YALE L.J. 499 (1961).

incompatible land uses will be neutral with respect to the goal of allocative efficiency. Under the hypothetical, since the farmer values the crops in the fire zone more than it would cost the railroad to prevent the fires, if the railroad is entitled to emit the sparks, the farmer will pay the railroad an amount between $50 and $100 per year to stop. Both the farmer and the railroad gain by this contract. On the other hand, if the railroad is liable for the damage from fires caused by its engines, it will install the necessary spark arrestors since this is cheaper than paying for the fire losses of $100 per year. In either event, the farmer ends up growing grain up to the tracks and the railroad installs the arrestors. But if the numbers are reversed, so that it costs the railroad $100 per year to maintain the spark arrestors and the farmer profits by $50 per year from the additional grain, then the grain will not be grown since, if the railroad is not liable, the farmer cannot afford to pay off the railroad, or, if the railroad is liable, the railroad will pay the farmer an amount between $50 and $100 per year for the right to cause fires along the tracks. As is seen, the party who values the entitlement most will end up with it, if necessary, by purchasing it from the owner.

The point of the Coase Theorem is that externalities are reciprocal in nature. To prohibit the railroad from freely emitting sparks is to inflict a cost on the railroad, while to allow the railroad to freely emit sparks is to inflict a cost on the farmer. Which is the negative externality, the farmer's fire losses from the emitted sparks or the railroad's impediment to emitting sparks? As Calabresi put it, the problem is what-is-a-cost-of-what? In the ideal market, allocative theory alone does not reveal which party should have the entitlement; it is a political issue. But the parties are obviously not indifferent to how the issue is resolved. Though the assignment of legal entitlements has no allocative consequences in theory, it does have distributive consequences. The person assigned the entitlement ends up wealthier, either from not having to pay the other party (when the assigned party values the entitlement more), or from being paid by the other party (when the other party values it more).

There are many considerations in deciding who should be assigned the entitlement. Which use came first, or "naturalness," may be telling. For example, we intuitively believe that river polluters generally should be liable for the damage to downstream owners. This is more "natural" -- clean rivers came before polluted ones. On the other hand, if the downstream user came after the pollution had begun ("coming to the nuisance"), our intuitions are ambivalent, although the available information may affect our thinking (*e.g.*, the nature of the pollution harms was unknown when she bought the property). In another example, we believe that negligent drivers should be liable for running into pedestrians, and not that injured pedestrians should be liable for the messes they make of the negligently driven cars. Several reasons support this. Corrective justice, whereby one should be liable for the harm one causes another through blameworthy conduct, points toward driver liability. It is generally easier for drivers to avoid being negligent than it is for pedestrians to avoid being hit by negligent drivers ("risk avoidance"). By making negligent drivers liable, drivers as a class will become less careless ("moral hazard") and accidents will decrease ("cost minimization" or "social efficiency").

In the railroad-farmer hypothetical, we must further consider that there are other farms along the tracks, so that the sale of the entitlement will involve many people. If, when the entitlement is more valued by the farmers, the railroad has the entitlement to emit sparks, the farmers must organize, which is a difficult endeavor ("transaction costs"), and each farmer must be willing to pay its share for the entitlement ("freerider"). On the other hand, if the farmers have the entitlement more valued by the railroad, the railroad's attempt to buy the entitlement from each of the farmers may be frustrated by the unwillingness of some farmers to sell it near fair market value ("holdout"). If litigation is employed to protect an established entitlement, vindicate an uncertain entitlement or get the attention of the other side ("nuisance suit"), then administrative costs are generated by the out-of-pocket expenses required for the litigation, and the time and effort ("opportunity costs") of the litigants. When the party with the higher administrative costs (here, the farmers with organization expenses and freerider problems) has the entitlement, it may be squeezed into a disadvantageous settlement by an opponent that resists compromise and threatens litigation. In addition, litigation is overused, arguably, because the parties do not pay its full costs. The fees and costs paid by the litigants to the court fall far short of the true expense of operating the judicial system, which is chiefly financed through taxes. Businesses generally take tax deductions for amounts spent on legal fees. To avoid these and related problems, it is important that the court or legislature make the proper, well-circumscribed choice in determining the original entitlement, since a later transfer is often costly and unlikely. Although assuming no transaction costs allows the Coase Theorem to make a convincing case in the abstract for free markets, reality is not nearly so simple nor efficient.

In determining the original entitlement, the court or legislature may choose to protect it by **property, liability and inalienability rules**. This distinction, first explicated by Calabresi and A. Douglas Melamed in 1972,[11] provides the decisionmaker formulating the entitlement with greater flexibility to accommodate efficiency and distributive concerns. An entitlement protected by a property rule grants the owner the power to exclude others or alienate it. The owner must consent beforehand to the use of the entitlement by others or its sale, as is the standard case regarding personal or real property, such as where the farmers in the hypothetical above may enjoin the railroad from continuing to emit damaging sparks. When an entitlement is protected by a liability rule, the owner has the power to obtain compensation from those who, without prior consent, take or interfere with it. Unlike protection by a property rule, forced transfers can occur under a liability rule, as where the injured farmers may recover damages from the railroad for the fire losses, but may not enjoin the railroad from continuing to emit sparks. An inalienability rule prevents transfers either by prior consent or subsequent compensation. For example, the entitlement to property is protected by an inalienability rule when the owner is incompetent, since the incompetent's sale may be disaffirmed. As the examples suggest, entitlements are typically protected by a variety of rules which depend on the circumstances.

Additional Concepts and Principles. An additional collection of concepts and principles are central to the economic analysis of law. Many of them have been mentioned already. The discussion here further elaborates some and introduces others.

Loss Spreading. Concentrated losses may cause serious diseconomies or dislocations. For example, a sudden liability for $50,000 may be altogether disruptive, whereas a liability of $50 would not be. The unprepared debtor may be required to forgo other plans, such as attending law school or opening a business. The debtor's family may similarly suffer. If the debtor is a firm, this may be the last straw, thereby precipitating bankruptcy and negative repercussions on employees and their families, suppliers, customers, etc. The economy suffers. In general, then, it is better to avoid the risk of these dislocations by spreading a loss. It can be spread either across time or across persons. The loss is spread across time by allowing the debtor to pay off the obligation over an extended period. The loss is spread across persons by, for example, imposing the liability on a large business enterprise. Products liability is a particular example. Providing legal relief to the consumer for her injury avoids concentrating

---

[11] *Property Rules, Liability Rules and Inalienability: One View of the Cathedral*, 85 HARV. L. REV. 1089 (1972).

losses on her. The producer's liability for the product defect will drive it to raise prices accordingly and effectively spread the loss across all its customers. Insurance is the prime example of a loss spreading device. When a policyholder's claims are typical, the losses are spread across time since in the long run the premiums will pay for the losses. When a policyholder's claims are unusually large, the losses are partially spread across persons, specifically, across the other policyholders in the insurance pool. Historically, firms, by passing costs along to their customers, were in a better position to spread losses than were individuals, but this advantage is dissipating as private insurance coverage becomes more diversified and pervasive.

Risk Attitude. An individual's risk attitude reflects her taste for risk. A person who is risk neutral is indifferent to risk. For example, this person would be indifferent to whether she is to be given $50 for certain, or $100 with a probability of 0.5. In either case the (average) expected payoff is $50 ($100 x 0.5). A risk preferrer is one who is willing to take risks despite the lower prospective financial payoff and a risk avoider is averse to risk and prefers the sure thing. To extend the prior example, the risk preferrer may opt for the 50% gamble for the $100 payoff rather than for a certain payment of $60 (*e.g.*, lottery ticket buyers), while the risk avoider may settle for a certain $40 rather than face the 50% gamble. Social scientists have found that an individual's risk attitude varies with the circumstances. For example, in general one is risk averse regarding prospective losses to what one already owns and is risk preferring regarding prospective gains. In other words, a person is more eager to keep what she has than to acquire what she does not have. Akin to this is the "endowment effect" whereby, assuming no depreciation, one would charge more to sell what one owns than one would pay to buy it originally. The economic analysis of the law normally assumes that persons are risk neutral. Since this is typically not the case, the assumption will effectively benefit some and disadvantage others because of their risk attitudes.

Moral Hazard. An apparent fact of human nature is that people are less careful when they do not have to pay for all the harm that eventuates from their conduct. Moral hazard is the misleading title of this notion. It plays a role in virtually all decisions regarding liability in insurance-type situations. Products liability may be invoked as an example. If the producer is not liable for injuries from product defects -- it is "insured" against them under a legal regime of *caveat emptor* ("let the buyer beware") -- it will be less careful about preventing them. It will not be indifferent to defects, of course, because it still is concerned about goodwill losses, but nevertheless, without liability it has less to worry about from defects and this will affect its economic choices regarding its level of care. On the other hand, if the producer is, say, strictly liable for product defects, this creates a moral hazard in the consumer. She is "insured" against product harms and will be less careful with the product. Like the producer above, the consumer also is not indifferent about her care for the product since her life and limb may be at risk and the filing of claims is not costless, but nevertheless, she will tend to be less careful. So it can be seen that moral hazard will arise somewhat irrespective of whether the producer or the consumer is responsible for product defects. The perverse incentives can be reduced to some extent, depending on the context. Fire insurance companies, for example, by limiting their coverage to less than 100% of the losses, require the policyholder to be a coinsurer, which, since she must partially pay for some losses, induces more care. The discussion of products liability reveals that other incentives (*e.g.*, to preserve goodwill or life and limb) may run counter to moral hazard. In the end, however, moral hazard hangs over every tort-like liability decision. An important policy consideration for a judicial or legislative rule is the minimization of moral hazard.

The Declining Marginal Utility of Wealth. The wealthier one is, the less one covets the next dollar. An individual, it seems, obtains less utility from each additional dollar she acquires. The same can be said for all goods, such as peaches or lawnmowers. How many lawnmowers can you use, after all? You only have two kids to run them and you live in an urban condo at that! That marginal utility declines is basically an intuitive supposition. It is not always the case, of course, as when the person driven to become a millionaire contemplates the last dollar of that goal. But because it is generally the case, it has far-reaching implications. For example, on this basis a utilitarian can argue that, all else equal, it is better that a rich person be liable for a loss than a poor person since the rich person will suffer less.

This **"deep pocket"** argument is an anathema to the libertarian right. They and other opponents attack the intuitive underpinning of the proposition with the observation that an **interpersonal utility comparison** is unrealistic. The utility one person obtains from each dollar cannot truly be compared to that obtained by another person. The frugal millionaire, for example, may procure more utility from her last dollar than does the religious ascetic from her first one. Hence, libertarians argue that redistributive decisions cannot be based on this utilitarian (or any other) reasoning. A common rebuttal to this line of attack includes these elements: (1) while there are exceptions to the declining marginal utility of wealth, utilitarianism is aggregative and we have substantial reason to believe, partially from empirical studies, in the usual validity of the supposition; (2) because the rich receive proportionally more benefits from society than the poor, as a matter of justice they owe it more in return; and (3) a modern developed society inevitably does make redistributive decisions and it is nonsensical to ignore this consideration. Rather, the task is to make rational redistributive decisions that improve upon private markets (correcting "market imperfections") or serve other valid social goals without unduly undermining the essential efficiency of the free market. The libertarian rejoinder to this criticism is suggested in Chapter Three on political theory.

Risk Avoidance. The principle of risk avoidance is one of the major themes in the economic analysis of law. While it was introduced above in the context of the Coase Theorem, more elaboration is necessary. Recall that transaction costs and other impediments to trades commonly prevent the transfer of an entitlement despite the logic of the Coase Theorem that, in theory, the person who values it most will end up with it irrespective of who owns it initially. Because, in practice, the entitlement often remains with the original owner, it is important that the decisionmaker properly designate the owner in the first instance. But determining which person values the entitlement most will often be exceedingly difficult. Resort to the uncertainties of a hypothetical market may be required. Owing to this valuation difficulty, among other reasons, further considerations come into play. The most important additional consideration according to many commentators is the principle of risk avoidance. The risk of particular losses should be allocated to the party in the best (cheapest) position to avoid them, or to do a cost-benefit analysis of whether they should be avoided and, if necessary, "bribe" the other party to avoid them. The air polluter, for example, is typically in a better position to avoid the pollution harms by means of a scrubber or precipitator on its smokestacks than are the many neighbors by means of individual house filters, etc. Since high organizational costs and freeriding will prevent the neighbors from buying the polluter's right to pollute, risk avoidance supports the initial determination that the neighbors should have the right to be free of pollution even though it may be unclear who values the entitlement more. The polluter may also be the best "briber" because, knowing what it spews out its smokestacks, it is better informed of the extent of the long-term pollution harms and thus, if necessary, is in a superior position to "bribe" the neighbors to take precautions. On the other hand, the principle of risk avoidance may not conclusively point to one party or the other. It may not be evident which party is the better risk avoider or briber, or whether cooperative behavior between the parties might be the efficient solution for a specific risk. For example, car-pedestrian accidents in the countryside might be avoided most efficiently by a combination of careful driving by the motorist and the wearing of dayglo attire by the pedestrian. Cooperative solutions are often difficult to implement by the courts or even by the legislatures.

Transaction Costs. The ideal market, it was noted, assumes the nonexistence of transaction costs (or perfect competition and zero externalities). Goods will not be moved to higher states of utility though trades if transaction costs consume the potential gains. Transaction costs appear in several forms. **Information costs** ensue from the collection and mastery of data. What is the durability of the models? What are their maintenance costs? How much energy do they consume? Which dealer provides the best service? What are the contract terms? The information may be divided into three types which hinge on the particular qualities of the goods or services. **Inspection** or **search qualities** are those that can be immediately judged, such as the sharpness of the television picture or the excellence of the perfume fragrance. **Use qualities** are those that require time to evaluate, such as the durability or energy consumption of particular goods. **Credence qualities** are those that are difficult to evaluate even after the passage of time, such as whether all the services of the doctor or lawyer were truly required or whether the car transmission actually needed replacement. The possibilities for deceit and nondisclosure obviously vary with the type of qualities. **Opportunity costs** follow, in this context, from the adage that time is money. The time a person spends to collect and digest information could instead be used for other activities. The general concept of opportunity costs is central to economic analysis. To elaborate, then, from an economic viewpoint, the cost of producing a product is the value of the other products that could have been produced instead with the needed resources. In other words, the cost of any product consists of the alternatives that must be foregone in order to obtain it. Money, from this perspective, is simply a common denominator for all relevant foregone alternatives. **Administrative costs**, which are sometimes distinguished from transaction costs as was done above in laying out the criteria of the invisible hand, involve the expenditures required to see the interaction or transaction through. Court costs, time in court, and lawyers fees are included. So too are other organizational costs such as registering title. In general, however, transaction and administrative costs are not finely delineated. Some claim that just about anything can count as a transaction cost. From another angle, one person's transaction cost is another person's livelihood. Lawyers, to pick an example not at random, would not exist in the world of the invisible hand where no grease is required to lubricate the gears of society.

Economic Rents. Sometimes the market price of a product is not governed by its production cost. When this occurs, economic rents accrue to the producer who has access to a resource at a lower cost than its competitors. The resource is then able to capture a payment in excess of what would be required to keep it in its present use. The reason for this is scarcity. For example, prime urban real estate is able to capture economic rents since other land cannot be moved in to compete. The realty's special location value provides the owner with substantially more income than she would earn by an alternative use that does not face this scarcity, such as farming. As another example, how much would Michael Jordan have earned if basketball was not a professional sport? (Former New York Jets quarterback Joe Namath used to say that if he had not played football he would have been pumping gas in his hometown of Beaver Falls, Pennsylvania.) The scarcity may be artificially created, as where a producer seeks to reduce competition by restrictive, government regulation. The attempt to procure economic rents is called "rent-seeking."

Cost Minimization or Social Efficiency. As seen in the discussion, many factors affect the degree to which a particular market works ideally. In general, when making social choices, it is better, all else equal, to establish rules by which desired goods are produced at a lower cost and with less waste. Social efficiency is advanced when people get what they want for less. Two of the most important considerations in meeting this goal are risk avoidance and transaction costs. Yet many other factors must also be weighed by the public decisionmaker when considering market regulation. The nature of the affected market should be examined, including the following factors: the types of affected interests of the parties (*e.g.*, liberty interest versus want satisfaction); the externalities and whether they can be internalized; the elasticity of the market (*i.e.*, the degree to which a change in the cost of the supply will affect the demand, *e.g.*, the demand for housing is fairly inelastic since people need it irrespective of its cost, and the demand for breathable air is entirely inelastic, whereas the demand for ordinary luxury goods is quite elastic and increases in proportion to price reductions); the returns to scale; the degree to which the market is regulated; the existence of a monopoly or oligopoly (*i.e.*, markets with one or a few sellers), or a monopsony or oligopsony (*i.e.*, markets with one or a few buyers); and the barriers to entrance to or exit from the market (*e.g.*, the very high startup costs for opening a RAM chip factory or losses from closing down an automobile production line).

To offer a glimpse of the potential complexity of these decisions, consider the case in which a court examines a tenant's common law rights against her landlord, irrespective of lease terms. It would properly appraise, among other things, the affect of the decision on the housing stock. To be more specific, if the tenant is required to make structural repairs, the landlord may build a less durable structure since it need worry less about later defects (moral hazard). The tenant, though, is unlikely to make durable repairs. She desires the repairs to last only for the expected length of her tenancy, so that later, avoidable repairs will follow, and she is unlikely to have the expertise and economies of scale of the landlord. If the landlord is required to make the repairs, it will generally do it at a lower overall cost and pass the costs of repairs along to the tenant, assuming that market regulations allow this and assuming that the landlord does not simply absorb the costs in light of any economic rents earned from the apartment. The increased rent will not drive away many tenants since the market is relatively inelastic. The tenant, however, being free of the duty to make the repairs, will be less careful about causing damage to the structure (moral hazard). This increases the need for repairs. Insofar as apartment ownership becomes less profitable, some landlords will leave the market and others will decline to enter, thereby reducing the overall housing stock and driving up the rent of that which remains. Other effects are also likely, but these are enough to reveal the difficulty in evaluating the overall tradeoffs ensuing from the court's decision.

The Theory of Second Best. In appraising a problem which stems from a failure of the market to work ideally, analysts often focus on a single factor and predict its linkage to a particular rule. For example, one might argue that X should be the rule to counter the effects of high transaction costs in a certain market. Because factors tend to interrelate in complicated ways, for the sake of simplification analysts typically isolate the one factor by arguing that, "all else being equal," or to put it in the commonly used Latin, "*ceterus paribus*," such-and-such will occur under the contemplated legal regime. Under the theory of second best, such strong predictions cannot be made. The "second-best" state of affairs will not track closely the first best in all ways but one. Instead, it will usually depart in several respects. When one of the conditions of the invisible hand is not satisfied, such as the where transaction costs exist as mentioned above, the effects of a proposed rule to cope with this defect are difficult to predict and, therefore, one cannot declare confidently whether it will result in a more efficient allocation of resources. In our highly imperfect world, one must be cautious when prescribing solutions based on theoretical analyses.

Economics is classified as a social or "soft" science since it involves human beings operating in weakly controllable environments (*i.e.*, society). In contrast, the "hard" sciences, such as chemistry or physics, involve physical phenomena in strongly controllable settings (*e.g.*, lab experiments), thereby allowing for greater replicability and predictability. Many economists argue, nevertheless, that economics has more rigor than other social sciences such as psychology or sociology. Without entering into this interdisciplinary squabble, one may note that physical science can also experience a version of the problem of second best. For example, efforts to predict weather are only partially successful even though the laws of physics govern. For weather systems, as for economic systems, one can never hold all factors but one constant. Under the chaos theory characterizing the weather, when a butterfly flaps its wings in Nebraska, it eventually affects the weather in New York in unpredictable ways. In much the same way, a single change in market behavior or government regulation can have unforeseeable ripple effects.

The Usefulness of Economic Analysis of Law. The world of the actual marketplace is far from the ideal construct of the invisible hand. For example, transaction costs always occur and available information is far from perfect. Therefore, the predictions based on the model which stem from the assumptions of the ideal marketplace are necessarily inaccurate to some degree. Even an analysis of an economic problem which relies on the relaxation of one or more of the assumptions faces the uncertainties of the theory of second best. Some considerations, such as the distributive effects of a particular contemplated rule, are inevitably omitted from the economic analysis. Despite this, economists defend their discipline by throwing down the gauntlet to critics. Modern economic analysis, though built on problematic assumptions, has been shown empirically to make useful predictions -- better predictions, economists contend, than any other model of the market. As in the "blackbox" theory of science, the realism of the model itself is irrelevant. What counts is whether the model (blackbox), when fed data, accurately predicts outcomes, or at least predicts them more accurately than competing models. That modern economic analysis does this is evident. Nevertheless, the underlying weaknesses should not be forgotten by public decisionmakers. Economics provides a powerful tool, but it is far from a perfect tool and must be used accordingly.

REFERENCES FOR FURTHER READING

DAVID W. BARNES & LYNN A. STOUT, CASES AND MATERIALS ON LAW AND ECONOMICS (1992).

GARY BECKER, THE ECONOMIC APPROACH TO HUMAN BEHAVIOR (1976); THE ECONOMICS OF DISCRIMINATION (2d ed. 1971).

ALLEN BUCHANAN, ETHICS, EFFICIENCY, AND THE MARKET (1985).

GUIDO CALABRESI, THE COSTS OF ACCIDENTS (1970); *see also The Point-
    lessness of Pareto: Carrying Coase Further*, 100 YALE L.J. 1121
    (1991); *Property Rules, Liability Rules and Inalienability: One
    View of the Cathedral*, 85 HARV. L. REV. 1089 (1972) (with A.
    Douglas Melamed); *Some Thoughts on Risk Distribution and the
    Law of Torts*, 70 YALE L.J. 499 (1961).

Ronald Coase, *The Problem of Social Cost*, 3 J.L. & ECON. 1 (1960).

JULES COLEMAN, MARKETS, MORALS AND THE LAW (1988); *see also*
    JEFFRIE MURPHY & JULES COLEMAN, THE PHILOSOPHY OF LAW:
    AN INTRODUCTION TO JURISPRUDENCE ch. 5 (2d ed. 1991) (brief
    introduction to Coleman's critique of law and economics).

ROBERT COOTER & THOMAS ULEN, LAW AND ECONOMICS (1988).

Duncan Kennedy, *Cost-Benefit Analysis of Entitlement Problems: A
    Critique*, 33 STAN. L. REV. 387 (1981); *Distributive and
    Paternalistic Motives in Contract and Tort Law, with Special
    Reference to Compulsory Terms and Unequal Bargaining Power*, 41
    MD. L. REV. 563 (1982).

Arthur Leff, *Economic Analysis of Law: Some Realism About Nominalism*,
    60 VA. L. REV. 451 (1974).

ROBIN MALLOY, LAW AND ECONOMICS: A COMPARATIVE APPROACH TO
    THEORY AND PRACTICE (1990).

HENRY MANNE (ed.), THE ECONOMICS OF LEGAL RELATIONSHIPS (1975).

Frank Michelman, *Norms and Normativity in the Economic Theory of Law*,
    62 MINN. L. REV. 1015 (1978).

A. MITCHELL POLINSKY, AN INTRODUCTION TO LAW AND ECONOMICS (2d
    ed. 1989).

RICHARD A. POSNER, ECONOMIC ANALYSIS OF LAW (4th ed. 1992); THE
    ECONOMICS OF JUSTICE (1981).

Symposium on Post-Chicago Law and Economics, 65 CHI.-KENT L. REV.
    1 (1989).

Symposium on Efficiency as a Legal Concern, 8 HOFSTRA L. REV. 485
    (1980); *Symposium on the Future of Law and Economics*, 20
    HOFSTRA L. REV. 757 (1992).

CHAPTER THREE

POLITICAL PHILOSOPHY AND LAW

- **Introduction**
- **The History of Western Political Philosophy**
    - **The Classical Age**
        - **Greece**
        - **Rome**
    - **The Middle Ages**
        - **Aquinas**
    - **The Modern Age**
        - **Machiavelli**
        - **Hobbes**
        - **Locke**
        - **Montesquieu**
        - **Rousseau**
        - **Burke**
        - **Bentham**
        - **J.S. Mill**
        - **Kant**
        - **Hegel**
        - **Marx**
        - **Nietzsche**
    - **The Twentieth Century**
        - **Dewey**
        - **Rawls**
        - **Nozick**
- **Contemporary Political Attitudes**
    - **Libertarian**
    - **Conservative**
        - **Lockean Conservatives**
        - **Smithean Conservatives**
        - **Burkean Conservatives**
    - **Liberal**
    - **Communitarian**
- **References for Further Reading**

Political philosophy examines the appropriate organization of individuals into groups. The views of proper political arrangements are generally based on notions of justice, which typically involve questions of security and property, and the means by which a social organization can bring about and maintain just conditions.

This introduction to political philosophy approaches the discipline in two ways. First, there is a survey of the history of Western political thought from the classical age until recent times. Second, there is an examination of the meaning of the common labels for general political viewpoints, such as "conservative" and "liberal."

The History of Western Political Philosophy.

Political philosophy has been driven by great thinkers. While these thinkers were not necessarily debating or responding to one another, the history of the discipline can be broken into periods and waves in which particular views emerged.

The Classical Age. The classical age begins in Greece during the fifth century B.C. and stretches to Rome through the first few centuries A.D. The purpose of political life, in the general opinion of the philosophers of this age, is to foster virtue.

Greece. Socrates, Plato, and Aristotle, the Athenian thinkers of the fifth and fourth centuries B.C., began the tradition of Western political philosophy. They were concerned with the Greek city-state, the polis, from which the term "political" is derived. Along with tyranny, they rejected democracy (roughly, government by the people, particularly, the rule of the majority), for it was the Athenian democracy that condemned Socrates to death. More to the point, they believed the goal of the state is to foster virtue rather than the freedom that is the objective of a democracy. Freedom must be rejected because it facilitates evil as well as good. Virtue entails wisdom, courage, moderation and justice, and is the true aim of the good life. An active rather than a passive quality, it is excellence in fulfilling one's function.

Notice that the term "function" implies a role that one plays with respect to a social situation. There was no room for modern notions of individualism, rugged or otherwise, in ancient Athens. The individual is not separate from the polis, but rather, as a political animal, is formed by and obligated to the community. Virtue is a quality instilled by education. This is not an easy enterprise. Proper character formation through education requires the leisure of both children and parents. Leisure, in its turn, requires wealth. Obviously, not everyone is wealthy. Since the goods of the earth are limited, not all persons can have the wherewithal to actively participate in the political system. The citizens cannot contemplate and implement the good life if they must attend to the fields. Justice, then, occurs in a political system in which each member does what she is best fitted to do. The result is a hierarchical society which, according to the Athenians, involves slavery and a subservient role for women.

In Plato's harmonious, utopian vision, it is the philosophers, the lovers of wisdom, who are fittest to rule.[12] Aristotle believed that conflict among the classes is inevitable, but is resolvable through politics with the upper class of aristocrats as the one to rule.[13] In both of their views, democracy, by enfranchising those who must be dutiful to their livelihood rather than the complexities of governance, is rule by the uneducated, a state of affairs that no reasonable person would favor. (As societies have prospered, universal education has tempered this objection, at least in principle. In practice, universal education does not necessarily mean proper education. The ancients would not approve of the current lack in the schools of the moral education needed to form virtuous character.)

Rome. Although the ancient Hebrews and early Christians scattered political seeds that were later to flower, the next systematic examination of the political life came from Rome.[14] The concept of natural law, along with the thoughts of the Big Three from Athens (Socrates, Plato and Aristotle), were central to Roman political philosophy. The origins of natural law are with Greek thinkers, the Stoics in particular. But in distinct contrast to the Greeks who found the small polis as necessary for meeting political goals, the broad idea of natural law is that there are certain eternal, universal moral principles common to all humans and nations which are in accordance with right reason. The realm under this everlasting, unchangeable, world-wide law is ruled by God. Because natural law aligns with reason, individuals, as rational beings, can know this law and must measure up to this yardstick irrespective of the declared (positive) law. In other words, there is a Law above the law that is grounded in nature, and all, individuals and the state, must obey it.

---

[12] Plato's most famous political tract is the REPUBLIC.

[13] Aristotle's main political works are NICOMACHEAN ETHICS and POLITICS.

[14] The best known Roman political tracts are from the stylus of Cicero, DE LEGIBUS (ON THE LAWS) (c. 46 B.C.) and DE OFFICIIS (ON DUTIES) (c. 44 B.C.).

The Middle Ages. From the fall of Rome in the fifth century A.D. and through the dark and middle ages, no new systematic political theory emerged. The works of the Greek philosophers were lost to the West for much of this period until they were reintroduced by Jewish and Arab sources. What speculation there was about political life came primarily from the Christian church.

      Aquinas. While St. Augustine (354-430) includes valuable political thoughts in his works, it is St. Thomas Aquinas (c. 1224-1274), an Italian, who left the more important political legacy.[15] Aristotle greatly stimulated his thinking, though many other philosophers also influenced him. As is true of other Catholic thinkers, his is a natural law philosophy. God and nature are all-encompassing and harmonious. A single grain of sand reflects the entire universe, the omnipresent principles of which can be discerned by human reason. Reason reveals that persons are naturally disposed, first, to preserve their own well-being, second, to satisfy biological drives, such as those to breed and nurture offspring, and third, to follow the inclination of reason towards universal goods, such as concern for others. These natural dispositions lead to rules of the natural law. Each being, of value in itself, fits into a hierarchy based on its degree of perfection. An individual, serving and guided by those above, contributes to the perfection of the whole while achieving the good life. This scheme, like all rational activities, is purposive, and is judged, as are individual actions, by its success at realizing its purpose as well as by the chosen means to this end. Even the ruler is judged by her contribution to the common good, which includes the effectuation of earthly happiness for her subjects. Though his theory of government is sketchy, Aquinas emphasizes the virtues of a limited monarchy, and condemns tyranny.

The Modern Age. The modern age of political philosophy begins with Niccolo Machiavelli (1469-1527), an Italian, in the early sixteenth century. He brought an end to the long consensus among political philosophers that the goal of political life is to instill virtue. The modern age has given birth to an array of political philosophies that reject the classical view as unrealistic.

      Machiavelli. This political thinker and politician believed that there is something basically flawed about a political scheme that, relying on

---

    [15]   His great systematic work on philosophy and theology is SUMMA THEOLOGIAE.

people's better nature, aims for a utopia.[16] The nature of humanity is to make the achievement of such an objective most unlikely. Politicians must be more realistic and account for the manifest qualities of the human character. Furthermore, though virtue may be a nice ideal, actual political realms pursue other goals. History reveals that states seek independence, stability, prosperity and glory. As a practical matter, virtue should be seen as the qualities needed to achieve these ends of civic selfishness. The furthering of these ends is in itself good and justifies whatever are the means.

As political communities are selfish, so are individuals. This disposition of the citizenry is bad and conflicts with the goals of the state. But since humans are malleable, they can be trained to be good. Yet, because the trainers are individuals who are bad themselves, how are the citizens to be properly trained? The answer is to make it in the self-interest of the trainers to do their job well. The passion for individual glory can be used to discipline the trainers. The prince is allowed to seek personal glory in order to motivate him to carry out his function of countering the inherent badness of his subjects. Under this vision, the prince, in dealing with his subjects and with other princes, may act if necessary with ruthless cruelty and unscrupulousness. For example, Machiavelli responded to the question of whether it is better for the prince to be loved than to be feared with a resounding "no." If the prince cannot be both, it is better to be feared than loved. To put the harsh gloss that some have placed on Machiavelli, in the end, the prince is distinguished from the criminal by successful opportunity alone.

Hobbes. There are various interpretations of Machiavelli's vision that make it more or less appealing. Thomas Hobbes (1588-1679), an Englishman, pursued its bright side through rehabilitation.[17] In mitigating Machiavelli's apparent oppressiveness, Hobbes takes up the duties of the citizen rather than the practices of the prince. He does not lose sight of justice and refutes the proposition that the state is essentially the result of a criminal enterprise. Justice is not merely a social product. As in the natural law tradition, there are natural rights. This idea of natural rights, which Hobbes is the first to advance, is a dramatic departure from Machiavelli. Still, Hobbes found Machiavelli correct in concentrating on

---

[16] His main works are THE PRINCE (written 1513, published 1532) and THE DISCOURSES (c. 1517).

[17] His great work is LEVIATHAN (1651).

practical schemes and rejecting utopian ones. The typical citizen is more concerned with life's immediate necessities than its distant ideals. Humans are more animal than angel. Self-preservation is the dominant impulse. In the state of nature, there is no property or justice, but rather a condition of war in which it is "every man against every man," along with "continual fear, and danger of violent death; and the life of man [is], solitary, poor, nasty, brutish and short." The state is founded under the white flag signifying the selfish fear of death, not behind the triumphant banner of glory.

To gain protection from the wolves at the door, the citizens give up their natural rights in the social contract and absolutely submit to the sovereign who can defend them, the Leviathan. The citizens are not to resist authority, except for the purpose of self-preservation. A defender of despotic government out of fear of anarchy, Hobbes declares monarchy, not aristocracy or democracy ("the government of a few orators"), to be the preferred political system. However, the problems of the citizen do not end with the creation of the state. Once the state is established and the wolves are kept from the door, the citizen must worry about the guard dog. The Leviathan itself threatens not only the instinct for self-preservation but also the acquired desire for comfort. Fortunately, the interests of the sovereign often coincide with those of the citizenry. For example, the sovereign gets richer if the citizens do. In the end, the name of the game is not glory, it is power. Glory is for the fortunate few, while the morally neutral and mundane need for the power to satisfy and preserve one's wants is for the many.

Locke. The utilitarian outlook o Hobbes was further developed and mitigated by John Locke (1632-1704), another seventeenth century Englishman.[18] He notices that the foremost instrument of self-preservation is not the sword, but rather it is the goods obtained from property, such as food. Acquisitiveness is the form in which the desire for self-preservation manifests itself. With this extension of Hobbes' lessons, political philosophy becomes remarkably practical and, in the Anglo-Saxon sphere, fully successful as is evidenced by the powerful Lockean undercurrents in the United States Constitution. Selfishness, when steered towards commerce, may be satisfied without bloodshed and to the advantage of all. In light of human characteristics, this indirection is the best way to advance the Good. The prince and citizens are to put down the war banner and pick up a primer on economics.

---

[18] Locke's main political work is the SECOND TREATISE OF GOVERNMENT (1690).

In the state of nature, Locke posits complete equality and freedom within the limits of the natural law discoverable through rational contemplation. Individuals must preserve the peace, and those who do not become outlaws punishable by others. Though, contra Hobbes, the state of nature is predominantly peaceful, the tensions among individuals stemming from human self-interest and the tendency to overreach are resolved by the formation of a civil government through a social contract. The contract is between the equally free citizens, not between the citizens and the sovereign. If the sovereign, whether a monarch or a legislative body, becomes tyrannical by depriving the citizens of their natural rights to life, liberty and property, the contract is breached and revolution is justified. In other words, under this sovereignty of the people, the citizens do not forgo all their natural rights by the social contract, instead they transfer the legislative and executive powers to the government on the understanding that the powers will not be abused. This is best accomplished through a legislative body regularly elected by majority vote providing checks and balances with the executive branch, the judiciary being neglected by Locke.

Locke's conception of property has been particularly influential. The natural right to property follows from its necessary linkage to the right of self-preservation. To live, a person must have the means to obtain food and shelter. Hence, property expresses God's dominion on earth, and the use of property evidences God's grace. An individual possesses herself absolutely, and thus owns that with which she "mixes" her labor. While the earth was originally owned by all in common, one may appropriate that which one removes from the state of nature by means of personal labor, so long as the goods removed do not go to waste and the removal does not deprive others of their means of self-preservation. The creation of money, which is a nondecaying medium of exchange, avoids the first limitation, that the goods do not spoil, and facilitates the accumulation of wealth. (The second limitation, that others not be unduly deprived (the "Lockean proviso"), is a rallying cry of environmentalists.) Locke places property at the core of his theory of political organization: "The great and chief end of men uniting into commonwealths, and putting themselves under government, is the preservation of their property."

Montesquieu. The eighteenth century, the age known as the Enlightenment, engendered many diverse political viewpoints. Historically important philosophers such as Voltaire, Montesquieu, Hume, Rousseau, Paine, Jefferson, Burke, and others, expressed their principles of political organization. Charles Louis de Secondat, Baron de Montesquieu (1689-1755), a Frenchman, was a follower of Locke who also influenced the

United States Constitution.[19] He perceives a conflict between the classical ideal that political organizations are to foster virtue, and the English ideal of personal liberty. Montesquieu finds the English ideal, which is materialized by trade and finance, to be less severe and more humane than Roman republican virtue. But the English design is not a product of pure rational thought. Individuals are subject to natural laws which determine their behavior and inform their moral beliefs. A complete empiricist, Montesquieu sees that the sociology and even the geography and climate of a people influence their political system. He is not, however, simply a relativist. He favors liberty as the better ideal, though it must be limited to prevent some from dominating others, as where commercial interests trample consumers. The law is to protect the common interest. Outside this declared sphere, individuals may do as they wish.

Rousseau. Born in Geneva, Jean-Jacques Rousseau (1712-1778), first stirred up the second wave of modern political thought which brought German idealism and Western romanticism.[20] Like Montesquieu, he is skeptical of progress and he believes that human nature has been corrupted by society. Disapproving the commercial world of the bourgeoisie, he looks back to the classical ideal of virtue. Like Hobbes, he posits self-preservation as the driving force of civil society, but, unlike Hobbes and Locke, he declares that a social order related to the classical republic is the best means to achieve this end. As is evident in what follows, it is not possible to expound Rousseau's thought in the straightforward, down-to-earth language traditional to Anglo-American philosophy. For this and the German idealists ahead, turn down the television set.

According to Rousseau, the positive law will align with natural law only when the general will of a society governs through the voice of the people. While the freedom in the state of nature is different from the freedom in civil society, the latter is also natural when the general will, the will of the collectivity, rules. Individual freedom must be maintained, because it is the essence of one's human quality and essential to morality. The general will, unlike the individual will, always steers toward the general good. When it holds sway, the actual coincides with the rational ideal. The just person allows every other person the same rights which she claims for herself, whatever the rights may be, by means of a self-enforcing

---

[19] Montesquieu's important work is DE L'ESPRIT DES LOIS (THE SPIRIT OF THE LAWS) (1748).

[20] Rousseau's most celebrated political book is DU CONTRAT SOCIAL (THE SOCIAL CONTRACT) (1762).

mechanism approaching the state of nature. Each person becomes truly free by obeying a self-prescribed law in a social situation of fraternity and equality with other accepting citizens. In Rousseau's scheme, the state, being the only setting in which individuals find true freedom, has claims against its citizens that most modern liberals reject.

Burke. Rousseau's speculations influenced the American and French revolutions, among others. The political philosophy of the American revolution, however, is best found in THE FEDERALIST, a collection of papers written in 1787-88 by James Madison, Alexander Hamilton, and John Jay. They espouse a just society which, rather than seeking the equality and fraternity of Rousseau, protects the weak from the strong. This is accomplished by a government which ensures the maintenance of liberty through the separation of powers within the federal government and a balance of power with the state governments.

Edmund Burke (1729-1797), a British statesman and political philosopher, championed the Americans against the British impositions leading to the revolution on the grounds that the traditional rights and liberties of Americans were being trampled. Like Locke and the authors of THE FEDERALIST, Burke advocates the protection of property interests, even when those interests are far from equally distributed. Harking back to the Greeks, he observes that the proper management of the government requires wisdom and experience. Substantial property owners and their executives are most likely to have been adequately schooled as managers. There is no room for the type of equality and fraternity promoted in the Rousseauist state.

Burke was not only convinced of this in theory, but also from the practice of the French Revolution beginning in 1789. Looking at it from across the channel, he was appalled at what he saw and wrote his most important political tract.[21] He agrees that the state is founded on a social contract, but this is a contract of a special sort, to be revered and observed beyond that of the workaday commercial agreement. In language closer to Rousseau's ideas than he would endorse, Burke states that "the great primeval contract of eternal society" constitutes a partnership not only with fellow citizens, but also with dead ancestors and unborn descendants. Revolution is, therefore, a breach with the past and the future. Change

---

[21] While, of Burke's many political writings, REFLECTIONS ON THE REVOLUTION IN FRANCE (1790) is best known, obviously, because of its date, it did not influence the American Revolution or Constitution.

within the state, if any, is to occur by incremental evolution rather than disruptive revolution. The inherited wisdom of tradition should be respected and preserved. Though tradition is not free of evil, the good in it should not be rejected for the sake of an unrealistic striving for perfection, as among the French revolutionaries. Evil is here to stay. Balance, compromise and tolerance are essential to political affairs, because the consequences of change are unpredictable.

Bentham. Jeremy Bentham (1748-1832), an Englishman, laid down the utilitarian end of political organizations: "It is the greatest happiness of the greatest number that is the measure of right and wrong."[22] Bentham was a lawyer who was appalled by the English legal system, which he found to be costly, harsh, unwieldy, and obscure. His major ambition was to reform both legal theory and practice. The utilitarian, pleasure-pain principle is the unifying precept of his political theory and guides his proposed legal reforms. In his view, for example, an individual should obey the laws so long as this produces more general happiness than does disobedience.

There is no room in Bentham's scheme for theories of the social contract, natural rights or natural law. The social contract is a legal fiction or, if considered merely hypothetical, should not be observed if it does not produce general happiness. The idea of natural rights, in turn, is "nonsense on stilts." It confuses what is with what ought to be. To object to a law on the grounds that a person has inalienable rights is false, since the law in question has in fact alienated those rights. Nor should a government strive to protect the supposed natural rights to life, liberty and property, for a necessary aspect of governing is to restrict some liberty, punish criminals and tax. Every law, for that matter, is a constraint on liberty. Bentham's theory of sovereignty is similarly pragmatic. A person has political authority when habitually obeyed by others. Under his theory of legal positivism (*see* the discussion in Chapter Six), the laws are the commands of the sovereign enforced by sanctions.

J.S. Mill. During his life, Bentham published very little. His followers, the Benthamites, were an effective political force that was quite successful in implementing some of his proposed reforms and spreading his views through the written word. One of his followers was John Stuart Mill (1806-1873), the most influential English philosopher during the nineteenth

---

[22] This quote comes from Bentham's FRAGMENT ON GOVERNMENT (1776). Better known is his INTRODUCTION TO THE PRINCIPLES OF MORALS AND LEGISLATION (1789).

century.[23]   He was a thoroughgoing utilitarian, but he was not beyond questioning the views of his famous father and fellow Benthamite, James Mill, as well as Bentham himself. For example, Mill sees in historical traditions a value that these two were uninterested in seeking. Favoring a representative democracy because it best fosters the development of constructive individuality, Mill believes that it works well only if the citizenry are reasonably well educated, committed and tolerant. His greatest fear is the propensity of majoritarian rule to suppress individuality and minorities. One might think that a utilitarian would be unconcerned about the invasion of individual rights. But Mill argues in his famed utilitarian defense of the precepts of justice that the means to general utility include the recognition of individual rights because the protection of people's sentiment of justice is socially expedient. In other words, people will be unhappy if justice does not prevail. The equal capacity of people for pleasure and pain calls for their treatment as equals ("everybody to count for one, nobody for more than one"). In order to promote happiness, individuals must have the right to choose what to believe and how to behave.

Under Mill's still prominent "harm principle," personal autonomy should be protected so long as it is not exercised in violation of the basic interests of others, for example, of their interests in personal security and property. Autonomy is not to be subordinated to the conventions of the majority. Conventional standards of what is offensive or disgusting, unless rooted in basic rights, cannot justify laws limiting individual freedom. In other words, while "other-regarding harm" -- harm to others -- is a justification for limiting individual liberty, "self-regarding harm" -- harm felt by a person when aware of another's offensive activities -- is not. The current battleground which most often hears the cry of Mill's harm principle, often shouted by both sides, involves clashes over the regulation of private sexual conduct between consenting adults. Finally, Mill is a strong advocate of free speech. "[F]reedom of opinion, and freedom of the expression of opinion" is necessary "to the mental well-being of mankind (on which all their other well-being depends) . . . ."

Kant. The chronological order of the presentation is disrupted by this examination of the political philosophy of Immanuel Kant (1724-1804), a Prussian contemporary of Burke. He is the founder of German idealism. Though his political philosophy, which follows the spirit of Rousseau, is not

---

[23]   Mill's most significant political works, sometimes published under a single cover, are ON LIBERTY (1859), UTILITARIANISM (1861) and REPRESENTATIVE GOVERNMENT (1861).

particularly important or lucid, he lays the groundwork for the momentous work of Hegel and Marx, among others. Like Rousseau, German idealism strives for the lofty level of classical political philosophy, but, very significantly, replaces the social goal of virtue with freedom. It emphasizes the fundamental importance of the philosophy of history, a study foreign to the classical age. German idealism also emphatically rejects utilitarianism and its pragmatism in favor of abstract philosophical reasoning. Kant's own political philosophy follows from his supreme ethical principle, the "categorical imperative" (*see* Chapter One on ethics), that persons are to be treated under universalized maxims as ends in themselves, and not as a means only to another's end. As a stern ethicist and legalist (one *must* do one's duty; the law *is* the law), he is an unbending retributivist in criminal matters. Paralleling Rousseau, he justifies political authority in terms of the general will of the people as well as social contract. With various beliefs ranging from the liberal to the reactionary, he favors a representative voice so long as the franchise is restricted to those who are independent and self-sufficient, thereby excluding most individuals, including all women. The aim of just political schemes is individual freedom, but to attain freedom persons must be subject to a master who forces them to be free. Under Kant's theory of history, that master is the general will.

Hegel. Georg Wilhelm Friedrich Hegel (1770-1831) was a German follower of Kant's idealist philosophy. He devised a comprehensive system that places all philosophical questions into an historical context.[24] In his world filled with dynamic concepts, reality is seen as a dialectic process which unfolds over time. Reality (the Absolute) is "mind" or "spirit." Hegel perceives contradiction to be inherent in the nature of things. The contradiction, whereby each thesis regarding ultimate questions generates a contradictory antithesis, reflects philosophical truth. The contradiction is an imperfect expression of a higher proposition, a "synthesis," which captures the genuine essence of both the thesis and the antithesis. The synthesis, in turn, becomes a thesis that generates its own antithesis which again yields a new synthesis at a higher stage. The process continues endlessly so that each point in history has its own truths. While objective, the "Absolute," the only concrete reality, is an unknowable ideal.

Hegel's political philosophy plays out this dialectic. From the individual to the three collectivities always imperfectly manifested in history

---

[24] While Hegel's main political work is THE PHILOSOPHY OF RIGHT (1821), his LECTURES ON THE PHILOSOPHY OF HISTORY (1837) is also relevant and accessible (for Hegel, that is).

(the family, "civil society," and the state), the "Absolute" unfolds through the dialectic to higher stages. Freedom, as Hegel conceives it, is the capacity to realize one's self. The person understands that, as a product of her cultural and social environment, she is part of an evolving community. She becomes free, realizes her self, when she identifies herself with the duties and responsibilities of a member of the state, the highest form of the social institutions. As far as the type of state, Hegel is no democrat. He is said by some to have been an apologist for the Prussian monarchy who rejects representative democracy because it recognizes citizens as autonomous individuals, and not as participant members in harmony with the collective.

Marx. Karl Marx (1818-1883), another German, was a philosophical radical not content with understanding the flow of history.[25] Instead, he wants to revolutionize its substance: "The philosophers have only *interpreted* the world, in various ways; the point is to *change* it." This is to be accomplished by producing a new kind of person with a new way of life. Marx, and his German collaborator Friedrich Engels (1820-1895), are severe critics, but followers, of Hegel. Marx was an important social scientist who objects to the theoretical speculations of Hegel that are barely attentive to social fact. Dialectics is not a law of thought, but is to be interpreted "materialistically" and used scientifically to understand the factual workings of historical evolution. Marx employs Hegel's dialectic against Hegel's analyses and finds some of his pivotal conclusions deficient. Although Hegel is correct in assigning civil society an essential economic role with, as now comprised, police powers, he wrongfully equates civil society with the existing capitalistic, bourgeois society. Civil society is not just guided by impartial authorities, as Hegel assumes, but rather is driven by individuals with economic power and interests. The economically dominant exclude others from political power who might challenge their interests. This creates class divisions. The state became necessary, then, not because it is intrinsic to social life, as Hegel would have it, but as an instrument of the dominant class, the bourgeoisie, the class that controls the instruments of production, to oppress the other class, the proletariat, the class that must work for the bourgeoisie at subsistence wages.

If the division between the classes would dissolve, the state would vanish for lack of oppressors. Only civil society would remain. This will occur in the following way. The development of the capitalistic state will

---

[25] Of the many political tracts written by Marx, the one best known is DAS KAPITAL (1867).

reach the stage where it is feasible and necessary for it to end. The contradictions inherent in a capitalistic society, including the growing antagonisms between the bourgeoisie and the proletariat, will, with dialectic inevitability, induce the proletariat to rise up in revolution and seize the means of production from the bourgeoisie, thereby eliminating class distinctions and the oppressive role of the state. Remaining to the classless state will simply be administrative functions. The principle of distributive justice in this regime, aiming for the happiness of the individual, is: "to each according to need, from each according to ability." Obviously history has not unfolded as Marx declared it would. However, this development has kept Marxian theorists occupied.

Nietzsche. The final German discussed, Friedrich Nietzsche (1844-1900), fomented the third wave of modern political philosophy which brought existentialism in its wake.[26] To Rousseau, nature and civil society are in opposition, but the sentiment of existence is to commune with nature, thereby situating the human condition in nature rather than in society and reason. Nietzsche agrees with Rousseau that there is such an opposition, but he declares the sentiment of existence to be terror and anguish, rather than peace and harmony. There is an historic consciousness, as asserted by the German idealists, but its sentiment is one of tragedy. The historic process is neither rational nor able to avoid the conflict between the genuine individual and the modern state. No one escapes the alienated, solitary unhappiness which is basic to the human condition.

Fundamental to Nietzsche's philosophy is his notion of the "will to power," a basic drive of all creatures. Power is the only thing desired for its own sake. The historically great individuals are the creators who, free of the resentment of others and overcoming the terror of life, steadfastly follow a law unto themselves and stretch the horizon with their creations. The existing path of history is at an end. Not as a product of Marxian necessity, but as a matter of free will, the towering individual (the "overman" or, though this translated label has taken on misleading negative connotations, the "superman") will prevail as humanity becomes the master of its own fate. Or, possibly, society will degenerate into a mindless, contented herd. Finally, under his doctrine of the eternal recurrence, the same events repeat themselves endlessly. One must exert and overcome oneself to give meaning to one's life and make the best of it, for it is to be relived

---

[26] A good taste of Nietzsche, a wonderful stylist, can be savored in THUS SPOKE ZARATHUSTRA (1885) or BEYOND GOOD AND EVIL (1886).

again and again. A defense of the fascistic state proceeds from a perversion of Nietzsche's vision.

The Twentieth Century. For much of the twentieth century, political philosophy languished in the Western world while related disciplines, such as political science (the study of the practice of politics) and sociology, flourished. In America, an important factor behind this drift is due to its general philosophical outlook, which is different from the European one.

Dewey. The divergence between the European intellectual traditions and the American perspective is evident from the writings of John Dewey (1859-1952), an American philosopher, educator, psychologist, and social critic.[27] He studied the European philosophers and ultimately found that they had little of use to teach him. As a youth, however, he was an avid Hegelian, convinced of the explanatory power of the emphasis on dynamic process. Before long he was put off by the abstract speculation of European idealism and began to articulate a philosophy that reflects the American interest in the practical. He subscribed to the philosophical movement called pragmatism, which also numbers Charles Pierce (1839-1914) and William James (1842-1910) among its American proponents. Two major threads tie together the political theory of pragmatism, though its espousers may occasionally break them. First, it is positivistic in that it accepts as valid knowledge, which philosophy should restrict itself to, only facts obtained empirically by the scientific method. This led to the ascendancy of political science, sociology, social psychology, and related empirically-grounded disciplines. American Legal Realism (*see* Chapter Six on jurisprudential movements) sprang from this orientation. Second, the underlying normative values of pragmatism are rooted in utilitarianism. Dewey, though never entirely spurning Hegelianism or the theoretical, champions a humanistic instrumentalism that aims at directing reason towards the actual consequences of proposed solutions to social problems, success being measured by the satisfactions produced. Good results count. Improvement in the human condition occurs step by step through the implementation, testing, and modification of practical measures, not by grandiose proposals or panaceas. Perhaps best known for his philosophy of education, he sees the school as the place where citizens can be morally and intellectually

---

[27] Dewey was a prolific writer, his bibliography extending beyond 150 pages. Because education is central to his philosophy, either DEMOCRACY AND EDUCATION (1916) or HUMAN NATURE AND CONDUCT (1922), which address the role of education in informing behavior, might be read as a good introduction to this thinking.

prepared and encouraged to openly address the evolving, dynamic developments and inevitable conflicts within modern democratic society.

Rawls. Just as some had rung the death knell for Anglo-American political philosophy, it leaped to life in resounding fashion with the publication by John Rawls, an American, of A THEORY OF JUSTICE in 1971. Rawls is a leader in the rebellion against the dominating influence of utilitarianism, which the pragmatists, Millians, and others had effectively promoted. That most normative philosophers today, like Rawls, are essentially Kantians, shows the success of the rebellion. Rawls presents his Kantian theory in a form more congenial to the Anglo-American mentality and traditions. He avoids the obscurities of Kant's "transcendental idealism" by relying on the "canons of a reasonable empiricism." The Kantian concerns for equality and personal autonomy can be satisfied, Rawls posits, by a hypothetical social contract in which all persons decide, as free and rational beings from an initial position of equality, "the principles which are to assign basic rights and duties and to determine the division of social benefits." With respect to Kantian and utilitarian morality (*see* Chapter One on ethics), notice the potential power of a social contract when it is actual, not hypothetical. The consent of each individual meets the Kantian concerns for autonomy and equality. Also, if the actual agreement advances pure utilitarianism as the basic principle, then it fully satisfies both Kantian and utilitarian mandates.

But Rawls, considering a hypothetical social contract rather than an actual one, insists that an utilitarian agreement would not be rational for all individuals. Being subject to demands for the sake of the overall social good, "[i]n a public utilitarian society men will find it more difficult to be confident of their own worth." Instead, in the "original position," in which the hypothetical social contract is framed, and behind the "veil of ignorance," which denies the contractors the knowledge of their particular circumstances, Rawls writes that two basic principles of justice would be chosen: first, a principle requiring an equal right to liberty; and second (the "difference principle"), a principle allowing social and economic inequalities only when they benefit the least advantaged individual and stem from opportunities that are fairly open to all. For example, the standard market economy is justifiable, even though it generates disparities in wealth, because it is open and benefits even the worst off more than would strict equality. Rawls, like most other modern Kantian liberals and utilitarians such as Mill, argues that the state, as much as possible, is to remain neutral with respect to declaring and establishing the precepts of the good life.

Nozick. Another American, Robert Nozick, responds to Rawls by striking out in a substantially different direction more akin to Locke. Nozick attacks the egalitarian thrust of Rawls' difference principle.[28] It is unjust because it requires, among other things, forms of redistributive taxation in support of an economic minimum and fails to take seriously the natural rights to one's body and to the product of the labor of one's body. For Nozick, principles of justice apply only to how goods are acquired, not to how they end up being distributed. Under the famous "Wilt Chamberlain hypothetical," injustice does not occur if Wilt is allowed to keep the proceeds from those who voluntarily pay to see him play basketball. If Wilt gets rich while others remain poor, that is no concern of the state. Rawls, on the other hand, insists that one deserves neither one's native endowments, initial starting place in society, nor even one's character, and therefore, to provide everyone with a fair opportunity, the state may make claims against the fruits of these attributes if they are assets, or may compensate for them if they are liabilities. Nozick argues for an entitlement theory of justice, according to which each person has natural property rights in her labor, body, and sentiments, and retains such rights except as one may voluntarily transfer these rights to another by contract, gift or bequest. Any coercive interference with such rights is immoral, including taxation ("on a par with forced labor") for any reason other than very restricted common purposes. In this libertarian scheme, the only justifiably organized government is a minimal state, "limited to the narrow functions of protection against force, theft, fraud, enforcement of contracts, and so on."

Political philosophy has again become a respectable discipline for deep thinkers. There are many who have recently produced important, thoughtful tracts on general political arrangements and on specific issues. The limits of this discussion prevent further examination. We may, in fact, be experiencing a golden age. But that question is for our descendants to ponder.

Contemporary Political Attitudes.

In the political arena, a person's political attitude may be characterized with a glib label. A person may wear such a label proudly, or may use it as a means to dismiss others. For example, during his 1988 presidential campaign, George Bush, quick to hold himself out as a "conservative," turned the term "liberal" into a pejorative epithet by

---

[28] Nozick's distinguished political work is ANARCHY, STATE, AND UTOPIA (1974).

refusing to utter "the 'L'-word." A close look at the meanings behind the labels reveals that, while they do have some use, each one may also represent a wide range of views that fit together uncomfortably. The meanings also have changed over time, and may differ from place to place. For example, a "liberal" party in Europe (*e.g.*, France) would be labeled as conservative or libertarian in America. The following discussion elaborates on four terms common in political discourse: libertarian, conservative, liberal, and communitarian. The roughly unifying feature in this panoply of political viewpoints is the attitude towards the role of government. As one moves from libertarian to communitarian, one generally finds more tolerance of increased governmental functions. But this rule of thumb must be applied cautiously. The discussion relies on generalities that some subscribers reject. Politics leads to curious alliances.

Libertarian. As implied by the label, libertarians stress the claims to personal freedom or liberty. They sometimes call themselves the "true liberals." They usually agree with Locke that individuals in the state of nature, that is, in a condition in which no state exists, are totally free and equal. Each has the natural right to life, liberty and property. Libertarians usually also are Kantians and urge respect for another individual's autonomy. Treat all persons as ends in themselves, and not as a means only to another's end. The Kantian vein leads libertarians to abhor the utilitarian claim that individuals may be used for the greater good of society.

A key question for libertarians is the justification of the state. They usually are skeptical of hypothetical social contracts that "rational" individuals would agree to, especially since these contracts are found by many commentators to demand much from the individual citizen. As for what can be demanded by the state, some libertarians would go so far as to say "nothing." These libertarians are anarchists, believing that no state that is forced on individuals, by means of a hypothetical social contract or otherwise, is legitimate. If a person does not actually consent to the state, it is unacceptable. These anarchists do not believe that interpersonal chaos would reign in this stateless society, but rather that people would be forced to get together and actually agree to form a government of sorts, perhaps by means of private protective associations. Moving away from this extreme wing of libertarianism, one finds those who would grant to a nonconsensual state the legitimate function of national defense only. A further step is exemplified by Nozick's minimal, "nightwatchman" state which, as quoted above, is "limited to the narrow functions of protection against force, theft, fraud, enforcement of contracts, and so on."

The centrality of liberty relates to the libertarian perception of responsibility and merit. Individuals are responsible for their actions. As self-made persons, they must accept the consequences, and reap the rewards, of their actions. The enforceability of contracts, for example, should not be undermined by the doctrine of unconscionability which, by not holding persons to all their contract terms, diminishes the idea of personal responsibility and autonomy. The libertarian attitude toward distributive or corrective justice is shaped by the individualistic conception of merit or desert.

As discussed in the chapter on ethics, there are many conceptions of desert, including virtue (merit), effort (labor), contribution to society, agreement with others, "the same thing" (equality), need(s), rank, and society's rules (legal entitlement). These conceptions are either liberty-oriented, such as virtue, effort, contribution to society, and agreement with others, or they are equality-oriented, such as "the same thing," need, rank and society's rules. The liberty-oriented ones posit that desert relates to actions, while equality-oriented ones seek parity within status classifications. Although most modern theories of distributive justice struggle with the conflict between the goals of liberty and equality, while pluralistically adopting more than one of these conceptions of desert, libertarians strongly or exclusively favor the liberty-oriented ones. For example, libertarians typically endorse Locke's opinion that a person owns that with which she "mixes" her labor. This articulates the effort or labor, liberty-oriented conception of what one deserves.

Conservative. There are substantial differences among those who hold themselves out as conservatives. Some common threads can be identified. Conservatives tend to be liberty-oriented, and hence anti-egalitarian, and advance an ordered, hierarchical view of society strongly supportive of private property rights. Though most generally favor a limited government, some conservatives would allow the government an expansive role. To better identify several of the varying themes under the umbrella of conservatism, the discussion is subdivided with labels that refer to differing guiding lights: Locke, Adam Smith, and Burke.

Lockean Conservatives. As among libertarians, Lockean conservatives underscore the importance of individual liberty. In practice, libertarianism and Lockean conservatism blur together at their common border. As one expands the proper reach of the government beyond the libertarian nightwatchman state, one merges into conservatism. While neither libertarian nor Lockean is generous in the space allowed the government, the libertarians paint the government into a smaller corner.

For the sake of liberty, Lockean conservatives are wary of the state because of their readings of the lessons of history. The employment of government intervention makes the government more powerful, thereby threatening individual liberty. Power corrupts. Agents of a powerful institution seek self-aggrandizement by enlarging their sphere of influence. When discretion is granted to an institution, history demonstrates that it will be abused. At the very least, the exercise of discretion suffers from the fallibilities of the decisionmakers. In sum, it is necessary to keep the government narrowly circumscribed and without discretion in order to prevent it from invading personal liberty.

Finally, Lockean conservatives, along with libertarians, tend to ascribe to the government a very restricted role regarding the legal enforcement of private morality. As previously noted, the debate whether morality, as manifested in the natural law, is supreme over positive law goes back to the classical age. Locke himself espoused a natural law discoverable through reason. But the question here is whether the government should detail the principles of private morality, irrespective of whether they are derived from a natural law, and implement them through legal enactment. A newsworthy example of this question is the issue of prohibiting certain private sexual acts between consenting adults. Lockean conservatives (though perhaps not Locke himself in this instance), would keep the sphere of individual liberty as large as possible, and therefore would tell the government to back off. The most famous defense of this position comes from the utilitarian, J.S. Mill, in the form of his "harm principle" which is discussed above in the section about him. Since private sexual conduct is not harmful to others, it should not be legally proscribed even if it is harmful to the consenters. Liberty must prevail.

Smithian Conservatives. These economically-oriented conservatives generally place the goal of efficiency before that of liberty. Like Adam Smith,[29] they believe that the invisible hand works quite effectively (*see* Chapter Two on economics). There is a limited role for the government under Smith's theory, because intervention is seldom necessary to improve efficiency. Yet certain governmental rules can improve it. Prime examples are the default rules for contracts. For the typical agreement, it is costly for the parties to expend the effort to detail the contractual effects of all possible contingencies, however remote (*e.g.*, What are the contractual rights and duties if the World Trade Center next door is

---

[29] Smith's economic tract, THE WEALTH OF NATIONS (1776), must certainly have been what made it's year of publication noteworthy.

bombed?).   Unless the contract is quite large, the costs of the details outweigh the benefits.   For this reason, the government, by furnishing proper rules to govern situations for which contracts do not provide, will increase efficiency by lowering the transaction costs of contracting. Proper rules are those that rational parties would adopt in normal circumstances. But the efficiency may be lost if the rules are not settled, clearly delineated, easily applied, or subject to modification by the parties.

Under the invisible hand, desired social goods will be produced as much as is possible and will end up in the right hands. Intervention often pours sand in the frictionless workings of the market. It can distort the market by dictating an advantage favoring the satisfaction of the preferences of government officials over the preferences of the market players. There are two main objections to this result. First, the distortion will impinge on the freedom of some persons to obtain what they desire through private contract. Second, the reduction in efficiency, by running up costs, will decrease the overall satisfaction of the preferences of the people. The first objection is liberty-oriented, with groundings in Locke and Kant. The second objection is utilitarian.

Some economists claim that economics is simply applied utilitarianism. It seems that when the market is defended in utilitarian terms, there is a greater willingness of the defender to allow government intervention when there is a perceived market failure. Markets fail when the presuppositions of the invisible hand do not hold under the circumstances, for example, with respect to the production of public goods, such as highways or information, which will be underproduced by the private market alone.   Actually, the invisible hand never works perfectly because its assumptions are too unrealistic for the actual world. For instance, people never have perfect information regarding a contemplated transaction and information costs are never zero. Nevertheless, a liberty-oriented Smithian who confronts this reality may still keep the government at bay since the interactors are formally free to do as they wish in the unregulated market, even if they might not know fully what they are getting into. The utilitarian Smithian, on the other hand, is more willing to do a cost-benefit analysis to see whether government intervention is worthwhile. The more (Lockean or, perhaps, Burkean) conservative the analyst, the more she tends to weigh the speculative costs of intervention heavily and the speculative benefits lightly. Based on a cost-benefit analysis of prior or existing intervention, these conservatives often favor reduced regulation or deregulation (*e.g.*, the airlines and trucking industry) and the privatization of many functions that have accrued to the modern state (*e.g.*, mail service and garbage collection). While Smithian and Lockean conservatives are extremely wary of public functions that redistribute wealth, they typically do not reject them all as seen, for example, in the "safety net" of welfare granted by the Reagan and Bush administrations. Adam Smith also favored welfare. The end result of the disposition to minimize government functions should be obvious: taxes are to be kept low.

Burkean Conservatives. Libertarians, Lockeans and Smithians have much in common. They have been distinguished by how much weight they give to their particular concerns and, except for some Smithians who may be less interested in liberty per se, how they would justify them. But in the political arena, they usually come down on the same side of the controversial issues. This is not the case when it comes to Burkeans. They are a breed apart. The term "conservative" applies to them in the sense that it derives from the root "conserve," meaning, to protect from loss or change, preserve.

The term "Burkean" alludes to the major theme of Burke's political philosophy as seen in the discussion above. Burke was a traditionalist. He sympathizes with the complaints from the American colonies because the British were curtailing their traditional rights and liberties. The social contract, as he sees it, obligates citizens to their ancestors, fellow citizens, and unborn descendants. There is inherited wisdom and value in the existing society that is worth preserving. Though the status quo is not flawless, the unpredictability of designed transformation often leads to worse consequences. Social change, if at all, is to proceed by incremental evolution.

Western social traditions reflect two diverse values: individualism as well as family or community. On the one hand, the rights of the individual are elevated. On the other hand, the responsibilities to the family and community are sanctified. Lockean conservatives give greater weight to the liberty interests grounding individualism. Burkean conservatives prefer family and community. This divergence manifests itself in the law and morality issues. The Burkean, for example, favors the regulation of moral standards by government decree. In particular, some private sexual conduct between consenting adults, such as prostitution, is intolerable when it disrupts family cohesion or runs contrary to the traditions and needs of the community. To allow society's sexual standards to change is to change society. Dramatic transmutations, which bypass the careful testing in the crucible of time, are unmanageable and abridge the social contract. The individual rights worthy of protection are only those that the community traditionally found acceptable.

In sum, the label "conservative" covers a broad range of political beliefs, some of which are incompatible and even quite opposed. That a single political party can retain the loyalty of the diverse groups of conservatives is a masterful feat of political tactics. Indeed, politics makes for strange bedfellows.

Liberal. The term "liberal," because of its linkage to the idea of liberty which is of prime concern to libertarians and Lockean conservatives, has been used to describe a broad range of political philosophies. To distinguish the right wing meanings from the left wing ones, the current use of "liberal" in America is often clarified by the label "welfare state liberal." This title cuts to the heart of the main unifying feature of this liberalism: it advocates a meaningful amount of welfare for those in need, significantly above the safety net of conservatism.

Liberalism, as exemplified in the writings of Rawls, rejects the strong libertarian notion of individual responsibility and merit. Persons are not entirely self-made, but rather owe much to nature and nurture. An advantageous genetic endowment is a gift of the fates, not an earned reward. Similarly, an individual does not deserve her initial station in life and the social and educational advantages it facilitates or thwarts. Nor does an individual even deserve the privilege or impoverishment that her caregivers provide as a result of their merit or demerit. These formative influences are morally neutral -- matters of moral luck. In light of this, society should be temperate toward a person's weaknesses (*e.g.*, expansive with the contract doctrine of unconscionability), and skeptical of a person's claim to her acquired wealth (*e.g.*, open to substantial or progressive taxation).

Under this reasoning, the primary principles of distributive justice adopted by Lockeans must be rejected. While there is room for liberty-oriented principles of desert, they must be based on the actual desert of the individual, as in the principle advancing virtue or excellence, and not on moral luck. Insofar as a person excels at elevating herself, pulling herself up by her own bootstraps from whatever level her initial endowments placed her, she is truly deserving. But the liberty-oriented principle of labor, for example, may not reflect a person's true merit, as where a hard-working, millionaire businessperson born with a silver spoon pays minimum wages to an equally hard-working household servant born with a plastic fork. Even when the invisible hand is efficient, it often is not fair. For example, the producer of product A may be as meritorious as the prosperous producer of product B, but go bankrupt simply because an unforeseeable breakthrough made product A obsolete, again this being a matter of moral luck.

As far as efficiency in the marketplace, the economic liberal is more disposed than the Smithian to intervene to correct perceived market failures and advance social goals. Furthermore, society must concern itself collectively with the distributive effects of the market as well as the allocative ones Smithians attend to. Redistribution is a legitimate governmental function. Some of the equality-oriented principles of distributive justice better respond to the vagaries of moral luck than do the liberty-oriented ones. For example, individuals should be entitled to government grants according to need or assured social equality ("the same thing").

This latter principle, equality, leads to the divergence between liberals and conservatives in questions of the proper reach of civil rights, among other issues. Libertarians and Lockeans are also concerned with civil rights, but they generally restrict them to negative civil rights against governmental organizations. They would agree, for example, that a school district should not discriminate on the basis of race. Liberals, to advance equality, are willing to institute positive civil rights against private groups as well, for example, to require a private employer to implement an affirmative action program. Mill's harm principle is one liberty standard on which liberals and Lockeans usually agree. When it comes to private conduct that has only self-regarding consequences, the state is to keep away. In general, the government is not to impose on its citizens any particular conception of what is good for them. To put this in current parlance, the liberal state is to remain neutral with respect to the Good.

Communitarian. Communitarians challenge the view that the state is to remain neutral with respect to the Good. First, neutrality is itself a value and thus implicates a value choice at square one. Second, communitarians take a step beyond the liberal critique of the notions of individual responsibility and merit. They see the individual as even further from totally autonomous, instead, as embedded in, and defined by, the community. A person is a product of her molding environment. Consequently, the justification of political organizations must acknowledge common aims (the Good). A person's very conception of herself must also refer to this relationship to the community, as a member of a group of people engaged in a common enterprise. Social value inheres in this community. Because it has a formative influence and is an object of personal identification, the community has legitimate claims against the individual.

There are overtones in communitarianism of classical republicanism and Burkean traditionalism. But communitarianism, like the other political labels, is an umbrella term that covers a wide range of beliefs. For example, republicanism and, to a lesser extent, traditionalism usually conceive of the central community, *i.e.*, the state, as the object of their principles. Yet as discussed in the chapter on ethics, communitarians may recognize attachments and responsibilities of varying degree to many communities, such as to the family, church, club, neighborhood, city, and hemisphere. Socialism and communism, and even possibly totalitarianism, are communitarian. So communitarians may be revolutionary radicals or stifling conservatives. Modern communitarian theorists are struggling to articulate their vision and agenda because of this broad range of political structures consistent with the basic tenets. Liberal communitarians, for example, reject the Burkean resistance to the formation of new, threatening groups, such as the gay and lesbian communities. While maintaining the Burkean position that tradition has value, they still tolerantly celebrate the emergence of new communities. Some favor strong constitutional rights to protect a sphere of individualism from an overreaching community. On the other hand, the communitarian arguments of some feminists against pornography because of its apparently harmful effects on women as a group are inconsistent with the current position of liberals on free speech. Communitarianism in its present incarnation is an emerging political school of diverse departments. Its impetus stems from the perceived moral decay of the modern age which is ascribed to the deficiencies of individualism and the inadequacies of the historical models of communitarian systems.

By way of summary, it must be reemphasized that the strains identified within the various political labels certainly do not make for unified political identities or parties. For example, persons or political parties may be conservative regarding economics, liberal regarding civil rights, and communitarian regarding pornography. As for whether these positions are compatible in principle -- well, no matter, consistency has never been a strong suit of the political animal.

REFERENCES FOR FURTHER READING

BRUCE ACKERMAN, SOCIAL JUSTICE IN THE LIBERAL STATE (1980).
HANNAH ARENDT, THE HUMAN CONDITION (1958).
SHLOMO AVINERI, HEGEL'S THEORY OF THE MODERN STATE (1972).
ALAN BLOOM, THE REPUBLIC OF PLATO (1968).
LAWRENCE BECKER, PROPERTY RIGHTS (1977).
ISAIAH BERLIN, FOUR ESSAYS ON LIBERTY (1969).
WILLIAM CONNOLLY, THE TERMS OF POLITICAL DISCOURSE (2d ed. 1983).
ROBERT DAHL, A PREFACE TO DEMOCRATIC THEORY (1956); DILEMMAS OF A PLURALIST DEMOCRACY (1982).

ANTHONY DOWNS, AN ECONOMIC THEORY OF DEMOCRACY (1957).

JON ELSTER, ULYSSES AND THE SIRENS (rev. ed. 1984); POLITICAL PSYCHOLOGY (1993).

JOEL FEINBERG, SOCIAL PHILOSOPHY (1973).

W. FRIEDMANN, LEGAL THEORY (5th ed. 1967).

DAVID GAUTHIER, MORALS BY AGREEMENT (1986).

FRIEDRICH HAYEK, THE CONSTITUTION OF LIBERTY (1960); THE ROAD TO SERFDOM (1943).

J.M. KELLY, A SHORT HISTORY OF WESTERN LEGAL THEORY (1992).

J.R. LUCAS, THE PRINCIPLES OF POLITICS (1966).

ALASDAIR MACINTYRE, AFTER VIRTUE (2d ed. 1984); WHOSE JUSTICE? WHICH RATIONALITY? (1988).

ROBERT NOZICK, ANARCHY, STATE AND UTOPIA (1974).

MICHAEL OAKESHOTT, ON HUMAN CONDUCT (1975).

SUSAN MOLLER OKIN, WOMEN IN WESTERN POLITICAL THOUGHT (1979).

MANCUR OLSON, THE LOGIC OF COLLECTIVE ACTION (2d ed. 1971).

J. ROLAND PENNOCK, DEMOCRATIC POLITICAL THEORY (1979).

J.G.A. POCOCK, THE MACHIAVELLIAN MOMENT (1975); THE ANCIENT CONSTITUTION AND THE FEUDAL LAW (1957).

KARL POPPER, THE OPEN SOCIETY AND ITS ENEMIES (4th ed. 1962).

JOHN RAWLS, A THEORY OF JUSTICE (1971); POLITICAL LIBERALISM (1993).

BERTRAND RUSSELL, A HISTORY OF WESTERN PHILOSOPHY (1945).

GEORGE SABINE & THOMAS THORSON, A HISTORY OF POLITICAL THEORY (4th ed. 1973).

MICHAEL SANDEL, LIBERALISM AND THE LIMITS OF JUSTICE (1984).

AMARTYA SEN, COLLECTIVE CHOICE AND SOCIAL WELFARE (1970).

A. JOHN SIMMONS, MORAL PRINCIPLES AND POLITICAL OBLIGATIONS (1979).

QUENTIN SKINNER, THE FOUNDATIONS OF MODERN POLITICAL THOUGHT (1978).

LEO STRAUSS, AN INTRODUCTION TO POLITICAL PHILOSOPHY (1989); HISTORY OF POLITICAL PHILOSOPHY (3d ed. 1987) (with Joseph Cropsey).

MICHAEL WALZER, SPHERES OF JUSTICE (1983).

MAX WEBER, THE PROTESTANT ETHIC AND THE SPIRIT OF CAPITALISM (1958).

ROBERT PAUL WOLFF, THE POVERTY OF LIBERALISM (1968).

CHAPTER FOUR

AMERICAN GOVERNMENTAL STRUCTURE: ITS IMPACT ON LAW

Politics and government have pervasive influences on modern life. Law is no exception. Chapter Three discussed the influence of political theory on law. As used in Chapter Three, we discussed politics in the broad sense: theories of interpersonal relations; the relation of persons to government; the distribution of power in society. In this chapter, we use the term politics in the narrow sense of referring to particular political arrangements or institutions used in operating a government. Specifically, we examine United States political norms, governmental structure, and political/governmental institutions that exert a strong pull on American legal theory, doctrine, and outcomes.

The United States was born in a burst of politics. In addition to the obviously military aspects of the American Revolution, the process of breaking away from England was spurred by political theory regarding governance and also eventually by well-conceived governmental institutions. The Founders did not wish to eradicate all traces of British influence. Quite the contrary -- the United States retained many aspects of the British legal system: powerful judges; the jury system; the adversarial system; and the common law (all discussed at greater length in Chapter Five). But much of the object of the Revolution was to be not only separate from Great Britain but also different. To that end, the Framers established a governmental

structure with distinct aspects that exerted influence on America's
subsequently developing legal establishment.[30]

A Sketch of the Constitutional Structure.

The famous American model of government institutions did not
develop overnight. The former colonies were initially resistant to the
establishment of any strong, central government, fearing that it might
possess the same disregard of local interests and rights they had seen from
the Crown. Consequently, the first step toward modern America was the
Articles of Confederation, a pact between the states proposed by the
Continental Congress in 1777, but not ratified until 1781. The Confederation was, of course, replaced by the Constitution (drafted in 1787), which
became effective in 1789.[31]

Despite its short tenure, the seldom-read Articles provide an
interesting window into the evolving views of the founders. Under the
Articles, there was national governance of sorts, but without the broad
powers found in the current Constitution. There was no national judiciary
and no real national executive, only a skeletal version of national government. For example, the national government could not directly levy taxes
or regulate commerce. Under the Articles, a Congress composed of state-
selected delegates met briefly each year and a congressionally selected
"Committee of the States" could exercise some quasi-executive national
power when Congress was not in session.

Although the Articles provided the national government with certain
enumerated powers similar to those provided today under the Constitution's
"necessary and proper" clause, which permits the federal government to
engage in activities essential to its function, any action by the pre-
Constitutional national government of the Confederation required a supermajority of nine of the thirteen states. As a result, the national government
was effectively disabled from taking action on most controversial issues.
Nonetheless, the Articles were an important advance in interstate coopera-

---

[30] *See generally* GORDON WOOD, THE RADICALISM OF THE AMERICAN REVOLUTION
(1992).

[31] For more extensive background on the establishment of the national
government, see GORDON WOOD, THE CREATION OF THE AMERICAN REPUBLIC 1776-
1787 (1976); BERNARD BAILYN, IDEOLOGICAL ORIGINS OF THE AMERICAN REVOLUTION
(1967).

tion and included, sometimes in clearer language, many of the individual rights and ground rules of government found in the Constitution: common defense against invaders paid for from a common national treasury with levies based on the respective states' property values; full faith and credit between states for the laws and judgments of one another; a right to travel between states; nondiscrimination against interstate commerce; immunity of the federal government from state taxation; cooperation in extradition; and a requirement that interstate agreements or "compacts" be approved by Congress. Within a decade, however, American leaders concluded that the unifying themes of the Articles were inadequate without an established federal government to administer the new nation.

While the Articles were in force, states themselves were developing political structures that in some ways presaged the later federal structure. The legislature was supreme and it was authorized to pass statutes and take action in response to perceived social needs, perhaps too much action. Although the notion of legislative supremacy in governance was established in England's "Glorious Revolution" of 1689 (which also ushered in, along with the famed Monarchs William and Mary, the modern notion of stable government as an aid to economic development), the state legislatures occasionally flexed their muscles in ways that would have made even Oliver Cromwell blush. For example, legislatures during the colonial and Articles of Confederation period frequently exercised powers of eminent domain to seize private lands for public uses, such as building bridges or roads, often with little or no compensation to the owners. Backlash against such episodes brought about the Takings Clause of the current Fifth Amendment, which provides that the federal government may not seize private property without paying the owner just compensation. This same restraint now applies to state governments through the Due Process Clause of the Fourteenth Amendment. State executive branches also developed during the Confederation period. Governors were elected and reasonably powerful, but subject to de jure and de facto political constraints. On the legal front, state courts and the local bars began to develop an American style of jurisprudence separate from the system initially imported from Britain.

Increasing desire to cure the shortcomings of the Articles led to the Constitutional Convention of 1787. The resulting Constitution differed from the Articles primarily by its establishment of a permanent national government with reasonably broad powers to raise revenue, wage war, and legislate regarding interstate and foreign commerce. It also established a Supreme Court for "refereeing" disputes between the national legislature, the executive, and the states.[32]   Although the Constitution continued to provide healthy "breathing space" for the state prerogatives that had spurred the Confederation, the new federal order provided the national government with substantial powers to override inconsistent state law, regulation, or custom.

Organizationally, the Constitution has three primary sections: Article I (the Legislative Article); Article II (the Executive Article) and Article III (the Judicial Article).   These Articles in turn establish the three branches of American government.   For example, Article I sets forth the organization and selection of the House of Representatives and the Senate and enumerates a long list of express congressional powers, such as the power to tax, declare war, and pass legislation in aid of interstate commerce.   Article II establishes the Presidency and outlines a number of the functions of the office (*e.g.*, select a cabinet, nominate ambassadors and judges, and grant pardons).

Article III, the portion of the Constitution that usually receives most attention in legal studies, establishes a Supreme Court and the federal judicial power to decide cases and controversies.   Note, however, that Article III does not establish federal trial courts or trial judges but merely permits Congress to do so.   The Judiciary Act of 1789 established federal districts and a district judge for each.   However, district courts had no general authority over questions of federal law until 1875, nearly a century after the Constitution took effect.   Other portions of the Constitution help to establish and secure the constitutional scheme of federalism, separation of powers, and checks and balances, which are discussed later in this chapter.   For example, Article IV promotes federalism (the shared power of the states with deference to the rights of the state most closely associated with a conflict) by providing that each state must give full faith and credit to the judgments rendered by courts in other states.

But even as the Constitution was ratified by the required number (three-fourths) of the thirteen states in 1789, the delegates and others acknowledged that it had shortcomings.   Most particularly, it was perceived as having recognized insufficient protection of individual rights from the strongly empowered central government.   By 1789, ten amendments to the

---

[32]   Under the Articles, disputes between the states were settled by a committee of congressional delegates in which the members of the congressional tribunal were chosen in a manner strikingly similar to the way in which disputants today select arbitrators under the Rules of the American Arbitration Association. *See generally* Chapter 5 regarding dispute resolution.

Constitution were drafted (collectively known as the Bill of Rights), with the requisite number of states ratifying them by 1791. These amendments establish most of the American freedoms so frequently debated by the public and invoked during political campaigns: freedom of speech, press, and religion (the First Amendment); right to bear arms (the Second Amendment); protection against unreasonable searches and seizures (the Fourth Amendment); the right to just compensation if the government takes private property (the Fifth Amendment); the right to due process of law before the government deprives one of life, liberty or property (the Fifth Amendment); the right to a fair criminal trial (the Sixth Amendment); the right to a jury for civil suits in federal court (the Seventh Amendment); and protection against cruel and unusual punishment (the Eighth Amendment).

The Ninth Amendment, which reserves rights to the people, and the Tenth Amendment, which reserves rights to the states, are regarded by most commentators as nice bits of political rhetoric but essentially legal dead letters. However, even these atrophied amendments occasionally have some bite. For example, the famous case of *Griswold v. Connecticut*,[33] which struck down a state law limiting use of contraceptives by married couples, did so in large part on the basis of the law's intrusion on a perceived constitutional right to privacy derived from the thrust of the First, Fourth, Fifth and oft-forgotten Ninth Amendments. Although controversial, *Griswold's* right to privacy has proven to be one of the more powerful constitutional developments. For example, it provided the main underpinning of the controversial decision in *Roe v. Wade*[34] limiting state rights to proscribe abortion. Although *Roe v. Wade* has been under attack since its inception, the notion of a constitutional right to privacy continues to enjoy wide public support. Distinguished former judge and law professor Robert Bork learned this when he disputed the existence of a constitutional right to privacy, this becoming what many regarded as the death knell of his unsuccessful nomination in 1987 to the Supreme Court.

Of the constitutional amendments enacted after 1791, by far the most important are those enacted in the wake of the Civil War. Many observers in fact view the Civil War and its aftermath as essentially a second American Revolution and a de facto second Constitutional Convention brought on by America's need to resolve the issues of union, rebellion,

---

[33] 381 U.S. 479 (1965).

[34] 410 U.S. 113 (1973).

slavery, and their continuing impact on the nation. The Thirteenth Amendment outlaws slavery and involuntary servitude. The Fourteenth Amendment extends the important protections of the Fifth Amendment to persons aggrieved by the actions of state government by providing that no state may deprive a person of life, liberty or property without due process of law. It also introduces the important concept of equal protection into American jurisprudence in stating that no state may deprive a person of the equal protection of the laws. The Fifteenth Amendment outlaws restrictions on voting rights based on race, color, "or previous condition of servitude."

In addition, these important post-Civil War amendments (all were enacted and ratified during the Reconstruction period from 1865 to 1870) provided Congress with power to enforce them through "appropriate legislation," a prerogative Congress exercised to enact the federal Civil Rights Acts (codified at 42 U.S.C. §§ 1981-1988). These statutes provide a number of private rights of action to persons injured by the discriminatory conduct of state governments, employers, and even other private citizens acting in concert. These laws, along with the anti-discrimination provisions of the Civil Rights Act of 1964 (which makes job discrimination illegal if based on race, gender, religion, or ethnicity) and the Voting Rights Act of 1965 (which requires nondiscriminatory election procedures in state and local government) provide the bulk of federal anti-discrimination law.[35]

To the extent that the Civil War, Reconstruction, and related events gave the United States a "Second Constitution," the new additions strengthened the individual rights aspects of the original constitutional scheme which, despite the Bill of Rights, was largely a Constitution of government organization, at least as applied by the courts. Even the new powers of the Civil War amendments saw limited application by the judiciary for many years. However, during the 20th century, particularly in the period from 1950-1980, the judiciary increasingly gave broader construction to the individual rights aspects of constitutional and statutory law. Since 1980, the federal judiciary has become increasingly resistant to this jurisprudence, but

---

[35] The 1964 Civil Rights Act was amended significantly, mainly to strengthen it, in 1972 and 1991. The 1991 Act was mainly a reaction to several 1989 Supreme Court decisions which Congress viewed as unduly narrowing the scope of both the 1964 Act and the Civil War era civil rights statutes.

Congress has often responded with new legislation specifically broadening the text of civil rights statutes.[36]

By noting the importance of the Bill of Rights and Civil War era amendments, we do not intend to denigrate the other amendments. Some are very far reaching. For example, the Eleventh Amendment provides that federal courts lack power to hear a suit against a state brought by a citizen of a different state. It has been broadly interpreted as constitutionalizing the doctrine of sovereign immunity (the sovereign can do no wrong, at least no wrong that can be righted by a lawsuit seeking damages in federal court).[37] In fact, the Eleventh Amendment can be characterized as an amendment born more of politics than sound legal policy. In *Chisholm v. Georgia*,[38] the Court permitted a nonresident to sue Georgia for overdue debts incurred during the Revolutionary War. Congress, understandably concerned that members' home states might have to pay the Revolutionary War debts they had largely ignored, quickly passed the Eleventh Amendment, relegating creditors to the more hostile arena of state courts. Despite its soiled pedigree, the Eleventh Amendment plays an important part in the federalism of the Constitution.

Other important amendments passed after the Civil War amendments:

• extend voting rights to women (the Nineteenth);

• extend the franchise to persons 18 or older (the Twenty-sixth);

• give the vote to District of Columbia residents in presidential elections (the Twenty-third, but the District still has no voting representatives in Congress); and

• permit the federal government to impose an income tax (the Sixteenth).

---

[36] *See* William N. Eskridge, Jr., *Overriding Supreme Court Statutory Interpretation Decisions*, 101 YALE L.J. 331 (1991); Jeffrey W. Stempel, *The Rehnquist Court, Statutory Interpretation, Inertial Burdens, and a Misleading Version of Democracy*, 22 U. TOL. L. REV. 721 (1991).

[37] *See* Hans v. Louisiana, 134 U.S. 1 (1890).

[38] 2 U.S. 418 (1793).

Although obviously important, many of these isolated or "ad hoc" amendments simply do not have as much impact (and certainly are not as widely litigated) as those in the Bill of Rights or the "Civil War package." Two are embarrassing: the Eighteenth Amendment instituted Prohibition (banning manufacture or sale of alcohol) while the Twenty-first repealed it.

Other amendments are essentially technical. For example, the Twenty-fifth amendment provides that the vice-president becomes chief executive should the president die in office. The Twelfth establishes the electoral college procedure for selecting a president. Even the Twenty-fourth amendment, which outlaws payment of a "poll tax" as a condition of voting, was arguably unnecessary since imposition of such taxes probably violated the Fourteenth Amendment, although courts were reluctant to so hold given the long history of the poll tax, which effectively made voting more difficult for poor people and racial minorities.

New constitutional amendments, however, whether momentous or technical, are few and far between, as one might expect of a system that requires a successful amendment to achieve a two-thirds vote of support from both the House and the Senate, signature by the President, and ratification by three-fourths of the states. In the modern era, two important amendment initiatives have been the Equal Rights Amendment ("ERA") and proposed statehood (or full congressional representation) for the District of Columbia. The ERA, which provided that law should not make distinctions based on gender, passed both houses of Congress but fell just short of the required thirty-eight states' ratification to become a constitutional amendment, even though Congress extended the time available for obtaining ratification. Full congressional representation for D.C. has been proposed for many years but has been resisted on partisan and racial grounds (some opponents fear that D.C., which is 75 percent nonwhite, would routinely elect African-American Democrats as Senators and Representatives). As a result, no amendment favoring the simple proposition of congressional representation for American citizens residing in the nation's capitol has ever been reported out of Congress.

Modern America was born via the Constitution, but in what ways did this birth shape ensuing legal development? The U.S. government structure results in major impact upon U.S. law because of the following aspects of the constitutional scheme:

   • Federalism (the division of authority between the federal government and the states);

• Separation of Powers (the division of spheres of authority among the executive, legislative, and judicial branches of government);

• Checks and Balances (the overlapping and mutual authority shared by two or more branches of government over the same subject matter); and

• Guarantees of Individual Rights, primarily those enumerated in the Bill of Rights and the Civil War amendments (*e.g.*, freedom of speech, religion, press; right to bear arms; protection against unreasonable searches and seizure; right to jury trial; equal protection of the laws; guarantee of due process of law).

Constitutional Concepts Impacting Law.

A number of important constitutional doctrines affect the law in ways beyond constitutional adjudication.

Federalism. The American Revolution began as perhaps the ultimate states' rights movement. The colonies chaffed under the yoke of the British Crown and wanted to escape. They were hardly in agreement, however, about what should happen if they won their freedom from England. When Benjamin Franklin admonished the bickering revolutionary leaders that they must all hang together (in the war effort) or hang separately (on the gallows), he not only correctly assessed the military situation but also reflected the internal disagreements among the colonies.[39] Not surprisingly, the newly independent but wary colonies chose an initial form of government (the Articles of Confederation) that gave each former colony as much autonomy as possible under the semblance of a national government. When the Confederation proved problematic, the new states were willing to compromise, but the desire for state autonomy remained. In the resulting constitutional scheme, states therefore retained substantial prerogatives except insofar as the new national government possessed express or strongly implied national powers.

---

[39] The colonies themselves where hardly uniform in political viewpoint. Each colony had substantial subpopulations of "tories," political conservatives who opposed the revolution against Britain. In some areas, such as Philadelphia and the planter South, tory sentiment was quite strong.

The judicial branch, in particular, generally requires some express textual constitutional authorization for the exercise of federal power over the states. But a sufficiently strong implicit case for federal power will occasionally carry the day.[40] The intervening 200 years have seen a substantial increase in the relative importance and power of the national government. Notwithstanding this, the states retain great powers. If anything, concern for states' rights may be at a higher level during the period of 1970-1990 than it was during the prior 40 years. During the earlier era, the concern over combating the Great Depression, the popularity of President Franklin Roosevelt and the New Deal, the confrontations of World War II and the Cold War, as well as the struggle for civil rights for minorities in the face of strong pockets of state opposition all led to greater solicitude for the federal government and perhaps more than a little distrust of state governments. After 1970, however, changes in the composition of the federal bench (more Republican appointees), the political climate (an upswing in conservatism), salient political issues (a sense of accomplishment in civil rights; adverse reaction to federally mandated affirmative action efforts; a strong anti-abortion movement), and perhaps the sense that the pendulum had swung too far in favor of federal power brought a renewed judicial solicitude for states' rights.

Whether it is at high tide or low ebb, the notion of formidable state autonomy and somewhat limited federal intrusion into areas of law traditionally dominated by the states is usually referred to under the rubric of "federalism," or (in the almost religiously reverential words of Justice Hugo Black) "Our Federalism."[41] In short, federalism means deference to states in many facets of the legal system and in adjudicating close questions of federal authority. Federalism has shaped many aspects of America's substantive and procedural law. For example, judicial power is divided into separate state and federal court systems that have essential autonomy over their respective spheres of authority.

Despite federalism, the systems abut against one another and overlap. For example, state courts provide the last word on the interpretation of state law subject to review by the Supreme Court for constitutional

---

[40] *See* Crandall v. Nevada, 73 U.S. 35 (1867) (finding American citizens enjoy an implicit but inherent right to travel between states); CHARLES BLACK, STRUCTURE AND RELATIONSHIP IN CONSTITUTIONAL LAW (1969) (approving *Crandall's* holding and reasoning).

[41] *See* Younger v. Harris, 401 U.S. 37 (1971) (federal courts generally lack power to enjoin ongoing state criminal proceedings).

questions.[42] However, federal courts have jurisdiction over many disputes simply because they involve parties who are citizens of different states even though their dispute invokes state substantive law rather than federal law. In these "diversity jurisdiction" cases, the federal courts must apply state law, but often find themselves without clear guidance from state court precedent in light of the novelty of the legal question. In effect, federal district courts are then "making" state law when they decide the case. Unless overruled by a subsequent decision of the highest state court or the state legislature, the federal court decisions will stand and tend to influence state court jurisprudence as well.

Technically, a federal court's interpretation of state law is not binding on the state courts, and state interpretations of federal law are similarly nonbinding on the federal courts. In reality, however, federal and state courts effectively share power over issues of state substantive law since the particular adjudications of each court system bind the parties to a lawsuit. The de facto split of authority continues to be an issue. There is substantial current debate over whether to eliminate diversity jurisdiction, which was established as a reaction to perceived local prejudice against nonresidents. In early America, as well, this issue was hotly debated. Federalists embraced the concept of diversity jurisdiction while anti-federalists thought it an unnecessary incursion upon state authority.

Consequences of Federalism. The very structure of the federal court system and its concepts of subject matter jurisdiction, personal jurisdiction, and venue reflect the underlying American notion of federalism:

• Subject matter jurisdiction is the authority of the court to decide a dispute. Federal courts may hear and decide disputes only where the plaintiff has raised a federal question or all plaintiffs and all defendants are citizens of different states and the amount in controversy exceeds $50,000.

• Personal jurisdiction is the authority of the court over a party. Objections in this regard are usually raised by the defendant, who is by definition an unwilling litigant. The plaintiff, by filing the suit, has consented to jurisdiction. Federal courts can exercise authority over a

---

[42] *See* Erie R.R. v. Tompkins, 304 U.S. 64 (1938) (federal court adjudicating a case on the basis of diversity jurisdiction must apply state law to decide the case rather than federal common law).

defendant only to the extent that the party has sufficient contact with the state in which the federal court is located.

• Venue is the place of trial, the state in which a federal lawsuit may be heard. The proper venue in federal courts is the state where all the defendants reside or a state that has a substantial connection to the litigation. If no other venue is available, a federal court may also hold trial if all defendants are subject to its personal jurisdiction.

Federal courts are organized along state lines. For example, there exists the U.S. District Court for the Southern District of New York rather than the District Court of the New York City Metropolitan Area (hypothetically encompassing New York City and its suburbs in New York, New Jersey, and Connecticut). Circuit Courts of Appeal also run along state boundary lines. For example, the Second Circuit reviews district court decisions in New York, Connecticut and Vermont. As late as 1800, Federalists proposed that federal judicial districts be drawn without strictly observing state boundaries, but these suggestions never came close to enactment. The issue continues to affect our thinking about judicial administration. For years, Congress has considered splitting the large Ninth Circuit (comprising the states of California, Oregon, Washington, Montana, Idaho, Nevada, and Arizona) into two separate courts but has hesitated largely because it is reluctant to "split ' California among two circuit courts.

Federalism thus cannot only mean state sovereignty in an area of state law but also that the national government can often "take over," provided that Congress acts with sufficient clarity. The most important areas of substantive law traditionally regulated by the states are torts, contracts, property, criminal law, family law, trusts and estates, and insurance. Unless Congress acts, disputes raising these concerns are ordinarily decided by state law, even if the dispute is tried in federal court. The presumption in favor of state sovereignty in these core areas is so strong that it is occasionally codified by statute. For example, the McCarran-Ferguson Act (15 U.S.C. § 1011 *et seq.*) provides that the insurance business is, absent certain limited exceptions, left to state regulation unless Congress intrudes in this area through legislation using the clearest of terminology.

A specific federal statute is not necessary to establish a "hands off" presumption regarding federal regulation of traditional areas of state law. For example, although federal courts could, by virtue of diversity jurisdiction, arguably take jurisdiction of more property, divorce, and estates disputes than they do, there have arisen a number of court-created doctrines causing federal courts to refrain from adjudicating certain of these disputes under many circumstances (*e.g.*, boundary lines, spousal status, child custody, will contests). Various other doctrines (usually referred to as judicial "abstention doctrines") may counsel federal courts to refrain from adjudicating disputes touching too closely upon state law or regulation because federal courts regard such decisionmaking as "imprudent," or excessively invasive even though it is arguably within the federal judicial power. Consequently, federal courts often refer to "prudential" doctrines that impose essentially voluntary (*i.e.*, the courts choose not to act) rather than mandatory limits on their power (*i.e.*, constitutional text or other factors bar the courts from acting). In similar fashion, federal courts generally refrain from deciding constitutional issues when adjudicating a dispute so long as there exist legitimate alternative bases for the decision. This prudential restraint derives not from our notion of national-state federalism but from separation of powers (discussed *infra*). By refraining from decision on constitutional grounds, courts are less likely to invalidate an act or initiative of Congress.

The deference of federal courts to state spheres of law should not seem surprising when one considers the scope of the initial federal jurisdictional mandate. The federal courts are often described as having limited subject matter jurisdiction. By this, we mean that federal courts ordinarily have authority to adjudicate a case only if expressly authorized by the Constitution or valid statute implementing Article III of the Constitution (the Judicial Article). The influence of constitutional federalism on federal courts extends to even the technical minutia of litigating in federal court. For example, a summons and complaint may be personally served upon a defendant or can be served pursuant to any measures allowed by the state in which the federal court is located.

The federal courts, because of the prevailing ideology of federalism, generally take a restrictive view of both subject matter and personal jurisdiction. They also tend to take a somewhat restrictive view regarding the applicable substantive law. Regarding the law to be applied in diversity cases, for example, the interest in national consistency held the edge over the interest in state prerogatives during the period of 1867-1938, resulting in the application by federal courts in diversity cases of a "federal common law" of torts, contracts, etc. Since 1938, state prerogatives have held sway and federal courts exercising diversity jurisdiction have been required to apply state law in adjudicating the dispute.[43]

The law of personal jurisdiction reflects similar tensions between state and national power. The Fifth and Fourteenth Amendments provide that one may not be deprived of life, liberty or property without due process of law. Federal and state court civil judgments certainly implicate the property interests of litigants and, as a practical matter, their liberty interests as well (particularly in cases involving injunctive relief). Consequently, the Due Process Clause applies. However, due process is measured by the defendant's contact with the forum state rather than through an exclusively practical assessment of the fairness or inconvenience faced by a nonresident defendant. This approach occasionally leads to results seemingly at odds with common sense. For example, the U.S. District Court for the District of New Jersey in Newark cannot extend its jurisdictional reach a mere 10 miles over a resident of Manhattan who never crosses the Hudson River. But the federal court for the Northern District of California in San Francisco can hear a case against a resident of San Diego, more than 500 miles away. This discrepancy is, of course, not explained by common sense, or the lack of it, but by Federalism.

Federalism notions are not historic relics but continue to animate modern debate over changes in federal law or rules of court. Perhaps the leading example is the long-running debate over the continued existence of diversity jurisdiction. Many argue that the concept has outlived its usefulness due to the increasing integration and homogenization of the nation. Others argue that state and local prejudices continue to persist and that state judges, most of whom are elected in some form and do not enjoy the job security of federal judges, are insufficiently independent or courageous to defuse such biases. The solution to date has been, perhaps to no one's surprise, a compromise between the warring factions. The required "jurisdictional amount" for a court to have diversity jurisdiction has been raised from $10,000 to $50,000, but diversity remains, in effect suggesting that the collective sense of Congress found it wise to maintain the availability of the "neutral" federal forum for sufficiently important cases (with importance measured in dollars).

Separation of Powers. While federalism addresses tensions in the distribution of state and national authority, separation of powers focuses on tensions

---

[43] *See* Erie R.R. v. Tompkins, 304 U.S. 64 (1938), *overruling* Swift v. Tyson, 41 U.S. 1 (1842).

in the distribution of the powers concededly held by the national govern-ment. A typical high school civics class posits that Congress makes laws, the President enforces laws, and the federal courts adjudicate disputes over the meaning and application of the laws. Although American government in practice is considerably more complicated, the basic tripartite scheme exerts a powerful pull on the behavior of federal courts. Whether Congress and the President (and other executive branch employees) have as healthy a regard for separation of powers poses a more vexing question. Courts, at least, have historically tried to "play it straight" in observing sufficient deference to the other branches. Although persons in disagreement with a recent case frequently complain about "judicial activism," federal courts usually encroach upon the arguable turf of Congress and the Executive only after considerable and self-conscious reflection. Much more commonly, federal courts defer to the other branches, perhaps far more often than is required in the interests of erring on the side of a constrained judicial role.

Perhaps judicial self-restraint remains fashionable because the federal bench appreciates its essential weakness should a free-for-all erupt. Alexander Hamilton described the Judiciary as the "least dangerous branch" in the sense that the bench cannot levy and collect taxes, raise an army, or directly reorder society.[44] In practice, of course, judicial decisions frequently play a substantial role in national policy and have palpable distributive consequences, affecting the redistribution of wealth in society. However, courts exercise less sheer brute strength upon their subjects than do legislatures or executives. For the most part, it is generally easier to disagree with and reason with a judge than a policeman, a tax assessor, or a legislator. Many argue that the flexibility one does occasionally find in executive branch officials stems significantly from the possibility of judicial scrutiny and legal liability.

If a real collision occurs between the branches, conventional wisdom holds that the court would lose to either the President or Congress provided that the other branches acted in accord with popular sentiment. To be sure, court decisions can influence popular sentiment, but only through their institutional reputation and respect as well as the persuasiveness of their reasoning, language, and result. In demarcating their sphere of authority,

---

[44] *See* THE FEDERALIST No. 78 (Alexander Hamilton) ("The Judges as Guardians of the Constitution") (one of a series of "Federalist Papers" authored by James Madison, Alexander Hamilton, and John Jay as political brochures designed to encourage ratification of the Constitution). The label has achieved long-lasting notoriety.

the courts have reduced what seemingly is a matter of politics, policy, and "feel" for the situation to a series of legal doctrines that operate at a seemingly objective, non-political level.

Standing. Foremost among these legal doctrines reflecting political constraints are "standing" and "justiciability," which has spawned subdoctrines of "mootness," "ripeness," "political question," and the prohibition against federal courts rendering advisory opinions. Virtually all state courts share these doctrines in a degree similar to federal practice. Two notable exceptions are Massachusetts and Maine, which permit their state supreme courts to issue advisory opinions. All of these doctrines are based, at least in part, on separation of powers concerns in that they seek to confine the judiciary to traditional judicial activity -- deciding cases -- and to prevent the courts from slipping into a more direct policymaking role.

The Supreme Court has stated, in fact, that the doctrine of standing rests *solely* on separation of powers concerns.[45] This seems an overstatement. Even absent separation of powers concerns, courts would probably adopt some version of a standing doctrine in order to conserve judicial resources and in order to be prudent: cases brought by persons lacking a sufficiently tangible stake in a matter are less likely to provide the optimal context for rendering sound legal judgments. The Court has itself acknowledged this in a number of opinions.

Standing requires that a party bringing a suit be sufficiently appropriate to prosecute the litigation. If the plaintiff lacks standing, federal courts will not hear the case. To have standing, a plaintiff must have a direct and palpable interest in the controversy out of which the case arises. A speculative, overly ethereal interest or one that is too attenuated from the focus of the harm alleged does not suffice to confer standing on a plaintiff. In typical private litigation, the standing analysis is easy: If A hits B, B has standing to sue A for the damages caused by the blow. B is directly and concretely affected by the incident and is financially and personally concerned about the outcome of litigation regarding the attack. B's friend C is not directly affected and therefore lacks legal standing to sue A, no matter how outraged or emotionally distraught C becomes as a result of A's aggression. But if C is a spouse or child of A or financially dependent on A, courts may view C as having sufficient standing to sue.

---

[45] *See* Allen v. Wright, 468 U.S. 737 (1984).

Standing doctrine gets tougher when suits are brought against the government. For example, to have standing to challenge a government policy, a plaintiff must be affected by the challenged policy in a manner reasonably concrete, direct, and nonspeculative. In many but not all instances, organizations have been permitted to raise claims on behalf of members or clients. The notion of organizational representation undergirds much "public interest litigation" in which associations seek to represent members or allied persons who would individually have standing but who as a practical matter lack the individual time or resources to pursue the required litigation. Suits by environmental groups such as the Natural Resources Defense Council or the Environmental Defense Fund are classic illustrations of organizational standing. On the conservative side of the political ledger, organizations like the Chamber of Commerce serve the same function.

Standing doctrine restricts political activists from pursuing a claim challenging the political status quo unless the activist is quite directly impacted or has the organizational proxy of one who is directly impacted. Consequently, standing doctrine tends to push more of the battles brought by political activists into the legislative or executive arenas. As one might therefore expect, most of the close, difficult, and hard-fought standing battles are waged over cases with political implications.

As in so many other areas of law, application of standing doctrine correlates with the personal political preferences of the bench. The relatively liberal Warren Court of 1953-1969 adopted a broad view of standing and for a brief moment even hinted at allowing a plaintiff's status as a taxpayer to confer standing in the politically sensitive cases discussed above.[46] The Burger Court (1969-1986) and the Rehnquist Court (1986-present) significantly restricted standing to those with a quite direct and immediate interest in challenging government action and clearly rejected any semblance of taxpayer standing.[47]

Justiciability and Related Doctrines. Whether Smith or Jones, or the Sierra Club or the National Association of Manufacturers, or whomever,

---

[46] *See* Flast v. Cohen, 392 U.S. 83 (1968).

[47] *See, e.g.*, Allen v. Wright, 468 U.S. 737 (1984); Valley Forge Christian College v. Americans United for Separation of Church and State, Inc., 454 U.S. 464 (1982).

has a claim that courts will adjudicate to a final judgment hinges on the doctrine of justiciability. The Supreme Court has stated that in determining whether a matter is justiciable, it looks for a plaintiff with standing and a matter traditionally viewed as capable of resolution by the judiciary in a manner which does not place the courts in a position of intruding upon the proper sphere of another branch of government. Although the issue of justiciability is considerably more complicated than our brief treatment here might suggest, a court's essential inquiry in determining justiciability asks whether the action walks, talks, and seems like a lawsuit seeking a traditional judgment (such as an award of damages or an injunction). If it does, the matter is ordinarily justiciable, even if it requires the court to pass judgment on actions of the other branches, so long as the court is legitimately deciding a concrete controversy over a subject that is not textually committed by the Constitution to either the legislative or executive branch. As Chief Justice John Marshall stated long ago, it is the province of the judiciary to say what the law is.[48] Implicitly, saying what the law is occasionally requires the court to say that Congress or the President has violated the law.

As in the case of standing, justiciability in the ordinary case is not a particularly difficult issue. When B sues A for hitting him in the hypothetical discussed earlier, the issue looks much like any tort case. One party seeks a judgment for damages against another party. Such a judgment will for all practical purposes conclude the matter, at least as far as the law is concerned. Rendering the judgment will not intrude upon either the legislative or the executive branch, absent unusual special factors.

As with standing, courts determining justiciability look for real rather than speculative disputes, using the concreteness of the situation as a signal that the matter is more like a typical lawsuit and less like an invitation to judicial policymaking or public criticism of another branch of government. Where a plaintiff requests nontraditional relief, such as a complex injunction, this may give rise to more serious questions regarding justiciability. For the most part, the novelty of the relief sought does not preclude adjudication, at least not if the suit is sufficiently concrete and the relief apt in relation to the harm alleged.

Ripeness, Mootness, Political Question. In determining a lawsuit's fitness for judicial resolution, courts apply subsets of justiciability: ripeness; mootness; and the political question doctrine. A case is not ripe

---

[48] Marbury v. Madison, 5 U.S. 137 (1803).

if the harm alleged is not sufficiently certain to occur. A case is moot if the harm alleged has been corrected by nonjudicial means before the case is heard. Federal courts will decline to decide a case that requires them to supplant either Congress or the Executive in an area of policymaking deemed committed by the Constitution to one of those branches in a manner precluding judicial review.

For example, under the political question doctrine, the Supreme Court has declined to decide cases where it has been asked to review a decision of the President to grant a pardon or grant diplomatic recognition to a country. The Court has also declined to adjudicate congressional election disputes (*e.g.*, did Smith or Jones win the nip-and-tuck election in the Eighth Congressional District), except insofar as it has set broad parameters on the grounds and procedures Congress must employ in determining membership.

Standing and justiciability doctrines would not exist in the American form were it not for concern over safeguarding separation of powers, which has led to more emphasis on judicial restraint in the U.S. than in other countries. For example, continental Europe has nothing to rival the American focus on standing and justiciability, although a weaker version of these doctrines appears to exist in order to conserve judicial resources and sharpen courts' decisionmaking. Even in England, the primary model of the American system, these notions are less important since England's notion of separation of powers is far more relaxed than that prevailing in the United States. The legislative and executive functions have been fused in Britain and the political system is unitary rather than federal. American notions of separation of powers are virtually nonexistent. The judiciary, although arguably similar to America's in terms of independence, simply has never been required to be as concerned with intrusion upon the rest of the political structure. In addition, as defenders of the British system are quick to point out, England fobs off fewer of its difficult public policy questions (*e.g.*, integration, abortion) on the judiciary.

American courts and commentators have also promoted judicial restraint more than have their counterparts in other countries. Unique features of the federal bench and American notions of separation of powers explain much of this concern as well. As compared to other countries, the U.S. bench (both federal and state) is unusual in that it results from a political, semi-partisan process in which judges are chosen at relatively advanced stages of their careers from various walks of the legal profession. By contrast, European judges train to be judges (rather than practicing lawyers), start at entry level judging positions, and advance (if they advance) upward in a bureaucratic system much like civil service in the United States. Thus, although federal judges, like European judges, are not elected, federal judges are more likely to behave like independent political forces than like bureaucrats.[49]   As noted above, most state judges in America must face some sort of election. However, for incumbent jurists, this usually involves a so-called "retention election," in which the judge does not run against a competing candidate but is ousted only if a majority of the voters give the judge a negative vote in the abstract.

In addition, the less centralized American model of electoral politics, with less discipline within political parties and less party loyalty among the voters, provides more occasion for people to approach courts with cases charged with political import. Under these circumstances, the constitutional structure, which envisions federal courts at least officiating between the other branches of government (often divided in control between Republicans and Democrats), permits courts more of a role in adjudicating cases with political implications. This larger judicial role, in turn, has led to more concern that it be exercised with restraint.

The Counter-Majoritarian Difficulty.   The so-called "counter-majoritarian difficulty" is typical of such concern for judicial restraint. The difficulty as generally identified is this: federal judges, who are not elected, are able to set aside or penalize the actions of elected representatives and the President. This seems inconsistent with the democratic principle that the will of the majority should govern policy outcomes. Most lawyers resolve the difficulty by concluding that the Constitution, which became law through super-majoritarian procedures, creates this situation. In addition, the bench is tinged with electoral accountability in that: judges must be nominated by the President and confirmed by the Senate; Congress and the President can respond to unfavorable court decisions by changes in the budget, jurisdiction, or other aspects of the courts; Congress and the President can also override disfavored court decisions through new legislation or (in extreme cases) constitutional amendment.

All of these responses, of course, fail to eradicate the counter-majoritarian difficulty but only make it acceptable (to Lockean conservatives

---

[49] *See* Mirjan R. Damaska, *Two Faces of State Authority: The Hierarchal and Coordinate Models*, 97 YALE L.J. 341 (1987) (suggesting that differences in systems explain why American judges are more prestigious and have more powerful impact on society as compared to European judges).

and welfare state liberals) or sufferable (to Burkean conservatives).[50] Federal judges remain unelected officials with substantial power who cannot be fired unless they commit a crime or something similarly disreputable. However, the difficulty is deemed by most as sufficiently muted to permit courts to venture significantly into charged political areas without serious political problems. Despite the oft-heard complaints about judicial activism and legislating from the bench, most political elites and informed people accept the active American judiciary, in part because there seems no realistic alternative.

As Alexis de Tocqueville wrote nearly 200 years ago, nearly every political issue in America ultimately becomes a judicial issue.[51] He was largely correct then and the sentiment remains largely correct today due to the constitutional structure, the American political system and culture (*see* Chapter Five regarding dispute resolution and the adversary system), as well as 200 years of historical reinforcement. In short, America has a politically involved judiciary because it has chosen it, although perhaps tacitly or even inadvertently. However, the United States attempts to keep the activist judiciary in check through doctrines like justiciability and standing as well as the notion of judicial restraint.

A particular example perhaps gives some flavor to the complexities of the issue. Traditionally, courts interpreting statutes have sought to effect the design of the legislature that drafted the statute. Judges, particularly in the modern era, have shown substantial disagreement over how best to accomplish this goal. Some argue that courts should be textualist in approach and focus, perhaps exclusively, on the plain language of a statute. Others argue that courts must also pay considerable attention to the indicia of congressional intent contained in the legislative history of the statute (*e.g.*, committee reports, hearing testimony, floor statements, failed amendments, adopted amendments, and so on). Others argue that courts should take even a broader view of effectuating congressional will and consider the overall purpose of the statute (*i.e.*, what the statute was designed to correct, what state of affairs Congress hoped to bring about) and interpret the law to achieve the purpose, even where this requires

---

[50]   Lockean conservatives generally subscribe to the views of political theorist John Locke (1632-1704), while Burkeans ally themselves with the thoughts of Edmund Burke (1729-1797). *See* Chapter Three on political philosophy.

[51] *See* ALEXIS DE TOCQUEVILLE, DEMOCRACY IN AMERICA (1832).

evolution of the law's meaning beyond the original specific expectations of the legislature.[52]

Jurists who profess a Burkean conservatism and greater concern for separation of powers and legislative hegemony tend to argue for greater reverence for text, viewing it as both the only "real" positive law before the court and the most precise embodiment of legislative sentiment. Lockean conservatives and liberals as well as pragmatists tend toward more eclectic approaches to statutory construction that blend analyses of text, intent and purpose. They see a greater judicial role in avoiding overly literal textual interpretation that may result in "poorer" law. They view this as helpful to the legislature. In addition, pragmatists emphasize that an overly grudging interpretation of a statute may only thwart legislative intent and increase the burden of lawmaking by needlessly forcing Congress to amend or reenact a statute.

Regardless of one's judicial politics, separation of powers concerns are important in framing the debate. In a system different from that of the United States, judicial statutory interpretation could logically be quite another story. Indeed, it appears that courts in continental Europe are relatively more inclined to pursue a "free inquiry" into statutory meaning and seek the "best result" regardless of the seeming views of the enacting legislature or the enforcing executive since European political systems are far less concerned with separation of powers than is the United States.

Checks and Balances. The notion of checks and balances is a refinement of the idea of separation of powers. The latter notion refers to delineated spheres of authority between the branches of government. In other words: what prerogatives belong (in the main) to which branch? Checks and balances, however, refer to the manner in which the various branches operate as a check on their own power and the power of one another regarding implementation of a single policy item. For example, Congress passes legislation (bicameralism -- the need for a bill to pass both the House and Senate is itself a check of sorts) but the President can veto the bill and prevent it from taking effect. Congress can then override the veto by a two-thirds vote. But the legislation may still be vulnerable to the Supreme Court holding part or all of it unconstitutional (or interpreting it more narrowly or broadly then expected).

---

[52] *See* WILLIAM N. ESKRIDGE, JR. & PHILIP FRICKEY, CASES AND MATERIALS ON LEGISLATION: STATUTES AND THE CREATION OF PUBLIC POLICY 569-638 (1987).

Thus, the branches check one another at various stages of the history of a single piece of legislation. This is different from, for example, the primary authority that the Executive has over waging war (separation of powers), the Senate's control over its own membership and procedures (separation of powers again), or the inherent power of courts to administer trial proceedings, holding parties in contempt if necessary (separation of powers once again). Checks and balances include not only the checking function placed in the linear path of a statute or policy but also involve a substantial element of colloquy between the branches. The checking function often operates as a circular weave rather than simply a series of hurdles.

For example, assume a suddenly radicalized Congress enacts massive land reform that takes significant parcels of real property from the rich and gives it to the poor. The President vetoes, wanting to protect wealthy persons, who have been a substantial part of his support over the years (his own family assets are also on the line). Congressional leadership plans a vote to override the veto.

Although the legislation originally passed by a 3-to-1 vote, the President can appeal to a number of legislators based on party loyalty ("if we decimate our biggest supporters, our party is history"), ideological persuasion ("they tried this in the former Soviet Union and Cambodia and both were disasters"), incentives ("vote with me on the veto and I'll see that the new agency headquarters is located in your district, employing your constituents"), or threats ("vote with me on the veto or your former law partner's nomination to the federal bench is out of the question"). The Presidential checking power extends well beyond the veto in this case. He may elect to veto all bills, even those he would otherwise support, until Congress repeals the objectionable legislation.

Nevertheless, if Congress is sufficiently firm, it overrides his veto, enacting legislation sure to face court challenge. Unless the hypothetical land redistribution scheme is accompanied by "just compensation" as required by the Fifth Amendment (note that the individual rights structure of the U.S. system, discussed below, also affects this dispute), the Supreme Court would probably hold it unconstitutional. At that juncture, the checked piece of legislation returns to the congressional forum, where Congress can either compromise (*e.g.*, by adding a provision to pay for land seizures at market rates, providing just compensation) or attempt to bend the Court to its will (*e.g.*, by restricting the Court's jurisdiction, enlarging it to permit the addition of new members favorable to Congress, trimming the Court's budget unpleasantly to the bone, etc.).

Which path it chooses depends on the situation. In this hypothetical, the prohibitively high costs of just compensation for massive land redistribution would probably make it a fiscal impossibility. How easily the Court might capitulate in the face of a congressional counterattack varies with other checking factors. The President in this example would likely help the Court by refusing to nominate to a newly enlarged Court any Justices favorable to Congress on this issue.

All of this constitutional sturm and drang undoubtedly would take some time, allowing for at least the cooling of political tempers if not a "return to normalcy" for political preferences. For example, House of Representatives elections occur every two years, making the land reform act a likely topic of a campaign in which wealthy citizens would presumably pull out all the stops to either unseat or reeducate Robin Hood representatives. In the House races, the views of the President and the Court would undoubtedly matter to at least some significant number of voters. Even if opponents of land reform were only partially successful, the combination of time, political opposition, and congressional exhaustion would likely lead to a compromise or the demise of the land reform idea.

No wonder American government and politics is inherently centrist and oriented toward the status quo! Apart from the personal opinions of the electorate, the very structure of American government makes it difficult to implement really radical or extremely divisive policies. This applies to radically conservative initiatives as well. Substitute the notion of repeal of Medicare or Social Security for the land reform scheme in the above example and a similar scenario would unfold. Federal courts, although they attempt to be non-partisan, play an important role in the structure because of their checking role on the other branches. Although it may at times function poorly in this role (through either inadequate resistance to bad ideas, excessive thwarting of useful reforms, or undue deference or hostility to another branch), the judiciary is still intimately involved in the checking system.

For clarity, this chapter has focused on the federal system and federal courts. Because most state systems mirror the federal in substantial regard, the relations between political superstructure and judicial role found at the federal level will also be largely true in the states. To the extent there exist differences, however, issues of localism (in lieu of federalism), separation of powers, checks and balances, and individual rights tend to be of less concern to states than to the federal government. This is because the federal government is designed under the Constitution as one of limited powers, whereas state governments have general and residual authority over the public welfare.

Guarantees of Individual Rights. As alluded to at various points earlier in this chapter, the American political structure has imbedded into it a baseline respect for individual rights. The Bill of Rights and the Civil War Amendments as well as other aspects of the Constitution establish certain rights by "superlaw" that cannot be curtailed. These individual rights are sacrosanct to whatever degree they are accepted and enforced by the judiciary. As a practical matter, however, individual rights can be diminished to the degree that the federal courts permit this to occur. In rarer cases, the other branches may override decisions of the courts favoring individual rights on the ground that they excessively privilege individual rights over other concerns. Where an anticourt reaction involves passage of a constitutional amendment, it is not only Congress and the President but also the vast bulk of the American polity (remember the necessary ratification by three-fourths of the states) that is required to thwart the Court when it rests its decisions firmly upon constitutional grounds. In the truly extreme case of interbranch conflict, something less than Constitution-amending consensus might roll back individual rights. For example, the U.S. Army might seize and assassinate the Justices for rendering a decision that displeases the President. Fortunately, such scenarios akin to totalitarianism or mob rule are farfetched as applied to the United States.

Although, as discussed above, a host of formal and informal political pressures can be brought to bear on the Court, the constitutionification of important individual rights, such as free expression, open assembly, freedom of worship, fair trials, jury trials, privacy, due process, and equal protection, gives the bench an important power for assessing the application and adequacy of the work product of other corners of government. As also noted, the Supreme Court and lower federal courts are usually sensitive to criticisms of judicial activism and painfully aware of the weaknesses of the judiciary. Consequently, they usually bend in part to pressures brought to bear by other parts of the system. As the saying goes, "the Supreme Court reads the election returns."

But reading the returns does not reduce the Justices to mere automatons. In many instances, the federal bench has resolutely enforced its vision of the law even in the face of popular resistance. For example, many federal judges in the American South displayed great courage and enforced the Fourteenth Amendment and civil rights laws despite the antipathy of the vast majority of white voters and powerful interests.[53] But, as we have noted, visions of the law in close cases vary with the viewer. Consequently, the most commonly effective means by which other branches alter the Supreme Court's view of the individual rights guarantees of the Constitution (as well as other aspects of constitutional jurisprudence) has been through a change in the Court's membership. For example, when the Court decided that the Constitution placed limits on state regulation and prohibition of abortion,[54] it met a firestorm of criticism. From 1980 through 1992, the Executive Branch (the Reagan and Bush Administrations) was committed to overturning constitutionalized abortion rights through appointing "pro-life" Justices. With the election of President Clinton, the Executive switched completely and expressed a commitment to nominating "pro-choice" Justices.

Despite the political pressures, it appears that no Justice participating in the *Roe* decision of 1973 altered his views on the subject in response to criticism or pressure. To be sure, some post-*Roe* abortion opinions can be read as bending to anti-abortion political forces in cases where the Court upheld state and federal restrictions on abortion funding, procedure, or the consent or notification of the parents of minors. In the main, however, it appears that the Court's drift toward increasing tolerance of abortion restriction during the period of 1973-1992 (with some concern that *Roe* would itself be overruled)[55] resulted from changing Court personnel (the substitutions of Justices O'Connor, Scalia, Kennedy, Souter and Thomas for Justices Stewart, Burger, Powell, Brennan, and Marshall) rather than changing constitutional views.

We present this detour into the abortion controversy not to suggest that law is only politics or merely the personal preferences of the Justices (although politics and personal judicial opinion are often determinative in close or difficult cases) but to underscore how powerful a resolute and

---

[53] *See, e.g.*, JACK BASS, UNLIKELY HEROES (1981).

[54] Roe v. Wade, 410 U.S. 113 (1973).

[55] *Compare* Planned Parenthood of Southeastern Penn. v. Casey, 947 F.2d 682 (3d Cir. 1991) (holding that Supreme Court has effectively overruled *Roe* and would explicitly overrule it if directly presented the question) *with* the Supreme Court's decision in the same case, 112 S. Ct. 2791 (1992), which, although upholding many aspects of Pennsylvania law restricting abortion, reaffirmed *Roe*.

unchanging judiciary can be when it acts pursuant to an individual rights guarantee of the Constitution. Whatever the ultimate fate of *Roe v. Wade*, it has had more than a 20-year "run" as the law of the land despite the best efforts of organized interest groups, state legislatures, and four presidents who opposed the decision.

The power of the federal courts regarding individual rights determinations is both a plus and a minus for the judiciary. On the minus side, these powers tend to be a lightning rod for critics and often engender efforts to punish the bench or restrict courts from what many regard as more appropriate tasks. On the plus side, the bulk of the profession appears to agree that the power to decide questions impacting on federal constitutional rights also implies that it would be unconstitutional to so fetter the federal courts that they are unable to perform this role. Certainly, the bulk of the legal profession and political actors have considered it unwise to attempt to destroy or diminish the institution of the federal courts as currently conceived despite disagreement with court decisionmaking. For example, efforts to strip the federal courts of jurisdiction over school busing for desegregation or enforcement of abortion rights have generally been unsuccessful. In a sense, then, both the American political structure (which is hard to change) and American political consensus (which, although relatively stable, could change in an instant) have combined to give the federal judiciary its current role in adjudicating disputes, maintaining political balance, protecting rights, and influencing the ongoing debate over national policy.

REFERENCES FOR FURTHER READING

BERNARD BAILYN, IDEOLOGICAL ORIGINS OF THE AMERICAN REVOLUTION (1967).

CHARLES BEARD, AN ECONOMIC INTERPRETATION OF THE CONSTITUTION (1913).

GUIDO CALABRESI, A COMMON LAW FOR THE AGE OF STATUTES (1982).

HAROLD W. CHASE & CRAIG R. DUCAT, CONSTITUTIONAL INTERPRETATION (5th ed. 1992).

EDWIN S. CORWIN, THE CONSTITUTION AND WHAT IT MEANS TODAY (14th ed. 1978).

ROBERT COVER, JUSTICE ACCUSED (1978).

KENNETH M. DOLBEARE & MURRAY J. EDELMAN, AMERICAN POLITICS: POLICIES, POWER, AND CHANGE (5th ed. 1985).

DAVID EPSTEIN, THE POLITICAL THEORY OF THE FEDERALIST (1981).

JOHN HART ELY, DEMOCRACY AND DISTRUST (1980).

WILLIAM N. ESKRIDGE, JR. & PHILIP P. FRICKEY, LEGISLATION: STATUTES AND THE CREATION OF PUBLIC POLICY (1987).

DANIEL A. FARBER & SUZANNA SHERRY, A HISTORY OF THE AMERICAN CONSTITUTION (1990).

THE FEDERALIST (Alexander Hamilton, John Jay & James Madison) (1788).

GERALD GUNTHER, CONSTITUTIONAL LAW (11th ed. 1991).

MAEVA MARCUS (ed.), ORIGINS OF THE FEDERAL JUDICIARY (1992).

THOMAS A. MASON, WILLIAM BEANEY & DONALD STEPHENSON, CONSTITUTIONAL LAW (7th ed. 1983).

WILLIAM NELSON, THE FOURTEENTH AMENDMENT (1988).

JOHN NOWAK, RONALD ROTUNDA & JOHN YOUNG, CONSTITUTIONAL LAW (3d ed. 1986).

JACK N. RAKOVE, THE BEGINNING OF NATIONAL POLITICS: AN INTERPRETATIVE HISTORY OF THE CONTINENTAL CONGRESS (1983).

LARRY SABATO & KAREN O'CONNOR, AMERICAN POLITICS: ROOTS TO REFORM (2d ed. 1993).

GEOFFREY R. STONE, LOUIS M. SEIDMAN, CASS R. SUNSTEIN & MARK V. TUSHNET, CONSTITUTIONAL LAW (2d ed. 1992).

CASS SUNSTEIN, AFTER THE RIGHTS REVOLUTION (1991).

LAURENCE TRIBE, AMERICAN CONSTITUTIONAL LAW (2d ed. 1989).

MARK TUSHNET, RED, WHITE, AND BLUE: A CRITICAL ANALYSIS OF CONSTITUTIONAL LAW (1988).

ROBERT WHEELER & CHARLES HARRISON, CREATING THE FEDERAL JUDICIAL CENTER (1989).

GARY WILLS, INVENTING AMERICA: THOMAS JEFFERSON'S DECLARATION OF INDEPENDENCE (1978); EXPLAINING AMERICA (1981).

GORDON S. WOOD, THE CREATION OF THE AMERICAN REPUBLIC (1976); THE RADICALISM OF THE AMERICAN REVOLUTION (1992); *see also* GORDON S. WOOD (ed.), THE CONFEDERATION AND THE CONSTITUTION (1978).
CHARLES ALAN WRIGHT, THE LAW OF FEDERAL COURTS (4th ed. 1983).

CHAPTER FIVE

LAW, DISPUTE RESOLUTION, AND THE ADVERSARY SYSTEM

To those studying the law and legal systems, it quickly becomes painfully obvious that American law is a discipline awash in text. Less obvious, however, may be the great degree to which nontextual influences shape law. As recounted in other chapters, legal structures and outcomes are shaped by the society's views on ethical philosophy (Chapter One), economics and commerce (Chapter Two), political theory (Chapter Three), its governmental structure (Chapter Four), history and, of course, its views on jurisprudence itself apart from the controlling texts (Chapter Six). Equally important, perhaps, is this chapter's subject: society's underlying model for resolving disputes and views about conflict resolution.

The Adversary and Inquisitorial Systems.

This section examines the major models of adjudication. Following a caveat, we discuss the Anglo-American adversary system and then contrast it to the system prevailing in continental Europe.

A Semantic and Historical Cautionary Note. The Anglo-American legal structure is generally deemed "adversary" or "adversarial" and is distinguished from the generally "inquisitorial" systems prevailing in Western Europe and most of the rest of the world, including Latin America. Under the Anglo-American model, the "adversaries take charge of most procedural action" while in an inquisitorial system "[government] officials perform most activities. Beyond this core meaning uncertainty begins."[56] For example, it is not even clear how countries should be classified according to this scheme. In the former Soviet bloc countries and much of the Third World, an arguably inquisitorial system design has been encrusted with elements of authoritarianism. These systems may at times function more like a dictatorial disciplinary board, especially when dealing with dissidents or disfavored parties. In other, less developed countries, tribal law and custom continue to be used for resolving many disputes. Arguably, however, even tribal systems could be classified as basically adversarial or inquisitorial.

The Anglo-American choice of the term "inquisitorial" carries connotative cultural baggage. The very word conjures up for many Westerners unpleasant, authoritarian, intolerant images of a tribunal that has prejudged the issues before it (*e.g.*, the Spanish Inquisition). Just as unsurprisingly, British and American lawyers, full of cultural pride, refer to their system under the relatively euphemistic rubric of adversarialism when words like "combative," "bellicose," and "minimally supervised" might be just as descriptive of what actually occurs. As one leading civil procedure treatise has noted, "some lawsuits are a quest for justice by neither side but rather a mutual vendetta by parties who are civilized only

---

[56] MIRJAN R. DAMASKA, THE FACES OF JUSTICE AND STATE AUTHORITY 3 (1986).

to the extent of refraining from physical violence."[57] Nevertheless, in this book we employ these labels because they are the prevailing terminology, at least in English-speaking countries. The reader should resist any tendency to view either system as inherently superior. Both are defensible and rational.

A "rational" dispute resolution system must be more than merely decipherable or explicable. For example, medieval Europeans once used trial by combat as a means of settling disputes.[58] Although this method can be understood both functionally (you can usually tell who won the fight) as well as anthropologically (it was the best society could do at the time), we shudder to call it rational. In a contract dispute between Arnold Schwartzenegger and Pee Wee Herman, there is no basis for assuming any relationship between the fighting ability of the parties and the merits of their legal positions.[59]

The same can be said of another ancient method of dispute resolution, trial by ordeal, in which the person accused (of theft, infidelity, whatever) undertook a painful activity, such as grabbing a hot iron (perhaps a crucifix or other religious symbol). If the accused showed no pain or no apparent damage, this was viewed as divine intervention to prove the innocence of the accused. In addition to the obvious due process problems of this approach (in effect presuming guilt or liability by requiring the painful procedure as a condition of exoneration), it fails the rationality criterion: only a religious fanatic would expect his or her God to intercede against the laws of nature across a range of private disputes. Even Mother Theresa's skin would probably become charred if she is forced to grab hot metal. Nonetheless, it took the Roman Catholic Church's announcement in

---

[57] FLEMING JAMES, JR., GEOFFREY C. HAZARD, JR. & JOHN LEUBSDORF, CIVIL PROCEDURE 7 (4th ed. 1992).

[58] This method appears to have been imported to England after 1066 by the Norman conquerors and used sparingly as a last resort. *See* STEPHEN A. LANDSMAN, READINGS ON ADVERSARIAL JUSTICE: THE AMERICAN APPROACH TO ADJUDI-CATION 3-4 (1988); Stephen A. Landsman, *The Civil Jury in America: Scenes from an Unappreciated History*, 44 HASTINGS L.J. 579, 582-87 (1993) (describing evolution of civil jury in part to replace trial by combat or by ordeal).

[59] Some commentators have suggested, however, that England and the United States adopted an adversarial method of dispute resolution in part because it serves as a pressure release valve that satisfies the human primor-dial instinct for combat and revenge. But other peoples who seem at least as combative as the British and Americans have opted for inquisitorial systems.

1215 that it would not permit clerical participation in such events to put these adjudication methods finally on the road to extinction.

Just this short glance at history suggests the great progress society has generally made toward more rational dispute resolution, whatever one's preferences among current systems. Over the past several hundred years, modern society has gravitated toward increased procedural protections for both the rights of accused persons (both criminal and civil) and more consistency and accuracy in dispute resolution. Although Anglo-American and other systems may have their drawbacks, few would trade them for a chance to settle things with a mace.

The Adversarial Model. An adversarial structure for dispute resolution is generally marked by several characteristics:

Direction by the Parties. A combat -- or perhaps sports -- analogy has some use in describing the workings of the adversary system, which is distinguished from the inquisitorial system primarily by the control which the disputing parties exercise over the matter at issue. In the Anglo-American system, for example, civil actions are usually commenced by the parties via the serving or filing of a complaint. This characterizes even the criminal system to a large degree. The government brings the action against the alleged criminal via a grand jury indictment or an information filed by the prosecutor. Even where administrative agencies are the front line for resolving disputes, the process is still largely structured as a contest between two different parties who each have respective control over what claims are made and seriously pursued.

Another key aspect of adversarialism related to "party control" is "party presentation": the disputants are largely responsible for the development and presentation of information about the dispute to the decisionmaker. For the most part, the parties are responsible for digging up evidence and determining how best to use it (or attempt to prevent its use). This is most obvious in American civil litigation where plaintiffs and defendants conduct "discovery" by asking each other for documents and other information, by examining prospective witnesses, and also by conducting their own extra-judicial investigations.

In criminal matters, the parties often investigate facts more informally. Of course, the government has a comparative advantage in the investigation process because law enforcement agencies assist the prosecutors. To a large extent, however, this advantage is canceled out by substantive legal rules requiring the prosecution to turn over to the defense any exculpatory evidence (that is, evidence tending to show that the accused did not commit the crime). In addition, the government must ordinarily make available to the defense any previous statements of a prosecution witness. Criminal defendants also enjoy some benefits of legal doctrine designed to adjust for the government's presumed advantages: 1) a higher standard of proof needed to convict (the "beyond a reasonable doubt" requirement); 2) the right against self-incrimination (expressly guaranteed by the Fifth Amendment of the United States Constitution); 3) constraints on the use of tainted evidence (grounded in the Fourth Amendment), and 4) a generalized fair trial guarantee, codified in the Sixth Amendment. Elements of adversarialism in criminal law have been constitutionalized in the United States but tend also to exist by custom, practice, or statute in other common law countries.

The basic adversarial pattern also holds for administrative agency proceedings, with some variation. Although there is little or no formal judicially supervised discovery as provided for under the Federal Rules of Civil Procedure, the U.S. Freedom of Information Act, 5 U.S.C. § 552, often serves this type of function. Similarly, there are fewer constraints on the manner in which information is presented as evidence.

At bottom, civil suits, criminal prosecutions, and agency determinations in America all look pretty adversarial: one side initiates the proceeding; both sides develop information; and the parties plan and execute strategies of presentation and argumentation designed to produce a favorable outcome.

A Neutral and Detached Adjudicator. In addition to party control, the second primary distinguishing feature of adversarialism is the neutrality and detachment of the decisionmaker. In Anglo-American litigation (both civil and criminal), the judge must not side with any of the disputing parties. Instead, her role is more that of an umpire or referee: she regulates the activity of the parties within certain ground rules to avoid unfairness (similar to a referee calling fouls) but essentially lets the parties "play their game" so long as counsel's representation of a party is not incompetent or at odds with important interests of the adjudication system. For example, a judge might well begin asking questions of a key witness for whom one side attempts no cross-examination. Similarly, the commitment to detachment and neutrality does not allow the American judge to sit idly by while one lawyer suborns perjury from a witness while the other lawyer does nothing to prevent it.

Thus, even in civil proceedings, the notion of a neutral jurist is neither simple nor absolute. In criminal proceedings, this norm is perhaps even less clear-cut because the judge and the prosecutor are both employees (in the larger sense of the term) of the government prosecuting the case. A similar twist often accompanies the adversarial adjudication process of an administrative agency, such as a review of benefit eligibility claims by the Social Security Administration: many disputes are decided by administrative law judges (ALJs) who are in a different division of the agency but still technically part of the same agency that is bringing an enforcement action or deciding a claim. ALJs are often in a potentially compromised position when they decide actions brought for or against the government. An anti-government ruling is technically a ruling against the ALJ's employer.

The Special Status of Administrative Agencies. We should stop here to distinguish administrative agency adjudication from administrative agency rulemaking. When adjudicating, an agency functions much like a court: it brings charges against a party and seeks a fine, imprisonment, secession of offending activity, or some other remedy (*e.g.*, when the U.S. Department of Agriculture acts to stop meat packers who fail to observe cleanliness standards at their packing plants). When an agency makes rules, it acts in something of a legislative capacity: it proposes new or amended rules, listens to objections and suggestions, and either withdraws the proposal, modifies it, or enacts it (*e.g.*, when the Agriculture Department decides that milk must be pasteurized if it is intended for sale to the public). In practice, of course, rulemaking can look quite adversarial. For example, the agency may propose new regulations opposed by industry. In such cases, public hearings on the proposal may sound like opposing arguments in private litigation. After a rule is established, it can usually be challenged in court so long as the complainant's attack is not frivolous.

Most agency adjudications are also subject to at least some level of judicial review. In reviewing either adjudication or rulemaking, however, courts will show great deference to the agency's determinations of adjudicative fact, public policy, and statutory interpretation. In short, private parties who lose before an agency in either rulemaking or adjudication are unlikely to obtain judicial relief. In any event, both systems are marked by an adversarial style of party control and presentation.

Protecting Neutrality. Regarding the criterion of neutrality, the American judicial and administrative systems attempt to alleviate the problem of potential bias favoring the government or powerful private interests by granting decisionmakers a substantial measure of independence and protection. For example, a United States judge (either appellate or trial) may not be discharged except for "bad" behavior such as the commission of a crime. Poor performance is not enough to get a judge fired. In addition, the salaries and compensation of federal judges cannot be reduced. Thus, Congress cannot punish or threaten the federal judiciary by cutting its pay or pensions. These protections are established in Article III of the United States Constitution. Hence, full-scale federal judges are often referred to as "Article III judges" because of the substantial protections they enjoy.

Other federal adjudicators and most state judges and ALJs have less protection but nonetheless enjoy significant job and income security that is designed to foster their independence and neutrality in decisionmaking. For example, United States Magistrate Judges and Bankruptcy Judges, who were established pursuant to Article I of the Constitution (and are hence called "Article I judges"), do not have the life tenure of Article III judges but are appointed for 10-year terms. ALJs, both federal and state, usually benefit from a similar arrangement, as do state court judges. Although the entire corps of Article I judges and ALJs could be abolished by the relevant legislature, this is unlikely as a practical matter. In essence, all of these decisionmakers have substantial protections of status and income that, in theory at least, should enable them to call the metaphorical "balls and strikes" of disputing as the judges see them.

Diffuse Authority of the Adjudicator: The American Jury. In the United States, there exists an additional important component of fact-finder neutrality -- the jury. Jurors, in both state and federal civil and criminal courts, are selected from the public at large from a broad list (*e.g.*, voter registration, driver's license registration). A sample of prospective jurors is presented to the court, oriented to the case set for trial, and scrutinized by the judge and the lawyers for the parties. Lawyers have a small number of peremptory challenges and unlimited opportunity to challenge the jurors for cause. A peremptory challenge is one that a party (through counsel unless representing himself) can exercise as a matter of right and is available without giving a reason for discharging the juror. Relatively recently, the U.S. Supreme Court invoked the equal protection guarantee of the Fourteenth Amendment to prohibit racially motivated peremptory challenges. Generally, however, peremptory challenges allow counsel to discharge a prospective juror for arbitrary reasons and are unchallengeable by the opposition or the court. Consequently, they are limited in number.

By contrast, when challenging a prospective juror for cause, the attorney must articulate a credible reason why the juror poses an unreasonable risk of being unable to decide the case fairly. For example, if Acme Corporation is a civil defendant and a juror was recently fired by Acme, counsel will be able to successfully challenge that juror for cause. In practice, peremptory challenges are usually rational rather than capricious. Usually lawyers exercise peremptory challenges when they suspect but cannot prove that the juror will be inclined to rule against them. For example, if a civil plaintiff is seeking a large damage award due to an automobile accident, he may well use a peremptory challenge to dismiss a juror who works for an automobile insurer on the theory that people in the insurance business generally are adverse to awarding substantial damages. Most judges will not consider this sufficient cause for the juror's discharge. However, if the juror works for the defendant's particular auto insurer, he may be successfully challenged for cause since the defendant's insurer has a direct financial stake in the case. Lawyers also use peremptory challenges to strike jurors who are thought by temperament to favor the opposing party.

The use of the jury of laypersons enhances neutrality because jurors are not regular participants in the justice system. To the contrary, jurors ordinarily want to end their participation in the system and return to their regular lives as soon as possible. Consequently, they have little to fear from rendering a verdict that displeases one of the litigants, the judge, or any government official. To assure this, jury tampering (either through intimidation or reward) is a crime. Jury duty is generally of short duration, usually limited to one case (although the case may occasionally take a long time to resolve) or one week of being considered as a potential juror. Being laypersons, jurors are also less likely to be influenced by the latest trends in law school education or the conventional wisdom of the bar. However, jurors may well be influenced by current events or public relations campaigns waged by classes of litigants.

The neutrality of the decisionmaker is buttressed to some degree by the division of roles between judge and jury. The oversimplified but basically accurate metaphor is that juries have dominion over factfinding while judges control the legal decisionmaking involved in a dispute. In the typical case, the judge makes pretrial rulings regarding the availability of information and may under certain circumstances terminate a case favorably for one of the parties prior to trial by making legal rulings on the basis of established facts. If the case goes to trial, the judge makes evidentiary rulings and participates at the margin in presentation of the case. She also instructs the jury as to legal issues but then stands back while the jury deliberates. After the jury has decided, the judge has considerable power to overturn the verdict, to reduce a damage award, or to order a new trial, but that power is relatively circumscribed. The judge cannot undo a verdict simply because of dislike for it but must show narrow legal grounds for changing the result or retrying the case. Thus, even a biased judge has limited power to dictate a result. Similarly, a biased jury has limited power to dictate a result; if it acts irrationally, the judge may upset the verdict.

By both historical accident and logic, juries are, for the most part, found in tandem with adversary systems of dispute resolution. In the main, this results because the jury is an English institution exported to its colonies. However, as described above, the jury also makes logical sense in an adversary system since it serves to give the adjudication machinery more independence and more neutrality -- it is an insurance policy of sorts against the potential failings of the government. In addition, the presence or absence of the jury tends to square with underlying assumptions of the respective systems. As noted, adversarial judges are idealized as referees who keep some distance from and perspective on the litigation. It therefore makes some sense to attempt to insulate the adversarial judge from the value judgments, credibility assessments, and making of inferences associated with factfinding. By contrast, the inquisitorial judge is presumed to be steeped in the unearthing and sifting of facts material to the dispute. Barring this model of judge from using this expertise to "finish the job" and find facts thus seems counterintuitive to policymakers in inquisitorial legal systems.

Both by history and function, the jury in the adversarial system is more frequently viewed as a bulwark or protection against the abuse of government authority. In one famous English case, for example, jurors refused to convict noted Quaker William Penn when the Crown charged him with trespass, contempt, and unlawful assembly in a case with obvious partisan political implications. The outraged, anti-Penn judge fined and jailed the jurors. One particularly brave juror, Edward Bushell, sought release through a habeas corpus proceeding and did not pay the fine. The reviewing Court of Common Pleas agreed with Bushell and held that jurors could not be punished for their verdicts unless they had engaged in corrupt behavior, such as taking a bribe. Mere disagreement with the Crown was not a crime.[60]

In contrast to the Anglo-American system, which venerates juror independence such as Bushell's, the inquisitorial system more often professes no need for such safeguards. The inquisitorial systems have generally embraced state authority in these matters both in the form of the different

---

[60] *See* Bushell's Case, 124 Eng. Rep. 1006 (C.P. 1670).

model of judge and the absence of the jury, particularly in civil cases. The state is seen as a consistent agent of justice rather than as a potential threat to justice.

In the United States, however, many observers see the benefits of the jury system as coming at a price. Juries make trials more expensive, slower, and less consistent. Scholars argue over the magnitude of these effects but almost all agree that they exist to some degree. Even those who believe that juries make trial outcomes more accurate may wonder whether the increased accuracy comes at too high a price. Many others, of course, argue that use of lay citizens is itself an important value (at even a high price) because it serves as a check which prevents government and the legal profession from becoming too insular.

Thus, despite the jury's positive attributes, it has been under attack and to some extent on the wane in the 20th century. For example, England has essentially eliminated civil juries except in a few types of actions, but retains the criminal jury. Both British and American courts appear to have expanded their ability to remove a case from the jury during the pretrial stage or to modify a jury verdict after trial. Nonetheless, the jury is certainly alive and well in the adversarial model even if less robust than before. By contrast, inquisitorial systems seldom use laypersons, even in criminal matters. To the extent they exist, these laypersons are usually confined to essentially an advisory role. Yet even in the citadel of reverence for the jury -- the United States -- much law is made or enforced by administrative agencies. Juries are not used at all in these proceedings.

Greater Procedural Structure. Many observers also find adversarial systems characterized by a "highly structured forensic procedure"[61] with more detailed and scrupulously observed rules about the conduct of litigation, the use of evidence, and the behavior of attorneys. To invoke the sports metaphor again, the judge in an adversarial system is expected to referee competing parties and counsel zealously. To keep control of "the game," referees are armed with a comprehensive structure of rules which they enforce stringently lest the participants and results get out of hand. By contrast, the judge in the inquisitorial system is a well-meaning participant in the development of the case. Restrictions on her access to information thus seem inappropriate. Since the lawyers are given less license to be adversarial and have no jurors to influence should they engage in grandstand

---

[61] *See* LANDSMAN, *supra* note 58, at 4.

tactics, the inquisitorial system perceives less need to keep lawyers, litigants, and witnesses on a short leash at trial.

The Background, Training, and Socialization of the Decision-maker. Another difference worth noting again stems from a combination of history and reason. Under the adversarial model, particularly in the United States, judges are selected in an eclectic, highly political manner. To be sure, ability plays a significant role, but it must compete with a host of other factors: political partisanship; political ideology; attempts to diversify the bench by race, ethnicity and background; personal friendship between judicial candidates and the executives or legislators responsible for their selection; and so on. In the continental legal world and even in Britain, these factors are greatly reduced.

In both the British and American worlds of adversarialism, judges typically ascend to the bench relatively late in their careers after having established themselves as "judge material." In the United States, judges tend to come from the ranks of prominent private practitioners, prosecutors, or academicians. When they take the bench, they in essence begin a second (or third or fourth) legal career. The process can work in reverse as well. During the 1970s and 1980s, a number of highly respected judges left the bench for private practice or other government service, a phenomenon generally attributed to frustration over static pay levels, burgeoning dockets, and other types of increasing dissatisfaction with the job.

By contrast, the inquisitorial judge normally plans to become a judge shortly after selecting law as a career, trains for a judgeship, and begins working as a lower echelon judge. If the new judge's work is viewed as good by more senior judges and government administrators, she is promoted to higher levels of judicial responsibility. In effect, the inquisitorial judiciary is part of the government civil service, while the adversarial judiciary is an amalgam of more independent and diffuse power centers.

In an insightful recharacterization of the traditional description of the systems, one commentator has described the inquisitorial judicial model as "hierarchical" while terming the adversarial judiciary a "coordinate" model.[62] He classifies the two models according to the respective degree of:

---

[62] *See* DAMASKA, *supra* note 56.

• Professionalization of officials (as discussed above, training for the inquisitorial judge is more rigid and consistent);

• Strict hierarchical ordering in the inquisitorial system with horizontal distribution of authority in the adversarial system;

• Technical standards for decisionmaking versus imposition of substantive justice (inquisitorial judges seek a more formalist resolution of the dispute with less freedom to render a result based on either sympathy or substantive justice);

• Lay officials (as noted above, America is the citadel of jury involvement);

• Reliance on oral testimony and the trial event, which is key in adversarial America but far less important in inquisitorial Europe; and

• Frequency and legitimacy of the privatization of disputes. For example, in America as contrasted to Europe, the parties control development of the case and have virtually unlimited authority to settle the case.

Despite the nomenclature, this commentator finds that judges in the coordinate adversarial system -- the supposed impartial referees -- have greater power and authority than do judges serving in the hierarchical model.

Whatever the terminology, it seems beyond debate that adversarial judges and inquisitorial judges are different in many ways. English and American judges differ markedly as well. The British selection system is less political and more focused on merit, with the trial bar of barristers largely controlling the selection process. The British bench, like the British bar and its system of legal education and apprenticeship, is generally more elitist and less open than its American counterpart. Although English judges do not work within a bureaucracy like their continental counterparts, the more closely knit English legal community may create a de facto bureaucracy of sorts. Certainly, the British and American systems are quite distinct despite both being adversarial.

The Inquisitorial Model. Thus far we have defined inquisitorial systems by indirection, primarily with reference to the traits of the adversarial system. We do not want to be so simplistic as to assert that inquisitorial systems are defined merely as those which differ from the adversarial model. Nonetheless, this type of taxonomy might be as good a classification approach as any. In general, inquisitorial systems are distinguished by the decisionmaker's greater involvement in the development and administration of the dispute, including the development of evidence. The decisionmaker is almost always a judge, usually the judge who developed the evidence and processed the case.

Lawyers in countries with inquisitorial regimes would probably argue that these judges are neutral, at least at the outset of the dispute, and that the judge merely investigates the matter, forming an opinion and developing proofs based upon judicially acquired knowledge rather than prejudice or favoritism. But the inquisitorial judge, whatever her neutrality, is still more actively involved in the processing of the case than her adversarial counterpart. Despite the differences, one noted authority has persuasively argued that most commentators have overly caricatured the distinctions between the systems. He argues that the primary difference is merely that inquisitorial judges actually develop the evidence but that they in other ways act much like adversarial judges dealing with lawyers who, despite working in an inquisitorial system, are quite active in initiating cases, proffering information for the court to consider, framing the issues, and arguing the case.[63]

In addition, the inquisitorial judge is ordinarily the last word on the matter, at least at the trial level, and is unencumbered by the jury. Both systems have appellate review. For the most part, it is arguably more searching in inquisitorial systems because inquisitorial appellate courts are permitted to review the matter and modify the result due to error as broadly defined. By contrast, American adversarial appellate judges are supposed to be more constrained: they can set aside a judge's factfinding only when it is clearly erroneous and upset a jury verdict only to prevent injustice or irrationality. In practice, of course, the scrutiny of appellate review in the two systems tends to converge. Inquisitorial appellate panels are more deferential to the trial bench than the superficial conventional wisdom might suggest while adversarial reviewing courts are more aggressive in scrutinizing jury verdicts.

As previously noted, the inquisitorial bench is different in its sociology and training. Despite these distinctions in judges and judicial function, the major point of departure separating inquisitorial and adversarial systems appears to be the degree of party involvement and autonomy

---

[63] *See* John H. Langbein, *The German Advantage in Civil Procedure*, 52 U. CHI. L. REV. 823 (1985).

in the processing of a dispute, particularly regarding the gathering of facts and evidence. Although, as noted above, adversarial systems tend to have a more stylized structure of procedure, evidence, and lawyer's ethics, this seems to be a less important distinction and one not inextricably linked to the adjudication system. One could argue, for example, that the inquisitorial system is really more rule bound to the extent it seeks judicial consistency/conformity and replicability. The procedural structure of inquisitorial systems may be less rigid but perhaps rigidity is unnecessary in view of the more structured judicial recruitment, selection, training, and promotion process.

Debating the Respective Merits of the Two Systems.

Which is preferable, an inquisitorial system or an adversarial one? We assume in this discussion a comparison between Anglo-American adversarialism and sophisticated inquisitorial systems such as those found in Western Europe. We would not argue that choosing between the U.S. court system and that of the People's Republic of China is a close question. Of course, even when confronted with the "best" inquisitorial model, the American legal profession has traditionally endorsed adversarialism. Perhaps this is out of self-interest since it is generally thought that U.S. lawyers are largely the best-paid and most prestigious in the world (but perhaps also the most vilified).

Whatever the relative merits of the two systems, increasing judicial power and diminution of jury authority during the past quarter century, including increased judicial support for aggressive "case management," suggests that the American system has moved toward the inquisitorial model in some degree. Similarly, more subtle understandings of the actual role of lawyers and the authority of judges in inquisitorial regimes suggest that continental systems are not as different from American courts as commonly supposed by Americans. One scholar has, for example, argued that the inquisitorial system of civil litigation in Germany is materially different from American litigation only in the area of fact gathering, which is judge-administered rather than lawyer-conducted.[64]

Whether the gulf between the adversarial and the inquisitorial is narrow or wide, most observers agree on the following pluses and minuses associated with the adversarial system.

---

[64] *See* Langbein, *supra* note 63.

Adversarial System

Pros	Cons
• gives parties strong incentives to develop evidence and police the opposition	• tempts parties to cheat; may make cheating harder to detect
• results are less suspect when reached by neutral, independent decisionmakers	• results may primarily reflect skill of counsel zeal or resources of parties rather than truth
• court system is more likely to protect individuals from government and to "take on" government policies	• may lead to excessive litigation and improper judicial meddling in public policy
• permits streamlined judicial system (fewer judges and government employees per case)	• may increase social cost of disputes because of high private costs of disputing
• respects party autonomy	• tolerates increased delay
• respects individual rights, even at the risk of inability to obtain truth	• may overvalue individual rights at the expense of fair outcomes
• party control leads to greater satisfaction to those involved in the dispute	• state control may be more satisfying to indirectly interested observers
• involves laypersons through juries	• avoids expense, delay, and uncertainty of juries

The benefits and drawbacks of the inquisitorial model are essentially the converse of this admittedly sketchy listing. In essence, the debate tends to turn on whether one sees American adversarialism as too much of an expensive game with insufficient benefits to justify the cost. For example, many Americans are not sufficiently afraid of government abuses or impressed by the positive worth of party control to strongly endorse adversarialism. But most Americans, nevertheless, support the adversarial model, primarily because they like the independence, the party autonomy, the deference to individual rights, and because they are not entirely sure they want to entrust the fact gathering function to a judicial officer. Adversarialism's supporters acknowledge that it carries a higher logistical price tag but claim it is one they are willing to pay.

The Role of National Culture. A good deal of the American preference for the adversarial model -- and continental resistance to it -- is probably explained by differences in national culture rather than any inherent superiority of either system. Although invoking the individuality of different nations and societies can become an excuse for clinging tenaciously to the status quo irrespective of the facts, there appear to be several valid reasons why the adversarial approach better comports with the American psyche. Some of the reasons, unfortunately, verge on caricature, but are nonetheless worth noting, to wit:

    • Americans endorse limited government and prefer a system that stands to some degree as a potential counterweight to government power. A less involved (theoretically) judiciary parallels the relatively smaller government superstructure found in the United States.

    • The checks and balances of the American political system (*see* Chapter Four) often result in policy stalemate (popularly referred to as "gridlock") or "buck passing" to the judiciary, which must grapple with substantive policy issues more often than its counterparts abroad. In Germany and France, for example, (and England for that matter,) the unitary and parliamentary forms of government ordinarily have more freedom to change substantive political and legal policy and react to current sentiment. Thus, litigation abroad is less often a vehicle for seeking social change, challenging authority, or enforcing policy preferences.

    • Americans generally have greater enthusiasm for market-based mechanisms than do other cultures. Party-controlled adversarial litigation parallels the more laissez-faire American economy, while inquisitorial centralization is consistent with the greater national economic planning found abroad.

    • Americans are less elitist (or at least like to think they are), making them proponents of a strong role for lay jurors in dispute resolution. Similarly, the American commitment to openness and egalitarianism (at least of opportunity if not outcome) lends support to adversarialism's coordinate model of judging and resistance to the more hierarchical and bureaucratic model of judging found under inquisitorial systems.

• History has made Americans comfortable with adversarial justice and hesitant to make major changes in the model, which has been essentially a popular one over the years.

To some extent, of course, cultural generalizations are almost always overbroad, as are the generalizations about the degree of difference between American adversarialism and continental inquisitorialism. We have already noted some tendency of the systems to converge in application, with the American system tending to look more inquisitorial over the past 25 years. For example, in late 1993, pronounced changes to the Federal Rules of Civil Procedure regarding discovery took effect. The proposed revisions are intended to make the process of litigation fact-gathering less adversarial in the hope that this will make litigation faster, less costly, and less determined by the resources of the parties. Despite the admirable goals of the proposed changes, many lawyers have great reservations about them, in large part because they attempt to reduce adversarialism in the civil discovery process without changing the American adversary system itself. Opposition to the changes has prompted some courts to abrogate the new provisions by local rule.

The role of the federal bench in pursuing these rule changes illustrates another potential evolution of the American system. Although judges operating under the adversarial model are stylized as passive, neutral umpires, American judges in fact play significant roles in shaping law as well as deciding cases. For example, federal judges acting as the Judicial Conference of the United States and sitting on various advisory committees dominate the process of rulemaking that governs criminal procedure, civil procedure, bankruptcy, evidence, and other aspects of judicial administration. To be sure, this power is shared with Congress and to some extent the practicing bar (although practitioners have only minority representation on the relevant committees that draft proposed rules). If Congress does not like a rule promulgated by the Supreme Court after Judicial Conference approval, Congress may prevent the rule from going into effect. If Congress does not act, the judicially created rule governs. Rule revision is relatively frequent. Consequently, the supposedly passive bench is often engaged in modification of the American adversary system on an ongoing basis.

Does the Adversarial System Affect American Case Outcomes? Of course, after having waded through the preceding pages delineating the distinctions between adversarial and inquisitorial models, a true pragmatist is most likely to ask "does it matter?" The answer, of course, is "yes" (otherwise we would not have forced you to wade through the preceding pages). But determining when, where, and precisely how it makes a difference involves considerable ad hoc analysis and investigation. Courts seldom say "the adversary system compels the following result" or "we base our decision on the implicit needs of the adversary system." Occasionally, however, judges come close to talking openly about the systemic force of the adversarial model on particular decisions. For example, in *United States v. Williams*,[65] a Supreme Court majority ruled on a legal issue and was met with strong protests by four dissenters, who argued that the issue was not preserved below and hence should not be reviewed by the high court out of deference to "the adversary process," an argument to which the majority devoted extensive discussion in attempted refutation. More often, the adversary system and its norms affect case outcomes in unspoken ways.

For example, capital punishment continues as an issue vexing both the legal profession and society at large. When eleventh-hour habeas corpus petitions assert the need for further scrutiny of the capital case (due to new evidence, past error, overlooked constitutional issues, etc.), the prisoner's counsel seeks to once again bring a judicial officer into a case the system thought was finally adjudicated. Increasingly, federal courts have resisted these efforts, with substantial support from the executive and legislative branches. Although more often implicit than explicit, the federal bench, particularly more conservative jurists, have essentially said that under an adversarial system, a prisoner -- even one sentenced to die -- has only a limited number of chances to attempt to make his case of innocence, extenuating circumstances, or unconstitutionality. If that case has been poorly presented or overlooked during the earlier stages of adjudication, courts are increasingly unlikely to permit review even at the risk of tolerating considerable substantive unfairness or mistake.

Conversely, supporters of more expansive habeas corpus review have often argued that the assumed efficacy of the adversary system is a farce if capital convicts are poorly represented during early proceedings. Consequently, they often support even eleventh-hour review that borders on the repetitive in order to correct deficiencies of adversarialism in practice or to ensure that goals of justice and accuracy are not undermined by the occasionally irreconcilable norms of finality and party control. In effect, strong adversarialists are willing to let litigants be their own worst enemies

---

[65] 112 S. Ct. 1735 (1992).

or to suffer the inequality that often accompanies autonomy. Others, although still basically committed to the adversarial norm, support greater judicial intervention to serve other goals. This is a divide unlikely to be bridged in the near future. The adversary system and differing enthusiasm for its effects will continue to play a role in these matters.

Courts are occasionally quite express in their invocation of the norms of adversarialism as a basis for decision. For example, in the famous Supreme Court case of *Hickman v. Taylor*,[66] one attorney sought access to witness statements compiled by opposing counsel in preparation for trial. The Court refused to compel the investigating attorney to provide his "work product" to his adversary except under narrow circumstances where an ironclad view of "finders, keepers" would work an injustice to either the system or other litigants. The spirit of adversarialism runs through Justice Murphy's majority opinion. "[I]n performing his various duties, however, it is essential that a lawyer work with a certain degree of privacy, free from unnecessary intrusion by opposing parties and their counsel . . . [otherwise,] [t]he effect on the legal profession would be demoralizing. And the interests of the clients and the cause of justice would be poorly served."[67] Justice Jackson's concurring opinion expresses his support for the adversary system more directly and with greater pith: "[A] common law trial is and always should be an adversary proceeding. Discovery was hardly intended to enable a learned profession to perform its functions either without wits or on wits borrowed from the adversary."[68]

The notion that parties rise or fall on their efforts and those of counsel serves in part to explain much of the jurisprudence of doctrines such as waiver, estoppel, laches, strict construction of limitations periods, the party admission exception to the hearsay rule, and the statement against interest exception to the hearsay rule. For example, a party may occasionally be stung by technically irrelevant or otherwise excludable evidence because its own conduct has "opened the door" to the court's consideration of the evidence. The old adage about being careful in what one says or does tends to take on particular meaning for lawyers. Although the pitfalls of foot-in-mouth disease are probably greater for litigation lawyers than the rest of the profession, nonlitigators are hardly immune. For example,

---

[66] 329 U.S. 495 (1947).

[67] 329 U.S. at 510, 511.

[68] 329 U.S. at 516 (Jackson, J., concurring).

statements made when negotiating a contract often have importance in subsequent litigation about the contract, even where the transaction is heavily documented with an eye toward limiting a court's consideration of extrinsic evidence.

Although this aspect of adversarialism is more prominent in civil litigation, it occurs in criminal law as well. For example, criminal suspects may waive their constitutional right to consult a lawyer. But criminal law often contains rules or norms limiting adversarialism to some degree. For example, the famous "Miranda warning" must be given to suspects in police custody to inform (or remind) them of their rights to remain silent and to see a lawyer. The requirement that prosecutors disclose exculpatory evidence to the defense is another example of the modified adversarialism often found in criminal law.

Administrative law resembles private civil adjudication, but with some interesting differences. For example, the general rule, one that is nearly absolute, holds that neither promissory nor equitable estoppel operates against the government. In other words, the government is not usually bound by the unauthorized or erroneous statements of its agents, even if relied upon by others. For an adversary system that prides itself on private citizens operating as a check on government power, this is a doctrine that probably should be more controversial than it has been in the hands of most courts.

On the whole, however, the unwritten consequences of the adversary system consistently pervade litigation and dispute resolution. Whether adversarialism's impact is express or implied, small or large, varies markedly from case to case. But in our view it is often there, at least as a background norm or judicial value of some import. The most effective lawyers and the wisest judges recognize this and shape their arguments and decisions accordingly.

Alternative Dispute Resolution (ADR).

Although lawsuits provide the paradigmatic model of dispute resolution in our society, the judiciary lacks a complete monopoly on disputing. To state an obvious fact often overlooked in current discussion about America's supposed "litigation explosion," nobody forces a plaintiff to resort to the courts. Aggrieved parties always have the option of forgoing the formal pursuit of recompense and "lumping it." Certainly, claimants make considerable use of informal methods to obtain satisfaction, such as oral complaints, threatening letters, exchange of merchandise, self-help repossession of collateral, holding back on the last installment until the contractor gets the bumps out of the new sidewalk, and so on.

Settlement or Default. Even after a lawsuit is commenced, it hardly need be pursued to the end. Parties can and do settle litigation. Although precise data are difficult to obtain, the conventional wisdom holds that 95 percent or more of litigation ends in settlement. One authority has characterized the American system as "one of compulsory bargaining in response to claims of right" where the courts provide an "arena" in which disputants are brought together with the judiciary tacitly hoping for private settlement and "litigation serving to resolve breakdowns in negotiation."[69]

In a sense, then, settlement (either informal or court-aided) is the most pervasive means of dispute resolution in the United States. Consequently, a completely accurate view might label litigation as alternative dispute resolution, since lawsuits are only used when informal settlement is impossible or elusive and are only adjudicated to conclusion in a small minority of cases. However, through accident of history and the legal profession's own self-absorption, we typically refer to nonlitigation methods of determining claims as "alternative dispute resolution" or "ADR."

ADR is a coat of multiple colors now routinely touched upon across the curriculum as well as itself being the subject of entire courses. Therefore, we attempt no comprehensive overview of ADR. Rather, we hope to alert the reader to jurisprudential issues lurking behind the black letter of ADR. For example, the previous comment that litigation is an option holds true for plaintiffs (they can decide whether to bring a claim) but not necessarily for defendants, who must respond with an answer and a defense or suffer default judgment. Default judgment is itself related to the adversary process. Our judicial system assumes that it is justified to impose liability on defendants who fail to respond to claims without requiring courts to undertake searching inquiry as to the merits of the claim. In the broadest sense, of course, defendants have some choice: they can always decide to do nothing and suffer the default. Where a defendant has no assets that can be reached by the claimant or where the court in which the suit is pending lacks jurisdiction (either subject matter or personal

---

[69] JAMES, HAZARD & LEUBSDORF, *supra* note 57, § 6.7, at 300; *see also* Lewis Kornhauser & Robert Mnookin, *Bargaining in the Shadow of the Law: The Case of Divorce*, 88 YALE L.J. 950 (1979).

jurisdiction), this may even be a rational strategy for defendants who hope to save on legal fees.

For most defendants, however, complete and immediate surrender is not the preferred option. Of course, defendants who wish not to fight still have an ADR option of sorts -- settlement. This can take the form of litigation cum settlement where the defendant answers and engages in other conduct (*e.g.*, propounding discovery requests, exercising self-help) designed to signal a tough defensive posture. With the battle lines so drawn, most litigants then engage in at least some settlement discussion. As the case ensues, the facts developed may move the parties closer to settlement or harden adverse positions, requiring trial for resolution. Even after trial, settlement remains a popular option. Many cases settle while on appeal after trial but prior to the appellate court's decision.

Arbitration. Increasingly, defendants have attempted to expand their ADR options through contract or statute. For example, many states require unresolved first-party insurance claims (those between the policyholder and the insurance company) to be submitted to arbitration either in lieu of litigation or as a prerequisite to litigation. Many commercial entities when entering contracts of any substantial import include a provision in the contract requiring the parties to submit any subsequent disputes to binding arbitration. Typically, arbitration works as something of a streamlined adversary proceeding without benefit of discovery, highly structured procedure, or jury deliberation. Nonetheless, it is still adversarial rather than inquisitorial in that the arbitrator or panel of arbitrators does not gather facts. The parties still control the presentation of claims, evidence, and legal argument. When the arbitrator or panel decides, there is usually less procedural structure as well. Whereas courts are generally required to issue findings of facts and conclusions of law in civil bench trials, arbitrators usually issue a one-page arbitration "award" declaring who won and how much. By statute, there is some judicial review of arbitration awards in both the federal and state systems but the review is highly deferential. Generally, arbitration awards will be vacated only where the arbitrators have exceeded their authority or where there is evidence of bias or prejudice on the part of the arbitrators.

Mediation. Many parties contract for mandatory mediation in lieu of, or as an adjunct to, arbitration. Mediation is an attempt to negotiate a resolution of a dispute through working with a third-party "facilitator" who is neutral (*i.e.*, without a financial or other strong tie to the disputants). Mediation is essentially an expert-assisted settlement effort. By definition, mediation is intended to be non-coercive; the mediator cannot force the parties to do anything, but attempts to persuade them to come together in a fair agreement. As previously noted, where two litigants have previously agreed to arbitration, mediation, or a variant of these major forms of ADR, either party can invoke the agreement and compel the dispute to be resolved via the chosen ADR method rather than litigation. Litigants dissatisfied with mediation can, of course, continue to litigate. Arbitration is by far the most popular alternative to litigation, particularly when attempts to invoke ADR are spearheaded by private parties. However, hybrid forms of ADR exist in significant degree, often with official involvement of the judicial system.

Court-Annexed Arbitration. One hybrid form of ADR adopted by many state and federal courts is "court-annexed" arbitration or mediation systems in which certain types of newly-filed cases (usually those of basic personal injury actions or contract disputes and involving only claims for money damages rather than injunctive relief) are automatically routed to an arbitration or mediation program administered by the courts. Even when mediation fails to terminate the litigation, it may succeed in culling some claims from the litigation or in improving the relations or clarifying the positions of the parties so that litigation proceeds more efficiently or effectively.

Participants in court-annexed arbitration can also demand trial if dissatisfied with the arbitration award. But litigants who have committed by contract to arbitrate disputes must abide by the award subject to the narrow grounds of judicial review available. Here, as in "pure" settlement negotiation, the judicial system is an important coercive backstop to ADR activity. For example, if the losing arbitrant refuses to pay the arbitration award, the winning party may come to court and request judgment on the arbitration award. Thereafter, the winner can enforce the award and collect upon it like any other judgment and use creditor's remedies such as attachment, garnishment, sequestration, and so on.

Additional Types of ADR. Other forms of hybrid ADR include the summary jury trial, in which litigants give a truncated presentation to a group of real jurors without binding authority. The theory of the summary jury trial is that it provides a dose of reality for litigants whose respective views of the merits of the lawsuit are too disparate to permit settlement. In addition, some administrative schemes can be viewed as forms of ADR. For example, every state has workers' compensation laws that essentially require employers to purchase workers' compensation insurance so that it is available to compensate employees injured on the job. Benefits are established by a schedule and are not individually valued. Workers need not prove employer fault to collect.

To illustrate, assume a worker who loses a finger in a punch press gets a certain amount; the worker who plays piano as his main hobby is not treated differently from one whose only avocation is reading. When an injury occurs and a claim is made, the employer may dispute the claim (*e.g.*, arguing that the injury occurred out of the workplace or that it is not as serious as claimed). For example, a warehouse worker may claim that he strained his back on the loading dock and is now permanently unable to work. The employer may dispute both claims. In such cases, most states provide an administrative agency proceeding (often called a hearing or hearing examination) which considers and decides the matter, subject only to limited judicial review such as that available for arbitration awards. Other examples include programs such as the Black Lung Benefits Review Board (30 U.S.C. § 932), which provides a type of federal backup workers' compensation for disabled miners, and the National Vaccine Injury Compensation Program (42 U.S.C. § 300aa *et seq.*), which abrogates private tort actions against vaccine manufacturers in lieu of an administration compensation system for injured parties. Note how in America even ADR is usually shaped by enthusiasm for (or reflexive tilt toward) the adversary system.

Broadly construed, one might also argue that other government programs can be a type of ADR. For example, approximately one-half the states have statutes establishing no-fault automobile insurance. To the extent that the mandatory no-fault policy precludes litigation of claims formerly heard by the courts, it can be said to be an ADR device. Normally, however, lawyers discussing ADR are referring to some sort of procedure specifically focused upon a pending dispute rather than a government program affecting a class of disputes. Perhaps this nomenclature only underscores how wedded American lawyers are to the ideal of bipolar adversarial adjudication or its close cousins. By contrast, the Western European nations using the inquisitorial model tend to have more extensive social programs and administrative agency activities than does the United States.

ADR has been a growth industry in the United States during the late 20th century and promises to continue to be an important aspect of social ordering in this country. Although adversarial litigation is likely to continue as the stock-in-trade of the American lawyer, continuing changes in adjudication and the expansion of ADR will require lawyers to advise clients and devise disputing strategies with a perspective extending beyond the traditional horizons of litigation.

Comparing Litigation and Its Alternatives.

The major forms of alternative dispute resolution are not radically different from litigation. All of them in fact build upon the litigation model to at least some degree, particularly in their continued use of the adversarial model of party control and party presentation of the dispute. Nonetheless, many lawyers and social scientists are engaged in continuing debate over the relative pros and cons of litigation and ADR.

Several legal scholars have suggested that ADR offers either lower quality justice or differs sufficiently from litigation as to affect case outcomes. For example, federal judges have life tenure and are screened by the Justice Department and the U.S. Senate. Courts operate with defined procedural rules as well. In addition, appellate review also acts as a quality control device. Critics of ADR see it as less likely to produce neutral or wise outcomes because it lacks these attributes. Consequently, they fear that winners and losers will be determined as much by forum selection as by the merits of the dispute, particularly if arbitrators or mediators tend to favor certain classes of litigants. To the extent that certain litigants can steer disputes to more favorable forums, they find this troubling. If, for example, large retailers or stock brokers can require consumers to sign arbitration clauses in order to do business and arbitration routinely favors the brokers and retailers, ADR has then become a means of redistributing wealth in society. Thus, these critics of (or skeptics regarding) ADR may argue that judicial scrutiny of ADR agreements and outcomes should be increased and that the current norm of judicial deference is unwise.

Defenders of ADR counter that the critics have either failed to prove that ADR results in different outcomes or have mistakenly assumed that the judicial result is preferable, making any distinction tautologically defined as "bad" or "inferior." Supporters of ADR often question whether court outcomes are correct. Many argue, for example, that arbitration generally brings better substantive results, particularly when the matter arbitrated involves technical disputes over patents, commercial practices, or the stock market. The arbitrators often have expertise judges lack. ADR proponents deny that arbitrators or mediators are more likely than judges to be biased. Other proponents of ADR acknowledge that devices such as arbitration have fewer procedural safeguards and may miss some information when compared to full-dress litigation but view this as a respectable tradeoff in light of the claimed lower costs and faster processing time of arbitration and other ADR hybrids.

Mediation critics and proponents also square off over slightly different issues. Proponents content that mediation is preferable because it permits disputants a last chance at amicable (or at least acceptable) accord, which can be especially important if the parties must continue to coexist in the future (regarding future contracts, child custody, employment, or other ongoing relations). Opponents of mediation charge that its informality stacks the deck in favor of the party that comes to the bargaining table with greater intrinsic strength: the larger corporation; the employer; the husband whose wife has relatively low wealth or earning power. Since mediators cannot order the stronger party around as can arbitrators and judges, critics see mediation as often only adding delay or a gloss of legitimacy to pre-existing social or economic inequality.

Both proponents and critics of ADR raise powerful conceptual points. Empirical work in the area is relatively limited but suggests that the overall fairness and efficacy of ADR as compared to litigation varies substantially according to the particular methods of the ADR device in question as well as the disputants involved and the subject matter of the dispute. Continuing research and experimentation by disputants will undoubtedly provide additional information as ADR continues to grow in use. Notwithstanding this growth, courts will likely retain a major role in dispute resolution and social ordering.

REFERENCES FOR FURTHER READING

JOHN J. COUND, JACK H. FRIEDENTHAL, ARTHUR A. MILLER & JOHN E. SEXTON, CIVIL PROCEDURE ch. 15 (6th ed. 1993).

MIRJAN R. DAMASKA, THE FACES OF JUSTICE AND STATE AUTHORITY (1986); *Structures of Authority and Comparative Criminal Procedure*, 84 YALE L.J. 480 (1975).

Owen Fiss, *Against Settlement*, 93 YALE L.J. 1073 (1984); *see also* Carrie Menkel-Meadow, *For and Against Settlement: Uses and Abuses of the Mandatory Settlement Conference*, 33 UCLA L. REV. 485 (1985).

MARVIN E. FRANKEL, THE SEARCH FOR TRUTH: AN UMPIREAL VIEW (1975).

MONROE H. FREEDMAN, LAWYERS' ETHICS IN AN ADVERSARY SYSTEM (1975).

Marc Galanter, *Why the 'Haves' Come Out Ahead: Speculations on the Limits of Legal Change*, 9 LAW & SOC. REV. 95 (1974).

STEPHEN B. GOLDBERG, ERIC GREEN & FRANK A. SANDER, DISPUTE RESOLUTION (1988).

GEOFFREY C. HAZARD, JR. & WILLIAM N. HODES, THE LAW OF LAWYERING (2d ed. 1990).

FLEMING JAMES, JR., GEOFFREY C. HAZARD, JR. & JOHN LEUBSDORF, CIVIL PROCEDURE (4th ed. 1992).

STEPHEN A. LANDSMAN, READINGS ON ADVERSARIAL JUSTICE: THE AMERICAN APPROACH TO ADJUDICATION (1988); *see also* Stephen A. Landsman, *The Rise of the Contentious Spirit: Adversary Procedure in Eighteenth Century England*, 75 CORNELL L. REV. 497 (1990) (tracing historical expansion of adversarialism in England and noting link to increased individual and political rights); *The Decline of the Adversary System: How the Rhetoric of Swift and Certain Justice Has Affected Adjudication in American Courts*, 29 BUFFALO L. REV. 487 (1980).

John H. Langbein, *The German Advantage in Civil Procedure*, 52 U. CHI. L. REV. 823 (1985); *see* Ronald Allen, Stefan Koch, Kurt Riechenberg & D. Toby Rosen, *The German Advantage in Civil Procedure: A Plea for More Details and Fewer Generalities in Comparative Scholarship*, 82 NW. U.L. REV. 705 (1986) (attacking Langbein's analysis); John H. Langbein, *Trashing the German Advantage*, 82 NW. U.L. REV. 763 (1988) (responding to Allen); Ronald Allen, *Idealization and Caricature in Comparative Scholarship*, 82 NW. U.L. REV. 785 (1988); *see also* Samuel R. Gross, *The American Advantage: The Value of Inefficient Litigation*, 85 MICH. L. REV. 734 (1987).

Arthur Miller, *The Adversary System: Dinosaur or Phoenix*, 69 MINN. L. REV. 1 (1984).

JEFFREY O'CONNELL & C. BRIAN KELLY, THE BLAME GAME: INJURIES, INSURANCE, AND INJUSTICE (1987).

Judith Resnik, *Failing Faith: Adjudicatory Procedure in Decline*, 53 U. CHI. L. REV. 494 (1986); *Managerial Judges*, 96 HARV. L. REV. 374 (1982).

William Simon, *The Ideology of Advocacy, Procedural Justice and Professional Ethics*, 1978 WIS. L. REV. 29.

CHARLES W. WOLFRAM, MODERN LEGAL ETHICS (1986).

CHAPTER SIX

HISTORICAL, JURISPRUDENTIAL, AND MULTIDISCIPLINARY INFLUENCES ON LAW

- **Introduction**
- **Whence Law Came**
- **What Is Jurisprudence and Where Did It Come From?**
  - ○ **Natural Law**
  - ○ **Positivism**
  - ○ **Formalism**
  - ○ **Instrumentalism/Functionalism**
- **Jurisprudence and Legal Structure**
- **Langdell and Legal Formalism**
- **The Vulnerability of High Formalism**
- **Holmes as Precursor to the Legal Realists**
- **Roscoe Pound's Critique and Sociological Jurisprudence**
- **The Legal Realist Movement**
- **The Empire Strikes Back (Sort of): The Harvard Legal Process School**
  - ○ **Another Strand: Analytic Jurisprudence and Debate About the Nature of Law in the Post-War Era**
  - ○ **Defending Progressive Adjudication: Fundamental Rights Jurisprudence**
  - ○ **Conservative Counterattacks**
- **After the Realist Revolution and the Legal Process Rehabilitation: Current Trends in Modern Jurisprudence**
  - ○ **The Law and Economics Movement and Public Choice Theory**
  - ○ **Multidisciplinarism, the Law & Society Movement, and the Core "Law ands" of Sociology, Psychology, and Anthropology**
  - ○ **Peripheral "Law ands"**
  - ○ **New "Law ands"**
  - ○ **Critical Legal Studies**
  - ○ **Law as Interpretation**
  - ○ **Feminist Jurisprudence**

○ **Critical Race Theory**
○ **Civic Republicanism**
○ **Postmodernism, Pragmatism and Related Concepts**
• **Does It Matter? An Illustration of the Impact of Different Jurisprudential Approaches**
• **Where Are We Now?**
• **References for Further Reading**

This book examines many of the forces that shape legal outcomes and legal doctrines. Not too surprisingly, one of those forces is the legal community's past. Also important is the currently prevailing set of attitudes toward jurisprudence. Theories of law and the legal process shape law and legal process. This is no secret.[70] What may surprise students or others unfamiliar with legal theory, however, is the degree to which jurisprudential attitudes have shifted over time. In addition, the intellectual legal community's overall consensus on legal theory is considerably fragmented once one ventures beyond the core areas of agreement.

This book has thus far tended to address these forces as background factors exerting a tidal pull on the law: philosophy; ethics; economics; politics; government; and dispute resolution structures. These factors influence the law even if lawyers, judges, and litigators never consciously reflect upon them. History, which could perhaps be defined as the sum of these and other social forces over time, has not be explicitly discussed, but it also has an obvious impact. In this chapter, we provide a very brief historical overview of the development of the law. Rather than seeking to review legal history per se, this chapter raises historical concerns and focuses on the modern intellectual history of Anglo-American law. The discussion covers historical developments in jurisprudence and the relation of law to other areas of learning.

This chapter also discusses significant movements in which nonlegal material is self-consciously examined with, or incorporated into, law. To a large extent, these efforts are not only efforts at multidisciplinarism but

---

[70] The legal community's acceptance of a particular brand of jurisprudence might also be considered a "paradigm" of law: a coherent model or framework of the legal world that establishes fundamental beliefs and permissible avenues of inquiry. *See generally* THOMAS S. KUHN, THE STRUCTURE OF SCIENTIFIC REVOLUTIONS (2d ed. 1970) (describing paradigms of different disciplines and changes in dominance of different paradigms).

also jurisprudential movements or subschools of their own. We generally (but not disparagingly) refer to them as the "law and . . ." movements or "law ands." The Law and Economics movement, having been accorded virtually its own chapter (Chapter Two), is touched upon only briefly. Perhaps a better title for this chapter would have been "Legal Anthropology and Epistemology."

Whence Law Came.

As the saying goes, "a page of history is worth a volume of logic."[71] Much of the state of current American law (or law anywhere), whether good or ill, can be explained better by historical referents than rational analysis. For example, prior to modern efforts to decrease jury size, twelve was considered the apt number of persons to constitute a jury in either criminal or civil cases. Although the number may have had some religious roots (*e.g.*, the twelve disciples of Jesus), no one is really sure why this size of jury arose in the English common law. Nonetheless, this historical practice became the norm. Consequently, a jury size of twelve carried a presumption of correctness that had to be overcome by arguments supporting the notion that smaller juries would be better (*e.g.*, less costly, more efficient) without any diminution of deliberative quality. In the 1970s, the American legal system, perhaps erroneously, accepted arguments in favor of permitting smaller juries.[72]

History is sometimes seen as its own rationale. For example, the Supreme Court has upheld a court's exercise of personal jurisdiction over a defendant solely because the defendant was handed a summons and complaint within the state (even if the instance of this "service of process" is the defendant's only visit to the state) simply because the practice is

---

[71] Or so thought Supreme Court Justice Oliver Wendell Holmes, writing in New York Trust Co. v. Eisner, 256 U.S. 345, 349 (1921).

[72] *See* Williams v. Florida, 399 U.S. 78 (1970) (six-person jury constitutional); *but see Ballew v. Georgia*, 435 U.S. 223 (1977) (five-person jury unconstitutional). Prominent social scientists have persuasively argued that the Court was wrong to accept juries as small as six. *See* Hans Zeisel, . . . *And Then There Were None: The Diminution of the Federal Jury*, 38 U. CHI. L. REV. 710 (1971); Michael J. Saks, *Ignorance of Science Is No Excuse*, 10 TRIAL 18 (Nov.-Dec. 1974). Perhaps the Ancients had stumbled onto something.

venerable, saying "its validation is its pedigree."[73] In a more controversial context, the Court upheld state laws criminalizing consensual sex by adult men in part because of historical condemnations of homosexuality.[74]

We cannot in this slim volume provide a comprehensive chronicle (or critique) of the ways in which historical norms or the status quo affect legal outcomes; the impact is omnipresent. Rather, we hope to remind the reader that the impact of history is sometimes so obvious that it is overlooked. Courts are seldom direct when basing decisions on historical practice or inertia in favor of the status quo. In addition, we emphasize a distinction between the impact of the status quo per se (the current norm) and the history of the status quo (the length and consistency of the law or society's use of the current norm). As an advocate, one almost always has an advantage defending the status quo. The advocate has even more of an advantage in defending a long-standing status quo that has been neither controversial nor criticized.

People seldom stop to ponder the origin of law. If they did, the answers would be pretty basic, at least at one level. Law arose as a means of organizing society and enforcing social norms for the benefit of the community. At its most rudimentary, law was simply a code of conduct or rules governing society. For example, the society may be a prehistoric tribe. When group norms were breached, intuition tells us that the tribe must have possessed some relatively institutionalized means for dealing with such problems. Societies without such means were probably not long-lived, although a tribe styled on "The Lord of the Flies"[75] is as least conceivable. Most likely, even primitive societies had at least a crude mechanism for adjudication. It may have been only the tribal shaman so often idealized in "B" movies, but that still counts.

It appears that more advanced ancient societies tended to have more of the trappings that modern lawyers tend to associate with due process: a right to make and respond to accusations; some consistent procedure for

---

[73] *See* Burnham v. Superior Court, 496 U.S. 604 (1990).

[74] *See* Bowers v. Hardwick, 478 U.S. 186 (1986).

[75] *See* WILLIAM GOLDING, THE LORD OF THE FLIES (1958) (British schoolboys shipwrecked on island begin to develop working society that degenerates into rival clans, with less "civilized" clan taking control by force, including killing).

hearing the disputants and gathering information; a neutral, established figure to hear and decide the case; a means of enforcing the decision. The "great" civilizations of the ancient world all appear to have met these criteria in some form. However, the operation of the ancient systems was often affected by its intertwinement with the ruling royalty or elite (even in Athens, which for much of its golden age was a democracy, but one with slaves and clear second-class status for women and noncitizens), the prevailing religion of the culture, or both. As a result, ancient adjudications would often fail to satisfy the modern standard of due process since decisions and remedies might well hinge more on the personal attitudes of the King or High Priest than on any legal precepts.

The role of religion in law is complex and neither completely understood nor consistent. Some societies, even modern ones, are theocracies where religious law and teachings effectively delineate the sphere of secular law as well. For example, in countries like Iran and Saudi Arabia, the making and enforcement of both civil and criminal law flows quite directly from religious doctrine. Other countries or cultures keep the secular and religious more separate. For example, parts of Nigeria are apparently governed primarily by secular law derived from French colonial law while both Islamic and tribal law dominate some matters such as domestic relations. In the United States, the aspiration is that religion, or at least advocacy of any particular religion, be separate from the government's legal authority. But prevailing religious beliefs have a substantial impact on legal rules and outcomes even in secular nations.[76] Although the influence of religion upon adjudication outcomes is seldom this overt, it is probably not infrequent. On the whole, however, it appears that religious influence over law was greater in the past than today.

The influence of religion -- like most anything else -- is subject to historical trends. For example, the early ancient Greek civilization appears to have been quite devout toward its assortment of gods, although Greek mythology reveals that they were deemed to hold a number of very human failings (*e.g.*, Zeus's jealousy, Apollo's ego, and the assorted scheming of the gods on behalf of their favorite humans, which among other things was

---

[76] For example, in one famous case, the U.S. Supreme Court held that a broadly worded statute banning the importation of foreign workers did not apply to a church's recruitment of a British minister, in part because the United States is a "Christian nation" that encourages rather than inhibits religion (at least favored religions). *See* Holy Trinity Church v. United States, 143 U.S. 457 (1892). Today's Supreme Court would almost certainly avoid the "Christian nation" rhetoric.

said to have started the Trojan War). Later in ancient Greek civilization came the era of the "Twilight of the Gods" when social and political leaders quite openly questioned or rebelled against the prevailing theology.

During medieval times, as the Roman Catholic Church consolidated its power, both religion and religious law were very important as means of social ordering. "Canon law," the legal rules and principles of the Church, not only governed the status of church members in matters such as marriage, paternity, or standing within the church, but also set forth a regime of rules governing ostensibly secular behavior, such as property law and commercial transactions. Over time, the authoritative sphere of canon law generally shrank to matters of personal behavior and morality while the lay government administered commercial, property, and public law.[77]

Although many readers might today regard canon law as old-fashioned, prudish, and rigid, both it and the Roman Code of Justinian (from whom the modern English word justice is derived) were in their day substantial advancements of the legal culture. They set forth comprehensive legal schemes, rules and regulations governing personal conduct and social organization. They were enforced by established institutions with an array of remedies. Although modern thinkers might not always agree with the substantive outcomes, they were substantial strides toward modern law.

The coming of the Renaissance increased interest in the secular and scientific in derogation of religious hegemony. Soon after, the Protestant Reformation questioned the Catholic Church itself. The split over religion ignited the bloody Thirty Years War (from 1618-1648), which was finally ended by the Treaty of Westphalia. In attempting to recover from the war, Europe was more receptive to a secular legal and political society, a major shift in thinking that hastened the degree to which Western thought differs from that of other cultures. To be sure, religion's hold remained substantial, often being intertwined with the monarchy (the so-called "divine right of kings" that now seems ludicrous, at least to Westerners, in retrospect). The revolutions of the 18th and 19th centuries (*e.g.*, the American, French, Industrial) moved Western society quite sharply toward greater secularization.

---

[77] *See* GEORGE H. SABINE & THOMAS L. THORSON, A HISTORY OF POLITICAL THEORY 215-308 (4th ed. 1973) (tracing greater secularization of political thought).

Modern examples also testify to the shifting balance of religious and secular law -- and the world-wide trend is not always away from religion. For example, Iran attempted a more Western secularization of law during the reign of the Shah (Persian for "king") (1953-1979), much to the resentment of many Iranians. During the early years of the Islamic Republic, dominated by Ayatollah Khomeini (1979-1987), religious law was reported to have taken over the secular. Although the Islamic Republic continued in the same form after Khomeini's death, some observers report a greater liberalization of the society, tending toward less theological dominance over nonreligious affairs. Some ancient societies provide contrasting examples. They are reported to have kept surprising distance (for the time) between the religious and the secular. But history is neither linear nor static.

Despite the twists and turns of history, there appears in Western society as a whole to have been a sporadic evolution away from theological doctrine or divine right of the rulers toward what we might now term a "rule of law" in which social norms are to be evenly applied regardless of the status of persons affected. The English legal scholar Sir Henry Maine wrote that modern legal society evidences a distinct movement from "status to contract,"[78] by which he means that the organization of society is increasingly based on agreements and laws of general application rather than class structure. Most scholars accept this view, although many argue that modern law continues the tendency to favor political and social elites. Nonetheless, even critics tend to see modern law as less protective of the ruling class than its predecessors.

While secularizing, Western societies have also moved toward separating the judicial function from that of the executive leader (be it king, president, or premier). Anglo-American law is also the product of the evolution of tribal and royal practices in England, a land dominated by the Anglo-Saxon ethnic group prior to 1066 when William the Conqueror and his Norman army triumphed at the battle of Hastings. The Normans, from what is now western France, brought with them many continental legal norms with Roman roots but did not supplant all existing English legal structures. Over the centuries, this fusion produced a number of effects that continue to influence Anglo-American jurisprudence. For example, the division between courts of law and courts of equity that was long important in America (and continues in some importance notwithstanding the merger of these two courts in the federal and most state systems), grew from

---

[78] HENRY S. MAINE, ANCIENT LAW: ITS CONNECTION WITH THE EARLY HISTORY OF SOCIETY AND ITS RELATION TO MODERN IDEAS (15th ed. 1894).

English roots. The British crown established parallel systems of courts, which themselves stemmed from the Norman system and the law courts operated by the Anglo-Saxons. It appears that jury trial was kept alive largely because the conquered Anglo-Saxons liked the institution and worked to keep it as a protection against the whims of Norman rulers. The King's chancellor, following the continental European tradition derived from Rome, made his determinations without a jury, in part to be able to more flexibly right the wrongs of the law courts and in part to maintain a measure of control over the largely Anglo-Saxon juries.[79] As discussed more fully in Chapter Four, the American colonies retained many aspects of the British system.

Despite these historical influences, American law had started to exhibit distinct differences from British law well before the Revolution. In addition to adapting to a different environment (one with more land, less civilization, more frontier threats, less class structure), American law was also differentiated because of its interaction with other legal cultures involved in the settlement of the United States: Native Americans; Dutch; French; Spanish. Even today, the law of Louisiana remains heavily influenced by the Napoleonic Code of France and is arguably a continental or code system rather than a common law system. The law of the western states, particularly California, reflects aspects of past Spanish colonization or influence. The institution of the district attorney or local prosecutor may be of Dutch origin.

During its history, United States law has frequently resulted from commercial, geographic, social, and political conflict. Some legal rules or systems reflect the non-legal dominance of certain groups, persons, or entities. As one leading authority has suggested, law and legal history are "mirror[s] of society."[80] Another important legal historian has theorized that law, particularly developments in the 19th century, reflects the ascendancy of capitalist business forces during the Industrial Revolution.[81]

---

[79] For an excellent brief introduction to Anglo-American legal history, especially as it affects procedure, *see* FLEMING JAMES, JR., GEOFFREY C. HAZARD, JR. & JOHN LEUBSDORF, CIVIL PROCEDURE §§ 1.3-1.7 (4th ed. 1992).

[80] *See* LAWRENCE M. FRIEDMAN, A HISTORY OF AMERICAN LAW 14 (1973).

[81] *See* MORTON HORWITZ, THE TRANSFORMATION OF AMERICAN LAW 1760-1850 (1977); *see also* MORTON HORWITZ, THE TRANSFORMATION OF AMERICAN LAW 1850-1960 (1992).

American legal doctrines and institutions, like those of other nations, have a history that has shaped them. Assessments of whether the outcomes have more to do with politics, religion, personality, war (*e.g.*, what would British law look like without the Norman invasion? Would Canon Law have remained dominant had the Reformation and the Thirty Years War not occurred?) or with mere accident varies with the portion of law at issue and also (frequently) with the viewpoint of the analyst. But today's law stems not only from the inexorable pressures of history and society but also from the intellectual efforts of those who reflect upon the law.

What Is Jurisprudence and Where Did It Come From?

Jurisprudence is traditionally defined as a "system of law," "science of law," or the study of legal principles and relationships.[82] More narrowly, lawyers may view jurisprudence as the "body of rules and theories which make up a certain field of law."[83] As used in this chapter, the embellished term "jurisprudence" pertains to particular theories of law or legal constructs. Consequently, we refer to a jurisprudence of legal formalism, one of legal realism, a feminist jurisprudence, and so on.

We also use the term "jurisprudence" to refer to the law in all its applications, including: adjudication; common law development; statutory interpretation; administrative agency rulemaking and enforcement; prosecutorial discretion; executive clemency. We also wish to avoid the loaded term "science" when discussing law or jurisprudence as this evokes an old and ongoing debate among legal scholars regarding the degree to which one might term law "scientific" and whether seeing law as a type of science invariably leads to a mechanical and formalistic view of the law.

We do not here attempt to review attitudes since antiquity toward law and justice. Instead, we begin with what should be most relevant for the modern era, which we define as roughly beginning with the start of formal legal education in America, generally ascribed to the opening of Harvard Law School in 1816. Establishment of a legal education infra-

---

[82] *See* BLACK'S LAW DICTIONARY 992 (4th ed. 1968); WEBSTER'S NINTH NEW COLLEGIATE DICTIONARY 655 (1984).

[83] JULES COLEMAN & ANTHONY J. SEBOK, SELECTED ESSAYS IN JURISPRUDENCE i (1993).

structure seems to us an important point of demarcation because established legal education also suggests institutionalized jurisprudential thought.

In modern Anglo-American jurisprudence (and perhaps since antiquity), there have been three primary (but often interwoven) strands of jurisprudence. Jurisprudential thought tends to try to achieve (1) a theory of law, (2) a theory of legal interpretation, or (3) a theory of adjudication.[84] Scholars working on a theory of law tend to focus on the nature of law, the separation or merger of law and morality, ethical questions, issues of justice, and moral philosophy. This type of jurisprudential enterprise is a fusion of philosophy and law. Scholars focusing on legal interpretation pay considerable attention to questions of interpretative authority and techniques, including problems of word meaning and interpretative convention as well as the degree of discretion or constraint affecting interpreters. Scholars focusing on the nature of adjudication tend more toward a socio-political jurisprudence, which focuses on the behavior of legal actors, social factors, and legal policymaking.

Core concepts of ethics have already been discussed in Chapter One. Although touching upon the nature of law and its interpretation, our chronological narrative in this chapter will concentrate most on the nature of adjudication and socio-political jurisprudence, which is the prime area of activity today. Questions about the nature of law and the degree of distinction between law and morality received considerable attention during the period of 1940-1980 and have by no means disappeared. Issues of interpretation are ever-present in law but often recede into the background. For example, statutory interpretation was widely overlooked during the period of 1960-1980 but experienced a considerable revival during the 1980s. As discussed below, scholarship on a wide range of legal interpretation issues also burst forth during the 1980s.

To some extent, issues of constitutional interpretation are different in America because they always are close to center stage, particularly since

---

[84] Or perhaps all three. According to Sebok, THE LEGAL PROCESS by HENRY HART & ALBERT SACKS (tent. ed. 1958) contains all three strands. *See* ANTHONY J. SEBOK, LEGAL POSITIVISM AND THE GROWTH OF TWENTIETH CENTURY AMERICAN JURISPRUDENCE 262 (1993) (unpublished Ph.D. dissertation, Princeton University). The Hart and Sacks book was an unpublished, but widely circulated and very influential, manuscript used by these two eminent Harvard professors as teaching materials.

the Warren Court and the decision in *Brown v. Board of Education.*[85] Many observers see much of the American jurisprudential debate during the period of 1950-1980 as focusing on questions of justifying the *Brown* decision (Did the Court, however enlightened its views, act as a super-legislature?). Because constitutional law receives much attention, the jurisprudential attitudes of constitutional scholars receive much attention. We try in this chapter not to be too "con law" driven in our explanation, striving instead to discuss jurisprudence as it affects law as a whole.

To be sure, there was jurisprudence before the 19th century and before there were full-time law schools. Jurisprudence results whenever the King, the Parliament, the Bishop, a philosopher, or a High Council thinks about law and advances a vision of law, a rule of law, an institution to apply the law, and so on. A system of law schools is not required. For example, in Great Britain today and in continental Europe, law is an undergraduate discipline.[86] Graduates further study on their own and through apprenticing to become a lawyer or the functional equivalent (in Europe, for example, notaries perform some of the functions that are performed by lawyers in America). Despite the absence of law schools as Americans know them, jurisprudence thrives in many places.

In the early and mid 19th century, legal education was largely the product of lectures, the reading of key legal texts (*e.g.*, *Blackstone's Commentaries*, the treatises of Supreme Court Justice Joseph Story), and apprenticeship. Although this period of legal education is not heavily chronicled, it appears that the prevailing jurisprudence was one of natural law, although it was beginning to yield to formalism which, by the late 19th century, became entrenched as the prevailing jurisprudence.

Natural Law. Natural law was the primary approach of William Blackstone, an English lawyer appointed to the first chair of law at Oxford in 1758. His "mission [was] to present the English law to educated nonlawyers [by which] he was forced to make an organized exposition of what the English law was, to the extent possible in lay terms, and to demonstrate why it was a legitimate 'science' or subject fit for academic

---

[85]   347 U.S. 483 (1954) (holding that racial segregation in public schools violated Equal Protection Clause of the Fourteenth Amendment of the Constitution).

[86] *See* JAMES HERGET, AMERICAN JURISPRUDENCE 1870-1970 12-22 (1990) (discussing impact of different educational systems on jurisprudence in Europe, Britain, and America).

treatment."[87]   Blackstone went at the task with relish, producing his famous *Commentaries*, which had great influence in America, perhaps even greater than its considerable influence in England. It was the most widely purchased law book of the late 18th and early 19th centuries.

According to Anglo-American norms of natural law jurisprudence, law is a product of natural reason as exemplified by the common law. But the notion of natural law predates the Anglo-American legal system. For example, natural law enjoyed favor with the ancient Greeks and Romans (but not consistent, unrestricted favor: remember what happened to Socrates, whose thinking on legal matters could be deemed natural law). Natural law thinking was also a centerpiece of much of the philosophy associated with the Renaissance and the Age of Enlightenment, both periods of comparatively free thought. However, natural law thinking has often derived from prevailing religious norms. The canon law of the Catholic Church was seen as rooted in divine principles of natural law. Consequently, natural law is often erroneously identified as part and parcel of a religious view of law and society. Some natural law writings do strike a moralist tone despite being largely grounded in a claim of substantive rationality or moral philosophy. But natural law need not be intertwined with religious precepts: a rational philosophical basis for positing natural law precepts and arriving at natural law conclusions is all that is necessary. But religious legal scholars of all eras would not see this as necessarily inconsistent with theological dictates since they view divine decrees as resulting from reason.

To Blackstone and others, the experience-based rationality of the common law was natural law that was not derived from religion. Ordinarily, posited Blackstone, the common law would be reasonable and moral, thus preventing any conflict between common law precedents and natural law. Yet Blackstone and most American lawyers of the time were not pure natural lawyers but instead had a statist slant: if there was a conflict between common law precedent and natural law reasoning, the judge was to follow precedent in order to vindicate values of stability, order, and predictability -- values based on reason. A pure natural law approach might suggest the uninhibited overruling or disregarding of any precedent in conflict with natural reason. Blackstone was quite self-satisfied with the English common law system, even smug according to many readers,

---

[87] *Id.* at 13.

perhaps because, as some said, he oversimplified or distorted portions of the law while overlooking its problems.

Positivism. In response to Blackstone's view, a number of strong critics emerged during the 19th century in England: Jeremy Bentham and his followers, John Austin and John Stuart Mill. Austin in particular is now seen as a leading founder of modern legal positivism. Positivism generally defines law not as the product of natural reason or moral dictates but merely as a command issued by a sovereign and backed by a sanction. Over the next two centuries, positivist jurisprudence in England became considerably more sophisticated as well as dominant, a phenomenon further discussed below. The United States, however, has tended to be less obviously in the positivist camp during the modern era. First, it is less clear that leading 19th century figures in America were postivists. Oliver Wendell Holmes certainly was and many give this characterization to Christopher Columbus Langdell, the influential Harvard Law School Dean and founder of the modern law school case method. Langdell never expressly identified himself in this way. He was, though, certainly a formalist.

Formalism. Under a formalist regime, the law is seen as a series of first principles laid down for application by society to recurring disputes or problems. Lawyers and judges are to reason deductively, from the general rules to specific conclusions, using these first principles in order to decide particular cases. Judges are to avoid making any moral or public policy decisions in rendering judgments. Rather, they are to constrict themselves to applying the rules. Langdell's case method stressed the derivation of the operative rules from appellate opinions, which seems quite positivist if one views the judges as Langdell's sovereigns giving Austinian commands.[88]

But to the extent that Langdell and other formalists treated first principles or rules as something "just there," the "brooding omnipresence in the sky" later mocked by Holmes, formalism can be said to have natural law aspects. In the late 19th and early 20th centuries, for example, politically conservative courts were often hostile to progressive legislation, striking it down as unconstitutional because it violated substantive due process, a now largely discredited theory. These conservative activist judges seemed just to assume that, for example, requiring an employer to limit workers' hours or participate in a social insurance scheme was an

---

[88] *See* SEBOK, *supra* note 84 (persuasively arguing that American formalists were positivists).

intolerable imposition on the employer's freedom and property rights.[89] Although the words "due process" are in the Constitution, it is far from obvious that they connote the meaning ascribed to them by these courts. Certainly, the due process clause hardly seems like a command from sovereign makers of this "superlaw" to strike down social legislation. This type of formalism, if it rests upon more than mere social prejudices, appears to result more from the judges' natural law reasoning that individual personal and economic liberties and contract flexibility are bedrock principles of our society because they are substantively reasonable.

Even as formalism took root in America, there remained a good deal of flex and unpredictability. However, legal positivism often aided the ascendence of legal formalism by providing a seemingly ready answer to the question of the proper source of legal rules and clothed the resulting rules in greater authority. The positivist defense of formalism nevertheless suffers from the weakness that many of the rules invoked for judicial decisionmaking were not clearly codified or otherwise enunciated by the political sovereign. They were seemingly drawn by judges from some background norms of thought. In addition, formalism and positivism are both weakened when the political process that supplies the rules for decision is flawed. For example, legal formalism in any totalitarian or authoritarian society is subject to reasoned challenge if the only basis for the rule invoked is a dictator's decree.

The possible tendency of legal thought to aid society's elites at the expense of the masses also cautions against the uncritical embrace of either positivism or formalism. For example, historians note that the reluctance to resort to natural law increased with the Industrial Revolution, which ushered in support for liberal/libertarian views that regard individual autonomy and contract as more important than other natural law precepts,

---

[89] *See, e.g.,* Coppage v. Kansas, 236 U.S. 1 (1915) (invalidating legislation prohibiting "Yellow Dog" contracts, which require workers as a condition of employment to agree not to join a union); Lochner v. New York, 198 U.S. 45 (1905) (striking down state law limiting bakery worker hours); Ives v. South Buffalo Railway Co., 200 N.Y. 271, 94 N.E. 431 (1911) (invalidating state workers' compensation law). In addition, many Supreme Court decisions reflect natural law bases for concern over property rights and liberty rights at risk from state government actions. Once armed with these views, judges can then often be seen as proceeding formalistically toward a decision. But the Just Compensation and Equal Protection Clauses of the Fourteenth Amendment also often provide a positivist base for these views, making it difficult to discern whether formalist judicial opinions are positivist or based on natural law.

and often more important than pre-contractual interests in property, dignity, family, or the like. Not coincidentally, the dominant legal norms assisted the ascendent social classes and their social and political views. Although this may be perfectly defensible as the proper stance of an evolving society, it simultaneously undermines the claim that formalism/positivism results in a legal regime that is completely neutral, detached, fair, and just.

Instrumentalism/Functionalism. Formalism is distinct from instrumentalism, which is sometimes called functionalism. Formalism attempts to apply rules through classification of the instant case under a general rule or principle and rigorous, deductive application of the selected rule for decision. Instrumentalist adjudication does not disregard the governing rule but application of the rule may be modified if strict application would undermine or fail to further the function intended to be achieved by the rule or the legal system of which it is a part. In interpreting statutes, for example, instrumentalists seek to find the legislature's intent or purpose and to render case results consistent with the goal of the statute irrespective of the literal terms of the statute. Some formalists may claim also to be vindicating legislative intent. These formalists tend to see this intent as reflected almost exclusively within the "four corners" of the statutory text, while the instrumentalist/functionalist is willing to consider other sources of information regarding the intent, such as the legislative history or the background of the law. Under some circumstances, the functionalist may arrive at a meaning for the statute which is seemingly at odds with a literal or strict textual construction. Other formalists disavow a search for intent in interpreting statutes and instead argue that the judicial task is limited to determining what the statute says rather than what the legislature meant.

Jurisprudence and Legal Structure.

As discussed more fully in Chapter Five, the legal infrastructure has substantial impact upon the processing and adjudication of disputes and reflects the society's jurisprudence. In the United States, for example, the common law system develops organically through the repeated process of judicial resolution of particular disputes brought before the courts. In the course of adjudicating these disputes, courts apply, modify, reject, and create legal rules, presumptions, and doctrines. Common law judges are to treat like cases alike, but results will often differ, at least at the margin, because cases are seldom exactly alike, even if similar. Because so much of the legal landscape is fleshed out by judicial decision, common law countries such as the United States and Britain tend to have fewer legislative enactments than other nations. In theory, common law systems would have few codified laws.

By contrast, in "code law" countries such as those in Western Europe (and other parts of the world influenced by its colonialization), the law is more comprehensively made by the legislature through greater use of ambitious statutes governing even private disputes over contract, tort, and property. The goal or ideal is more limited judicial lawmaking than occurs under a common law system. In Code countries, judges are visualized as adjudicating factual disputes with more circumscribed powers to create law. They are only to apply the comprehensive legal codes.

In practice, the two spheres tend to converge or overlap with Anglo-American judges increasingly bound by statute and continental judges increasingly being recognized as law creators even though they are interpreting codes rather than applying and establishing case law precedent. Whether bound by statutory text or case law precedent, the judge must make interpretative decisions that in practice affect outcomes and modify the ostensible rules of the legal system.

The common law judge has freedom to expressly modify or reverse common law rules. In the United States, judges also have the additional power of striking down or modifying statutes that are deemed to violate the Constitution. The continental judge cannot reject a statute outright. She must attempt to thwart legislation regarded as mistaken, foolish, or outmoded by using more indirect methods. Whether the judicial activism of either aggressive interpretation or invocation of the Constitution is glorified or vilified varies according to the jurisprudential winds of the time and society involved.

The common law/code distinction is not as important as it once was due to the increasing "statutorification" of American law, which has been described as being revolutionized by an "orgy" of legislative activity during the past century.[90] The same can largely be said of the United Kingdom countries as well. Consequently, more of the Anglo-American judge's work has become similar to that of the continental judge. However, much of this statutory growth has come in public law areas where the legislature has established a new program or responded to perceived social needs.

---

[90] *See* GRANT GILMORE, THE AGES OF AMERICAN LAW 91-98 (1977); *see also* GUIDO CALABRESI, A COMMON LAW FOR THE AGE OF STATUTES (1982).

Although some of the responses undoubtedly affect previously private behavior (*e.g.*, The Civil Rights Act of 1964 outlawed job discrimination by employers), the United States still leaves proportionately more of its private law matters to the common law than do code law countries or even other English-speaking countries, which have by regulation removed some issues from the realm of private law.

The distinctions between common law and code countries are, like most everything, rooted in history as well. Continental Europe was heavily influenced by the statutes found in the Roman codes of law and canon law of the Catholic Church. Britain developed the common law in isolation from the continent and exported it to its colonies, which have largely retained the system despite increasing codification of their own laws. As detailed in Chapter Five, the common law countries tend toward an adversarial model of dispute resolution while code nations are more inquisitorial. To a large extent these differences are structural and historical; but they are also jurisprudential. What we expect of and tolerate from our judges reflects society's views of the role of judges in administering the law. Where, for example, one finds common law judging frequently used, one would (all other things being equal) expect to find somewhat less positivism and formalism and a jurisprudence that tends to empower the judges to make the "just" decisions.

Langdell and Legal Formalism.

Despite common law adjudication and Yankee independence, the law in America shortly after the Revolution can be broadly classified as tending toward the formalist. How formalist is subject to debate (for example, some critics of formalism labeled it mechanical). How dominant is subject to less debate. By the latter part of the 19th century, the triumph of formalism became more apparent. In 1870, Christopher Langdell became Dean of Harvard Law School, establishing the case method of legal instruction and an enduring type of legal formalism. The case method involves the use of appellate opinions for studying and learning law. The opinions are assimilated by the students to allow them to distill legal rules and learn to make fine factual distinctions between the leading or controlling cases and future situations. The Langdellian method was formal: read the case; distill the rule; apply the rule to future cases. Once students discovered the immutable axioms of the legal "science," law became like mathematics, a rational process of deduction leading to objectively verifiable results.[91]

Under Langdell, law also aspired to be scientific by virtue of using real cases, but only a limited number of "leading" cases, as its data base. Rather than drawing legal axioms from the writings of Blackstone or the musings of a lecturer, students and lawyers were to derive legal rules from the actual operation of the courts. As most lawyers now acknowledge, Langdell overstated his case. Appellate opinions can be unrepresentative of day-to-day adjudication, which often is resolved by settlement or without written opinion. In addition, Langdell (or at least his most ardent disciples), assumed an unrealistic consistency, predictability, and detachment in legal outcomes. To the classic Langdellian, if Case A (a breach of contract case) had a different outcome than Case B (a breach of contract case involving similar facts), this must result from some distinguishing characteristic or a change in the operative legal standard. Cases were not supposed to differ because of differences in the identity of the parties, the composition of the bench, the quality of legal representation, or mere human inconsistency. Since the revolution brought by the Legal Realists (discussed below), these presuppositions of what might be termed "high Langdellianism" seem almost amusing and quaint.

Although some elements of formalist jurisprudence have long been attacked and perhaps even discredited, Langdell's case method nonetheless continues to dominate legal education. While modern legal educators frequently teach through problems, clinical experiences, exercises, examination of legal texts other than cases and also lecture, the stock-in-trade of law school continues to be the analysis of appellate cases through a Socratic dialogue between students and teacher. Although that discussion is now infused with the influence of post-formalist jurisprudence, the case method procedure by which law is learned continues to exert a subtle but strong pull that can lead students, lawyers, and judges toward the view that law is more self-contained, scientific, neutral, and predictable than is actually the case.

Of course, one must avoid caricature. Langdell and his peers and disciples were undoubtedly more formalist in their approach than most modern lawyers: a rule was a rule was a rule. However, modern defenders of formalism have argued that it has been unfairly treated as a synonym for

---

[91] *See* Michael H. Hoeflich, *Law and Geometry: Legal Science from Leibnitz to Langdell*, 30 AM. J. LEGAL HIST. 95 (1986).

rigidity or injustice through rigidity. For example, Professor Frederick Schauer, a leading proponent of a modern version of a "kinder, gentler" formalism, has argued that formalism could be defined as simply a method of decision that starts with rules and attempts to adjudicate consistently with the rules, absent strong reasons to the contrary. So defined, formalism is hardly the behemoth of rigidity characterized by its detractors.[92] Similarly, Schauer suggests that it is inaccurate to see common law judging as ever having been excessively rule-bound. The essence of the common law system is to empower judges to modify, avoid, or disregard rules as they see fit in particular cases. He also suggests that even highly rigid legal formalism can be defended as preferable to excessive judicial discretion.[93] This observation may be well-taken, but most scholars agree that the post-World War II bench has been less constrained by overarching legal rules than its predecessors from 1870 to 1937, but has rendered better, sounder decisions. Despite this, formalism may be making a comeback in the late 20th century.

The Vulnerability of High Formalism.

Describing legal thought in broad strokes, though it may not be strictly accurate, can often serve to illustrate or better describe jurisprudential trends. The legal formalism of the 19th century was less hidebound than often supposed but was often rigid and was nonetheless a formalism: it began with the notion of first principles rather than individualized justice; it saw these rules as fixed and not subject to modification based on individual circumstances; it assumed that all cases could be consistently decided under a set of rules; it often viewed fidelity to the structure of the rules as important and worth maintaining across-the-board in case outcomes regardless of the consequences for individual cases and affected parties. For example, many in the legal profession (even some like Harvard Law Dean Roscoe Pound who disclaimed formalism) favored strictly adhering to the scheme of bequests set forth in the text of a will even where the beneficiary had murdered the decedent and thereby profited

---

[92] *See* Frederick Schauer, *Formalism*, 97 YALE L.J. 509 (1988); *accord* SEBOK, *supra* note 84.

[93] *See* FREDERICK SCHAUER, PLAYING BY THE RULES: A PHILOSOPHICAL EXAMINATION OF RULES-BASED DECISION-MAKING IN LAW AND LIFE 179, 214 (1991).

from the crime. The modern approach, one which began while formalism was still dominant, is to deny the inheritance to the murdering heir.[94]

The legal system and legal thought remain substantially formal today. Rules are established and generally followed. The formalism of the 19th century differs from today's modest formalism because it was insular. Langdell made law a somewhat more "scientific" undertaking, but one that examined a relatively small universe -- written appellate opinions. Lawyers and law students were to derive legal answers and understanding through rigorous study of the reported cases without regard for other factors potentially affecting judicial outcomes. The legal establishment of 1870 did not worry about whether the reported cases reflected litigation as a whole, whether litigation reflected social disputes generally, whether judges and jurors were affected by factors other than legal doctrine, whether legal rules had distributional effects for society as a whole, and so on.

Holmes as Precursor to the Legal Realists.

The Legal Realist movement of the period of 1920-1940 exposed the vulnerabilities of formalism and to some extent dethroned it. But well before this period, a Harvard intimate, Oliver Wendell Holmes (who practiced in Boston, taught on the faculty and later sat on the Supreme Judicial Court of Massachusetts) began to criticize the scientific formalism of Langdell for being inbred. In his famous book, THE COMMON LAW (1881), Holmes began a recognizable drive toward a less insular view of law when he stated:

> The life of the law has not been logic; it has been experi-
> ence. The felt necessities of the time, the prevalent moral
> and political theories, intuitions of public policy, avowed or
> unconscious, even the prejudices which judges share with
> their fellow-men, have a good deal more to do than the
> syllogism in determining the rules by which men should be
> governed.[95]

---

[94] *See*, *e.g.*, Riggs v. Palmer, 22 N.E. 188 (N.Y. 1889).

[95] OLIVER WENDELL HOLMES, THE COMMON LAW 1 (1881). The pithy aphorism was first used by Holmes in a book review of a contract textbook authored by Langdell. *See* 14 AM. L. REV. 233, 234 (1880).

Holmes's commitment to using facts outside the law in making legal decisions was more clearly articulated in his major article, *The Path of Law*, published near the turn of the century,[96] in which he argued that the "black letter" student of the law will eventually be eclipsed by the lawyer who possesses more varied and modern learning in economics, politics, statistics, and other social sciences.

We do not suggest that Holmes was a lone voice against Langdellianism. His work, although especially important in America, has been described as derivative of that of other scholars.[97] Regardless of whether one sees Holmes as original, he was clearly not alone. He also was clearly not a radical revolutionary but a rather charter member of the legal establishment. There is much in his writings consistent with formalism. But his criticisms of Langdell have had a more long-lasting bite than his comments that square perfectly well with formalism. Holmes' career as a state court judge and Supreme Court Justice reveals considerable use of formalism as a means of deciding cases. But Holmes is nonetheless remembered as something of an iconoclast because his reformist comments seem so much more quotable than his more conventional views.

In sum, it would be wrong to view Holmes as an early Legal Realist storming the barricades of the establishment. He was the establishment. But perhaps that made him even more important. He provided a high-profile and respected source of criticism of the overly formal and narrow view of law as library science. In retrospect, this can be seen as part of the evolutionary trend in which law became much less insular and considerably less formal throughout the 20th century. This itself is no small achievement and could justify the assessment of Karl Llewellyn, perhaps the most prominent Legal Realist, that "we [the Realists] all derive" from Holmes.

Roscoe Pound's Critique and Sociological Jurisprudence.

A younger contemporary of Holmes, Roscoe Pound, Dean of Harvard Law School, can be seen as part of this trend against formalism even though he later behaved with some hostility toward the Realists, whom

---

[96] *See* Oliver Wendell Holmes, *The Path of Law*, 10 HARV. L. REV. 457, 469 (1897).

[97] *See, e.g.,* Neil Duxbury, *The Birth of Legal Realism and the Myth of Justice Holmes*, 1991, ANGLO-AMERICAN L. REV. 81, 88. In particular, Sir Henry Maine's book, ANCIENT LAW, seems to have influenced Holmes.

he apparently thought went too far in deformalizing and demythologizing law. Pound spoke of a "Sociological Jurisprudence," which he outlined as emphasizing: 1) The study of the "actual social effects of legal institutions and doctrines"; 2) Use of the scientific method of inquiry into legal issues as preparation for responsive legislation; 3) Study of the actual application of law in practice rather than the focus on doctrine alone; 4) Study of the actual effect of law over time; 5) "[E]quitable application of law" in which legal precepts and doctrine function more as guides for decision rather than as rigid rules of decision; and 6) Efforts to make law more effective as an instrument of social policy for the improvement of society.[98]

Pound particularly criticized the hostile reaction of the courts to progressive legislation of the early 20th century, such as laws on workers' compensation, protection for labor organizers, and antitrust.[99] For Pound, the best law was law that worked with society's preferences rather than against them. Law can legitimately be used as a method of setting social policy. He viewed the bench as too hostile to progressive legislation because of its excessive and narrow commitment to formalism and the bedrock assumptions underlying formalism, such as the sanctity of freedom of contract.

Pound did not spare lawyers from his criticism. He found the bar insufficiently helpful to society as well. In 1906, Pound gave a speech at the American Bar Association annual meeting that was a memorable slap in the face of the legal establishment. The speech, "The Causes of Popular Dissatisfaction with the Administration of Justice,"[100] continues to be cited today as illustrative of the ills and waste often attending American adversarial litigation. In the speech, Pound inveighed against excessive posturing and hypertechnicality that impeded both the search for truth and the economical pursuit of dispute resolution. Pound criticized the "sporting theory of justice" as elevating the competitiveness of the adjudication system

---

[98] Roscoe Pound, *The Scope and Purpose of Sociological Jurisprudence*, 25 HARV. L. REV. 489 (1912). Pound also emphasized the divergence of legal rules and actual legal results. *See* Roscoe Pound, *Law in Books and Law in Action*, 44 AM. L. REV. 12 (1910).

[99] *See* Roscoe Pound, *The Scope and Purpose of Sociological Jurisprudence*, 25 HARV. L. REV. 489 (1912); *Common Law and Legislation*, 21 HARV. L. REV. 383 (1908).

[100] Roscoe Pound, Paper Presented to the ABA (Aug. 29, 1906), in 40 AM. L. REV. 729 (1906).

to the detriment of its value to society. Although Pound's criticisms are usually viewed primarily as an indictment of the adversary system and judicial inefficiency, his comments can be more broadly read as a plea for less formalism and more instrumentalism/functionalism/realism in the American bench and bar.

As two scholars have observed, "[m]any of Pound's views have become so widely accepted that today they are regarded as commonplace."[101] Today, both reformers who seek greater equality and social engineering through law and those who seek streamlined, cheaper litigation to aid commerce -- two camps often at loggerheads over particular issues -- are the progeny of Pound's Sociological Jurisprudence. Also commonly seen as derived from Pound's approach is a standard legal process tool of much of the 20th century: the balancing of interests when rendering a judicial decision.

The Legal Realist Movement.

Notwithstanding the views of Holmes, Pound and others in the legal establishment (epitomized by Harvard Law School), law teaching, legal scholarship, and the legal enterprise in America remained largely formalist. Law school teaching remained (and remains to this day) a "cult of the judge," particularly the appellate judge, in which law students focus most energy on reading cases and learning doctrine rather than examining the work of lawyers, legislators, bureaucrats, and other legal actors. In opposition to this status quo arose a Legal Realist movement, principally centered at Yale and Columbia Law Schools. From a broad perspective, this movement can be seen as part of a revolt against formalism occurring throughout the intellectual community -- not just in law -- during the late 19th and early 20th centuries. The Realists took issue with Langdellianism and highly formalist thought, particularly at Harvard Law School.

Harvard's Joseph Beale was a special target. Beale was a conflict of laws scholar who advocated the "lex loci delicti" theory under which the state in which an injury occurred provided the applicable substantive law for adjudicating the dispute -- with no ifs, ands, or buts. Although the basic lex loci rule seems sensible as a presumption or consideration, Beale venerated it as an ironclad rule. For example, if a California plaintiff and a New

---

[101] JOHN MONAHAN & LAURENS WALKER, SOCIAL SCIENCE IN LAW: CASES AND MATERIALS 14 (2d ed. 1990).

York defendant crashed on a New Hampshire road, New Hampshire law would apply to all aspects of the case, even to questions of damages. Beale and his ultra-formalism thus became a lightening rod for the Realist's criticisms, and even their ridicule. Some members of the Yale Law faculty even penned a mocking poem about Beale and posted it in the faculty lounge.[102]

Many of the Legal Realist criticisms were reminiscent of those of Holmes, Pound, and others. What differentiated the Realists in large part was their approach to criticism and the depth of their critique. Many Realists did not appear to be working to become reformist members of the establishment. Rather, they attacked the establishment, sometimes with ferocity. Although Pound's views were not that disparate from those of the Realists, he was a target as well. Conversely, Pound was surprisingly hostile to the Realists in view of the often marginal differences of views. For example, Pound and Karl Llewellyn engaged in years of correspondence that can be read as a never-ending series of "potshots" or "digs" at one another over often trivial differences in thinking and scholarship.[103] As the cynical saying goes, the battles in academia are so fierce because the stakes are so small.

The Realists also gave more extra-legal explanations for the degree to which the judicial system seemed to be resisting progressive change. While Pound tended to blame the problem on the profession's excessive intellectual commitment to formalism, adversarialism, and other professional ideology, the Realists suspected that the conduct of bench and bar often derived from their own self-interests or those of their class, which opposed restrictions on corporations and capital while resisting workers' rights. In other words, the bench resisted progressive change not because of outmoded syllogism but because it was fighting, perhaps subconsciously, a judicial rear-guard action against policies it had unsuccessfully opposed in the legislature or society at large.

---

[102] *See* LAURA KALMAN, LEGAL REALISM AT YALE 1927-1960 26 (1986).

[103] *See, e.g.,* N.E.H. Hull, *Some Realism About the Llewellyn-Pound Exchange over Realism: The Newly Uncovered Private Correspondence, 1927-1931,* 1987 WIS. L. REV. 921; Roscoe Pound, *The Call for a Realist Jurisprudence,* 44 HARV. L. REV. 697 (1931); KARL N. LLEWELLYN, *Some Realism About Realism -- Responding to Dean Pound,* 44 HARV. L. REV. 1222 (1931).

The aggressive tone of many Realists created clearly delineated battle lines which forced the legal community to face more directly the contentions of the Realists. As a result, their ideas got attention. Because many were good ideas, they also became accepted to varying degrees. Some Realists were marginalized by part of the establishment due to perceived incivility. Many of the Realists were criticized. Realism was often wrongly characterized as tending toward anarchy because its proponents asserted that law was simply the result of individual caprice, social power, and serendipity -- "what the judge had for breakfast" as one wag suggested.

Llewellyn himself was more than a little dismayed at the broad, inaccurate brush with which traditional critics attempted to caricature the Realists. He saw Realism as "an effort at more effective legal technology" and not as a "philosophy." Llewellyn was particularly angry that so many critics had seized upon his statement that "[w]hat [government] officials do about disputes is, to my mind, the law itself"[104] and attempted to paint it as the credo of a result-oriented nihilist. As even this sketchy chapter shows, Legal Realism was not a call for legal anarchy, which perhaps explains why Llewellyn was so disturbed at the charge. Just the same, we take issue with him: Realism was a good deal more than a mere effort to sharpen legal technology.

Whatever the interpersonal tensions, the Realists were so successful that they shifted the orientation of the legal community beyond the point of no return, in effect creating a new legal establishment, or at least forced the establishment to modify itself in order to accommodate (some would say "co-opt") the Realists. Realists not only dominated some prestigious schools like Yale and Columbia but also captured large segments of the legal literature while penetrating with its adherents both the practicing bar and even the bench. For example, Yale Law School Professor Jerome Frank, an ultra-Realist, became a Second Circuit Judge,[105] while his colleagues William

---

[104] *See* KARL LLEWELLYN, THE BRAMBLE BUSH x-xi (3d ed. 1960) (the statement appeared in his introduction to the second edition).

[105] Frank also brought together law and Freudian psychoanalysis in his book LAW AND THE MODERN MIND (1930), in which he argued that formalism was infantile or childlike in its reverence for rules, much like a child reveres authority figures.

To the extent that non-Realists equated Frank and Llewellyn with Realist philosophy, this probably increased the controversy of the movement since these two were perhaps the most provocative of the Realists. *See*

O. Douglas and Abe Fortas became Supreme Court Justices. Part of the judicial success of the Realists resulted from their influence in the executive branch during the lengthy administration of Franklin Delano Roosevelt. Frank, Douglas, Fortas and others, including their students, were substantial figures in Roosevelt's New Deal and its "alphabet agencies," as well as the federal courts.

What did the Realists say that was so provocative? To oversimplify, the broad theme of Legal Realism posited that law is not an activity rendered in isolation from society. Rather, law consistently reflects historical, social, political, anthropological, economic, and other events, theories, and trends. To some extent, then, legal doctrines and outcomes will vary according to the identity of the decisionmakers and the cultural influences bearing upon them. Today, that proposition seems almost too obvious to discuss. Modern lawyers think this way today, however, because of the Realists. Prior to that movement, large elements of the legal community adhered to the formalist theology and pretended that law was more self-contained and immutable than it could actually be in any complex or diverse society or in any system dependent upon human beings for its operation.

Beyond this broad proposition, the Realists also expanded upon the Holmesian observation that legal doctrine had more value if it truly reflected the real world. In order to create and administer a legal system, lawyers must have concrete knowledge rather than simply rely on syllogistic speculation. This led to the plank of the Realist platform that emphasized empirical research and the use of it to evaluate and modify the law. Although there was a great range in Realist writings, they can all be roughly grouped by their demands that the legal system become less insular and more linked to current social and political realities.

However, there was little or no empirical body of legal scholarship nor even an established system of empirical measurements regarding law. Consequently, would-be empiricists and other Realists tended to import the learning and investigative techniques of other disciplines into legal study. Critics argued that the Realists often proved that a little knowledge of other fields was a dangerous thing. For example, in one frequently ridiculed project, a Yale Realist observed cars and drivers in New Haven to measure

---

MONAHAN & WALKER, *supra* note 101, at 16. In addition, Frank's arrogant demeanor annoyed many in the legal establishment.

the impact of traffic laws on driving behavior. Critics made the effort sound more ridiculous than it was by terming it "counting cars in the parking lot." But whatever its excesses or opportunity for comic relief, Legal Realism went well beyond Holmes in putting empiricism and multidisciplinary study onto the legal agenda. The growth of modern "law and . . ." movements are in that sense direct descendants of Realism.

The Realists criticized exclusive reliance on the case method or any form of teaching or scholarship that was too doctrinaire, abstract, or formalist. Realists modified the traditional casebook to include statutory materials, law review articles, and the professor's own notes, questions, or problems. But although these new collections of "cases and materials" were distinct from casebooks, they were still primarily designed for teaching through a modified case method. The Realists changed legal education substantially, not drastically.

Realists also did not forsake treatises. For example, Yale contracts scholar Arthur Corbin, generally viewed as a Realist, wrote one of the two leading multi-volume contracts treatises of all time (the more formalist Samuel Williston of Harvard wrote the other). But, a Realist's treatise was less likely to recite rules without comment and criticism. Modern treatises tend to follow this vein. Nevertheless, the Realist revolution may have made treatises permanently less important by making the very notion of legal categorization and certainty less accepted.[106]

Thus, despite criticism, Legal Realism took root in academia, government, the judiciary, and in practice. Modern lawyers expressly tailor legal arguments according to the social context of a dispute and the personal background and predilections of the decisionmaker, judge or jury. For example, a number of jury research firms now assist lawyers in attempting to pick the most favorable jury from the available pool arriving for voir dire. In addition, modern lawyers are more likely than their earlier counterparts to include empirical or multidisciplinary data in their arguments. The "Brandeis Brief," filed by future Supreme Court Justice Louis Brandeis in *Muller v. Oregon*,[107] was at the time considered a pathbreaking innovation because it included social science factoids in support of upholding a state law limiting the working hours of women.

---

[106] *See* A.W.B. Simpson, *The Rise and Fall of the Legal Treatise: Legal Principles and the Forms of Legal Literature*, 48 U. CHI. L. REV. 632 (1981).

[107] 208 U.S. 412 (1908).

Today, most lawyers frequently make more sophisticated use of such extralegal data than did Brandeis. As the adage goes, "we are all Realists, now."[108]

The Empire Strikes Back (Sort of): The Harvard Legal Process School.

One perceived problem with Realism was its indeterminacy. The supposed determinacy of formalism is usually overstated in view of the judicial tendency toward creative characterization of facts and manipulation of the applicability of the rules in order to render decisions that square with the personal preferences of the bench. Nonetheless, the success of the Realist enterprise is often accused of having left the profession with a longing for a more predictable jurisprudence, one that is more carefully protected from results flowing from personal or political preferences.

In addition, external events undermined the popularity of Realism. The spread of German Nazism and similar fascism, fanaticism, and racism in Italy, Japan, and other areas during the period of World War II sent shivers up the figurative spine of America, particularly its intellectual community. It suddenly seemed as though truly ugly political movements were possible even in the United States. To the extent that Realism was viewed, often incorrectly or with exaggeration, as a movement that tore down the protective cocoon of rules or supported moral relativism, some members of the legal establishment were bound to wonder whether the popularity of Realism made law too malleable, lest it should be molded by the likes of Hitler.[109]

America's legal establishment wanted to reassure itself that it was sufficiently protected from the specter of murderers becoming judges. These fears, like other criticisms of Realism, tend to be either overstated or blind to the vulnerabilities of non-Realist thought, as well as improperly commingling Realism with positivism. Nazism certainly can be viewed as the horrible consequence of having a legal system insufficiently constrained

---

[108] *See* MONAHAN & WALKER, *supra* note 101, at 27.

[109] *See* F.A. HAYEK, THE CONSTITUTION OF LIBERTY 236-46 (1960); LON FULLER, THE LAW IN QUEST OF ITSELF 122 (1941); Ben W. Palmer, *Holmes, Hobbes, and Hitler*, 31 A.B.A.J. 569 (1945); Gary Peller, *Neutral Principles in the 1950s*, 21 U. MICH. J.L. REFORM 561 (1988); Edward A. Purcell, Jr., *American Jurisprudence Between the Wars: Legal Realism and the Crisis of Democratic Theory*, 75 AM. HIST. REV. 424 (1969).

to follow neutral rules evenhandly.[110] On the other hand, Nazism can also be viewed as having traveled its hideous road so far and so fast because of a formalist positivism: seemingly decent citizens forgot or ignored right and wrong in blindly following rules decreed by the controlling hierarchy.

In the post-War period of the 1950s, the major counter-attack on Realism -- and it was something of a friendly one -- came from a new generation of Harvard law faculty, particularly the writings of Professors Henry Hart and (later Dean) Albert Sacks. In 1958, Hart and Sacks completed a "tentative" draft of a legal process text that, despite having the decidedly unsnappy title of *The Legal Process*, has been highly influential, earning the description as the most frequently cited unpublished manuscript in the world. The Hart and Sacks/Harvard Legal Process approach acknowledged the insights of the Realists but emphasized institutional division of authority, adherence to fair procedure, and mandated reasoned elaboration as key bulwarks against law becoming too ad hoc and arbitrary. The Legal Process School seeks a studied effort at rational decisionmaking as the means to prevent post-Realist law from lapsing into erratic determinations by judges who have eaten different things for breakfast.

Hart and Sacks contend that such rationality, restraint, and fairness could be achieved through the appropriate "black letter" distribution of institutional power and the adherence to evenhanded procedure coupled with the inculcation of jurists into a proper culture. For example, the Process School emphasized judges should articulate reasoned decisions, believing that this both improves the quality of analysis and prevents bad decisions, which are defined as those incapable of receiving credible rational support. To achieve this, the Process School emphasized a litigant's rights to notice, a hearing, and an explanation of a court's disposition.

The Legal Process School aims to resolve the conflict between the recognition that law was another form of social policy (Realism) and the notion that to be truly legitimate, the law must strive for objectivity distinct from pure politics (Formalism). By seeking systemic constraint and procedural fairness, the Process School seeks to depoliticize law as much as feasible while permitting law to reflect organic changes in social policy.

---

[110] *See* IAGO MULLER, THE NAZI JUDGES (1990) (conservative judiciary taking its traditions from Imperial Germany of the Kaisers silently rendered decisions that undermined the Weimar Republic, helping to set the stage for Nazi takeover).

"Hart & Sacks welcomed legal change . . . but . . . valued private expectations and legal determinacy. . . . 'Orderly change' was the ideal."[111]

Related to but distinct from the Process School was support for the precept that "neutral principles" of decisionmaking are to be followed by judges even where the results of a particular case conflicted with their personal preferences. To the neutralists, a principled decision was "one that rests on reasons with respect to all the issues in the case, reasons that in their generality and their neutrality transcend any immediate result that is involved."[112] The neutral principles thesis is, on one level, beguiling. Who can quarrel with the notion that law should be objective? But it became controversial and ostracized by many American legal scholars and indirectly diminished the influence of the Legal Process School as well through the unfortunate equating of the two theses.

The trouble began at the outset when the creator of the neutral principles school opened himself to criticism with an excessively formal, cold, and unrealistic view of law's actual impact and ability to perform objectively. In his famous article on neutral principles, Professor Herbert Wechsler (a superstar of the American legal establishment as a professor at Columbia and long-time director of the prestigious American Law Institute) attacked the Supreme Court, particularly the Warren Court, on a range of issues dear to many moderate and liberal lawyers: the invalidation of the white primary;[113] the refusal to enforce racially restrictive covenants;[114] and, most important, the *Brown* decision outlawing public school segregation.

Even the small details of Wechsler's article seemed designed to rankle civil libertarians. For example, he prided himself on representing the U.S. government as an Assistant Attorney General during World War II in

---

[111] WILLIAM N. ESKRIDGE, JR. & PHILIP P. FRICKEY, CASES AND MATERIALS ON LEGISLATION: STATUTES AND THE CREATION OF PUBLIC POLICY 247 (1988) (citing Robert Weisberg, *The Calabresian Judicial Artist: Statutes and the New Legal Process*, 35 STAN. L. REV. 213 (1983)).

[112] Herbert Wechsler, *Toward Neutral Principles of Constitutional Law*, 73 HARV. L. REV. 1, 27 (1959); *see also* Kent R. Greenawalt, *The Enduring Significance of Neutral Principles*, 78 COLUM. L. REV. 982 (1978).

[113] Smith v. Allwright, 321 U.S. 649 (1944).

[114] Shelley v. Kraemer, 334 U.S. 1 (1948).

the infamous *Korematsu* case despite his personal opposition to the government's policy (challenged in *Korematsu*) of incarcerating Asian-Americans simply because the U.S. was at war with Japan.[115] In a decision long seen as one of America's most embarrassing, the Court upheld this internment without due process as justified by the War, even though German-Americans and Italian-Americans were not imprisoned.[116] Although Legal Process thinking is a clear advantage over decision by brute force (Hitler and Stalin would probably never have even permitted the *Korematsu* case to begin, much less reach the Supreme Court), it, too, is vulnerable to the Realist critique. To many, Wechsler's neutral principles thesis made Legal Process theory look like a more stylized and palatable formalism that brought equally unjust results.

Attacks directed at neutral principles led to the "Fundamental Rights" school discussed below, which in its success in attacking neutral principles also undermined the Hart and Sacks version of Legal Process theory. Nonetheless, Legal Process thinking is influential in the legal academy and dominated during the 1950s and 1960s. Today, it still comes as close as anything to representing mainstream legal thought and continues to enjoy substantial tacit support by lawyers and judges, who almost reflexively use this style of thinking in framing arguments and rendering decisions. Much like Pound's influence, that of Hart and Sacks so permeates the profession that it is frequently overlooked. During the last quarter-century, however, the Process school has been wounded, particularly in the academy, by a number of criticisms from a variety of sources, most of which are descended from Legal Realism.

Another Strand: Analytic Jurisprudence and Debate About the Nature of Law in the Post-War Era. Contemporaneous with the rise of the Harvard Legal Process School came a renewed interest in neo-positivist

---

[115] *See* Korematsu v. United States, 323 U.S. 214 (1944). To be fair to Prof. Wechsler, we note that the conflict between personal preferences and the perceived need to "play by the rules" has long vexed society. *See, e.g.*, PLATO, CRITO (c. 399 B.C.) (in which Socrates, about to be unfairly executed, refuses to attempt to escape and explains to his friend Crito that it is more important to follow the laws of society than to avoid individual injustice -- but Socrates was making a personal sacrifice rather than advocating the enforced sacrifice of others).

[116] Forty years later, the judicial system gave some concrete acknowledgement of this unfairness by granting to Korematsu and others a post hoc writ of *coram nobis*, which in essence concludes that the earlier decision was a mistake. *See* Korematsu v. United States, 584 F. Supp. 1406 (N.D. Cal. 1984).

theories of the law. This work was a substantial refinement of positivism and a sustained defense of "the law" as an objective and autonomous system. These views gained increased attention because they clashed to some degree with those of leading American scholars of the time. The most prominent "analytic" positivist was Oxford's H.L.A. Hart (not to be confused with Henry Hart of Hart and Sacks Legal Process writings), who dueled with Harvard's Lon Fuller, a natural law advocate.[117]

Ironically, legal positivism in Europe had not suffered in reputation due to World War II's fascism as did positivism in the United States. In fact, one of the leading analytic jurisprudence scholars and positivists, Hans Kelsen, was a refugee from Nazism who was a student and teacher in Germany and Austria before fleeing to Switzerland in 1933. He later was a visiting professor at Harvard and then joined the political science faculty at California-Berkeley. Although he had done his major scholarly writings prior to World War II, they were not translated into English until the 1940s, and he thus was associated with the Hart-Fuller, positivism-natural law debate of the 1940s and 1950s.

Kelsen labeled his view of law as the "pure theory of law." It sought to avoid any infusion of politics or morality. He self-consciously aimed to distinguish "pure" law from the morality that he ascribed to natural law. He also rejected the Realist notion that law was the result of political preference, social values, or the psychology of decisionmakers. Kelsen saw law as truly its own discipline or subject area which employed its own normative concepts (similar to the "rules" of Langellian formalism) to be rigorously enforced through logical application. Kelsen's arguments are abstract and formalist and seem to ignore the concerns of Legal Realism. Some of this undoubtedly resulted from the delayed English consideration of Kelsen. During the bulk of Kelsen's writing (1906-1934), the Realist movement was in its infancy domestically or had not penetrated Europe. But the European positivists proved more resistant to Realism later in the 20th century as well.

---

[117] *Compare* H.L.A. Hart, *Positivism and the Separation of Law and Morals*, 71 HARV. L. REV. 593 (1958) *with* Lon Fuller, *Positivism and Fidelity to Law -- A Reply to Professor Hart*, 71 HARV. L. REV. 630 (1958). Hart also debated critics other than Fuller. *Compare* Edgar Bodenheimer, *Modern Analytic Jurisprudence and Its Usefulness*, 104 U. PA. L. REV. 1080 (1956) and Carl Auerbach, *On Professor Hart's Definition and Theory in Jurisprudence*, 9 J. LEGAL EDUC. 39 (1956) *with* H.L.A. Hart, *Analytical Jurisprudence in Mid-Twentieth Century: A Reply to Professor Bodenheimer*, 105 U. PA. L. REV. 953 (1957).

In the post-War years, H.L.A. Hart developed a more comprehensive positivist vision of law that self-consciously sought to answer the charge of Americans, particularly Fuller, that a strong positivist view of law made societies vulnerable to fascism.[118] Like Kelsen, Austin, and other positivists, Hart distinguished law from morality.[119] He also differentiated between "primary rules" -- specific rules governing specific behavior, and "secondary rules" -- those that determine the rightful "sovereign" and proper methods by which the sovereign might create positive law. A key secondary principle of Hart's was the "rule of recognition," which is a given society's norm for deciding whether to recognize a sovereign as legitimate and therefore capable of promulgating valid law. Perhaps today's leading figure in this tradition is Joseph Raz, a former student of Hart's who has defended modern positivism against American attack,[120] continuing to some degree the Hart-Fuller schism of jurisprudential scholars regarding issues of the nature of law and legal theory.

Fuller argued that law and morality were inevitably intertwined to the extent that an acceptable legal system must also be an acceptable moral system. Fuller contended that every legitimate legal system includes a minimum set of morally significant features, such as a ban on secret laws and *ex post facto* laws (which later criminalize conduct that was legal when undertaken). Enforcement of such laws is obviously immoral to any reasonable person, argued Fuller. Taking this into account, a judge having a limited range of discretion to invoke natural law principles can distinguish between acts of the sovereign that create law and those that are lawless acts of political power or unprincipled exercises of brute force.

Fuller differed from pre-20th century natural lawyers like Blackstone by not having the disdain for legislation or law as a social tool that characterizes Blackstone (who stated that "statutes [positive law] in derogation of the common [natural] law should be strictly construed").

---

[118] *See* H.L.A. HART, THE CONCEPT OF LAW (1960).

[119] In addition to his debate with Fuller, Hart is well-known for his debate with British Judge Sir Patrick Devlin, in which Hart defended the Wolfenden Report, which recommended that Britain decriminalize homosexuality. Hart reasoned that anti-gay laws codified the majority's morality but were not legitimately defensible as "laws." *Compare* H.L.A. Hart, *Immorality and Treason*, 62 LISTENER 162 (1959) *with* SIR PATRICK DEVLIN, THE ENFORCEMENT OF MORALS (1965).

[120] *See, e.g.*, JOSEPH RAZ, THE MORALITY OF FREEDOM (1986); THE AUTHORITY OF LAW (1979).

Fuller supported the introduction of natural law as a check on the power of the modern nation-state. Because of his views, Fuller fit rather comfortably with his Harvard Legal Process colleagues Hart and Sacks. Thus, when Fuller and H.L.A. Hart debated, the American legal profession generally saw it as a battle between the then-dominant Legal Process school and a more traditional British positivism, such as that of Austin or Bentham. But Fuller and Hart's disagreements were arguably not that pronounced since Fuller was not a complete natural lawyer and Hart's positivism was considerably different from the Austinian version. Nonetheless, like the Pound-Llewellyn debates of a generation earlier which overstated the differences between Sociological Jurisprudence and Legal Realism, the Hart-Fuller debate drew battle lines of sorts. In the next generation, the fight was pressed by the advocates of fundamental rights, principally Ronald Dworkin, who graduated from Harvard Law School in 1957 and became one of the leaders of an emerging fundamental rights school of neo-natural law thinking.

Defending Progressive Adjudication: Fundamental Rights Jurisprudence. The emerging fundamental rights scholars reacted not only to H.L.A. Hart's writings but also to Herbert Wechsler's neutral principles article, which had spurred a general firestorm of criticism even as it garnered admiration in many quarters.[121] Realists saw it as naive, arguing that the notion of truly neutral decisionmaking by judges divorced of their own value preferences was impossible to achieve.[122] Conservatives saw it as continuing to place too much power in judges to act as philosopher-kings.[123] Friendly critics from the Legal Process school found little fault with Wechsler's general principles but considered them misapplied, arguing that the Supreme Court decisions criticized by Wechsler were eminently defensible on Legal Process grounds.[124] Liberal critics argued that

---

[121] *See* Kent Greenawalt, *The Enduring Significance of Neutral Principles*, 78 COLUM. L. REV. 982 (1978) (discussing both supporters and critics of Wechsler's thesis).

[122] *See, e.g.*, Addison Mueller & Murray L. Schwartz, *The Principle of Neutral Principles*, 7 UCLA L. REV. 571 (1960).

[123] *See, e.g.*, ALEXANDER BICKEL, THE LEAST DANGEROUS BRANCH (1962).

[124] *See, e.g.*, Louis Henkin, *Some Reflections on Current Constitutional Controversy*, 109 U. PA. L. REV. 637 (1961); Louis Pollack, *Racial Discrimination and Judicial Integrity: A Reply to Professor Wechsler*, 108 U. PA. L. REV. 1 (1959).

Wechslerian neutral principles, like formalism, elevated method over substance and that the true goal of constitutional law in civil rights matters was the reasonable protection of the inherent civil rights of individuals.[125]

The liberal critics grew and developed into an important jurisprudential school that dominated American academic legal-philosophical thought during the late 1960s and 1970s. The group's thought is diverse enough to make labeling difficult but has persuasively been labeled a "Fundamental Rights" jurisprudence because of its emphasis on higher principles, such as the promotion of human dignity and welfare and the achievement of justice, principles that to this school outweigh the values of predictability, strict neutrality, constrained judicial role, and other notions thought by conservatives properly to limit the power of courts to do justice in a general sense.[126]

Fundamental rights theorists include some of the most prominent names in American legal scholarship: Thomas Grey;[127] Kenneth Karst;[128] Frank Michelman;[129] Michael Perry;[130] David A.J. Richards;[131] Laurence Tribe;[132] and, perhaps most prominently, Ronald

---

[125] *See* SEBOK, *supra* note 84, at 141-67; *see also*, *e.g.*, Arthur S. Miller & Ronald F. Howell, *The Myth of Neutrality in Constitutional Adjudication*, 27 U. CHI. L. REV. 661 (1960).

[126] *See* SEBOK, *supra* note 84, at 161-94; WALTER MURPHY ET AL., AMERICAN CONSTITUTIONAL INTERPRETATION 929-30 (1986).

[127] *See, e.g.*, Thomas Grey, *Do We Have an Unwritten Constitution?*, 27 STAN. L. REV. 703 (1975).

[128] *See, e.g.*, Kenneth Karst, *The Supreme Court, 1976 Term -- Foreword: Equal Citizenship Under the Fourteenth Amendment*, 91 HARV. L. REV. 1 (1977).

[129] *See, e.g.*, Frank Michelman, *In Pursuit of Constitutional Welfare Rights: One View of Rawls' Theory of Justice*, 121 U. PA. L. REV. 962 (1973); *The Supreme Court, 1968 Term -- Foreword: On Protecting the Poor Through the Fourteenth Amendment*, 83 HARV. L. REV. 7 (1969).

[130] *See, e.g.*, MICHAEL PERRY, MORALITY, POLITICS, AND LAW (1988).

[131] *See, e.g.*, David A.J. Richards, *Commercial Sex and the Rights of the Person: A Moral Argument for the Decriminalization of Prostitution*, 127 U. PA. L. REV. 1195 (1979).

[132] *See, e.g.*, Laurence Tribe, *The Puzzling Persistence of Process-Based Constitutional Theories*, 89 YALE L.J. 1063 (1980).

Dworkin. Dworkin first gained widespread attention by attacking the positivism of the British analytic jurisprudence school, particularly H.L.A. Hart's concept of law.[133] He continued to publish numerous articles, and provided what might be termed the manifesto of the Fundamental Rights school.[134] These scholars largely defended the Warren Court against the charges of "judicial activism" leveled against it by political and intellectual conservatives. In particular, they defended the broad Warren Court notions of individual rights *(e.g.,* the rights to challenge government policies, to free expression, to civil liberties, and to be protected from overly aggressive police conduct) against the charge that such decisions had insufficient support in the Constitution.

Dworkin acknowledged that judges often decide cases in the absence of clear textual commands from the sovereign, particularly in the less codified area of constitutional law. But rather than being apologetic, Dworkin celebrated this aspect of American adjudication and argued that it was not the product of excessive discretion or rampaging judicial activism. Rather, judges rationally apply principles inherent in the structure and text of the law, principles given greater certainty through court precedent and shared social understanding as revealed through searching interpretation. Although judicial results rendered under this scenario are not initially obvious and require hard work by the courts, Dworkin argued that the legal system nonetheless provides objectively "right" answers even in hard cases. Decisions are thus not the product only of the political preferences of legal actors.[135]

Also important to this school were the writings of nonlawyer John Rawls. The philosophy set forth in his pathbreaking book *A Theory of Justice* (discussed in Chapter One), which is "Neo-Kantian" and closer to natural law than positivism, stresses many of the same values promoted by Fundamental Rights scholars. Although Dworkin and others in this school

---

[133] *See, e.g.,* Ronald Dworkin, *The Model of Rules*, 35 U. CHI. L. REV. 14 (1967).

[134] *See* RONALD DWORKIN, TAKING RIGHTS SERIOUSLY (1978). Ironically, although Dworkin's reputation began with attacks on Hart, Dworkin was Hart's successor in the jurisprudence chair at Oxford.

[135] *See* RONALD DWORKIN, LAW'S EMPIRE (1986); A MATTER OF PRINCIPLE (1985).

deny being natural law advocates,[136] we disagree and see them as the logical descendants of Lon Fuller, continuing Fuller's attack on positivism, but with a more pointed focus in view of the controversy surrounding the Warren Court and civil rights issues like antidiscrimination law, affirmative action, voting rights, and abortion.

Conservative Counterattacks. The conservative reaction to the neutral principles and Legal Process Schools also achieved considerable prominence. Alexander Bickel suggested that the Supreme Court employ "passive virtues" to reduce controversy over its role.[137] Bickel's view itself became controversial,[138] but retained considerable impact. In subsequent writings, Bickel suggested that the Court should not only avoid controversy but also avoid making policy-laden, legislature-like decisions.[139] But Bickel was not completely at odds with Fundamental Rights thinking or aggressive Supreme Court adjudication: he successfully represented *The New York Times* in its battle to publish the government's secret "Pentagon Papers" during the midst of the Vietnam War,[140] although his argument and the decision are arguably based more on a broad reading of First Amendment text subject to balancing against government interests rather than bedrock notions of unfettered expression. A prominent compatriot of Bickel who was a more severe critic of both the Legal Process and Fundamental Rights schools was Robert Bork. He argued that constitutional rights did not exist unless they could be inferred in an unattenuated manner from sufficiently clear language in the Constitution.[141] This view led Bork to conclude that the Constitution did not create a right of privacy that could support rights to abortion or immunity from government regulation of

---

[136] *See, e.g.*, Ronald Dworkin, *"Natural" Law Revisited*, 34 U. FLA. L. REV. 165 (1982).

[137] See ALEXANDER BICKEL, THE LEAST DANGEROUS BRANCH (1962); Alexander Bickel, *The Supreme Court, 1960 Term -- Foreword: The Passive Virtues*, 75 HARV. L. REV. 40 (1960).

[138] *See* Gerald Gunther, *The Subtle Vices of the "Passive Virtues," A Comment on Principle and Expediency in Judicial Review*, 64 COLUM. L. REV. 1 (1964).

[139] *See* ALEXANDER BICKEL, THE SUPREME COURT AT THE BAR OF POLITICS (1970).

[140] *See* New York Times Co. v. United States, 403 U.S. 713 (1971).

[141] *See* Robert H. Bork, *Neutral Principles and Some First Amendment Problems*, 47 IND. L.J. 1 (1971).

contraceptives, positions that worked to defeat his nomination as a Supreme Court Justice in 1987.

The Fundamental Rights school and the Bickel-Bork conservative school continue to have substantial support and to exert considerable influence in academia, politics, and adjudication. Writings in these traditions have reduced prominence in academia since 1980 but cannot be viewed as discredited or supplanted. The changing profile of the Supreme Court and its issues have reduced the focus on the areas of constitutional law addressed by these scholars. In addition, a variety of newer jurisprudential movements discussed below have stolen the academic spotlight. But both viewpoints continue to have substantial influence on the bench, with politically liberal judges attracted to the Fundamental Rights School while politically conservative judges are attracted to constrained constitutionalism.

After the Realist Revolution and the Legal Process Rehabilitation: Current Trends in Modern Jurisprudence.

Today, American law is taught largely within a Legal Process framework. Within that framework, however, several substantial jurisprudential movements have made intellectual inroads, although none has established itself as dominant. In addition, a number of important trends in legal scholarship could be characterized as mini-movements or emerging movements. We briefly review these schools, roughly in chronological order of their emergence.

The Law and Economics Movement and Public Choice Theory. Law and Economics theory, discussed at length in Chapter Two, has been the most influential of the post-Legal Process trends in the law. Economic analysis of law arguably has supplanted the Process school to some degree. In most institutions and in the judicial system, however, economic analysis has been engrafted onto Legal Process analysis as a means of assessing the objectivity or wisdom of decisions resulting from the more traditional approach.

The L & E movement took significant shape and began to hold the status of a full-fledged movement in the 1960s, with strong impetus given from influential scholarly articles by Ronald Coase (*The Problem of Social*

Cost)[142] and Guido Calabresi (*Some Thoughts on Risk Distribution and the Law of Torts*).[143]   L & E did not become firmly established in the legal academy until the publication in 1973 of Richard Posner's *The Economic Analysis of Law*.   Coase and Calabresi had focused microeconomics on property and tort law rather than only antitrust law and commercial disputes (as was the case prior to the L & E movement).   Posner went further and utilized microeconomic theory for assessing virtually all aspects of law.[144] During the 1970s, L & E gained increasing stature and even a near-dominance during the 1980s.   At the outset of the movement's recognition, it was associated with the "Chicago School" as a politically conservative approach emphasizing efficiency in both substantive and procedural law. It tended to favor markets and limited government.   L & E was also linked closely to Judge Posner's utilitarian view that the object of law should be the maximization of social wealth, even if the relentless pursuit of that goal harmed some individual litigants.

In the matured L & E movement of today, there are more voices. Some L & E scholars argue for active government involvement to either correct market imperfections or compensate for market-based harms.   Many are critical of some work of the first generation of the Chicago School for being either too affected by the authors' political conservatism or insufficiently appreciative of the complexities of real life.   The new generation of L & E scholarship attempts to account for the glitches of reality.   In doing so, it has made L & E seem less like a self-standing scheme of jurisprudence and more like a variant and descendent of Realism.[145]   The latter

---

[142]   3 J. LAW & ECON. 1 (1960).

[143]   70 YALE L.J. 499 (1961); *see also* GUIDO CALABRESI, THE COST OF ACCIDENTS (1970) (applying economic analysis to a wide range of tort law issues).

[144]   Including criminal law.   In later writings, Posner applied microeconomic analysis to such seemingly "off-limits" topics as child adoption.   Another University of Chicago academic, Nobel Prize winner Gary Becker, has also been influential in expanding the scope of L & E's domain.   He is most known for writing on the economics of marriage and the family.

[145]   *See* Gary Minda, *The Jurisprudential Movements of the 1980s*, 50 OHIO ST. L.J. 599 (1989) (describing Chicago School and others in L & E movement) (hereinafter Minda, *Jurisprudential Movements*); *see also* Gary Minda, *Jurisprudence at Century's End*, 43 J. LEGAL EDUC. 35 (1993) (hereinafter Minda, *Jurisprudence*) (describing shift in L & E focus from efficiency to practical reason).   There has also long been a "Yale School" of L & E less deferential to preexisting entitlements and markets, the logical progeny of Calabresi's early work.   *See* Bruce

1980s also saw some subsidence of the legal academy's emphasis upon (some would say its obsession with) L & E writings.

But without doubt, L & E continues to have a major impact on legal thinking and the judicial process. Economists have also demonstrated entrepreneurial or proselytizing spirit as well, which is reflected in the growing importance of "public choice" scholarship. In essence, public choice thinkers attempt to apply microeconomic axioms to government, politics, and social behavior. They assume that politicians and bureaucrats are self-interested actors who seek to advance their own positions through rational behavior. This explains the allegedly poor product of American government: its members are often (perhaps usually) more concerned about getting (re)elected, wealthy, or popular rather than making good public policy, especially if this entails controversy or the wrath of powerful interest groups. This has been described, not surprisingly, as the "interest group" branch of public choice theory. Its other branch, which flows from the work of Nobel Prize winner Kenneth Arrow, is sometimes called the "agenda control" or "Arrow's Theorem" branch. It focuses upon the way in which organizational structure and procedures affect government, particularly legislative outcomes, by producing laws and policies that often do not represent the cumulative preferences of the majority.

Public Choice has obvious implications for facets of law quite far afield from what has traditionally been considered the domain of even modern L & E. For example, adherents to public choice theory may argue that government is so inherently dominated by well-positioned minority interests as to justify only strictly limited government power and more reliance on the supposedly less corruptible market. However, public choice insights can also be used to justify more aggressive judicial review of the legislative product (a/k/a statutes) as well as government reforms aimed at reducing the influence of powerful but unrepresentative interest groups. Public choice may similarly suggest certain government reforms aimed at reducing problems of agenda control, policy logjams, and so on. Public choice inquiry has focused on the legislature with comparatively little study of executive and judicial behavior. Judges and executive officials are presumably governed by the same amoral, utility-maximizing behavior that allegedly characterizes legislators. Neither the implications of this insight nor its accuracy has been extensively tested through either theory or empiri-

---

A. Ackerman, *Law, Economics, and the Problem of Legal Culture*, 1986 DUKE L.J. 929 (1986).

cal study. To persons familiar with the American political process, the interest group public choice theory makes much intuitive sense. It seems to explain much of the behavior we see regularly reported in the newspapers.

Multidisciplinarism, the Law & Society Movement, and the Core "Law ands" of Sociology, Psychology and Anthropology. During roughly the same time period as the L & E movement, beginning with the 1960s and accelerating in the 1970s, the legal profession saw a distinct upswing in conscious efforts to incorporate theories and empirical data from disciplines outside the law. These efforts are descendants of both the Realist movement, Pound's Sociological Jurisprudence, and Holmes' interest in matters outside pure doctrine. Describing these various "law ands" is difficult. Perhaps most prominent among them is the Law and Society (L & S) movement, which has its own association composed of lawyers and nonlawyers not only in the U.S. but also in many foreign countries. It publishes a quarterly journal (the *Law and Society Review*) and holds a large, well-attended annual meeting at which dozens of scholarly papers are presented.

The very breadth and institutionalization of this movement suggests that it is perhaps an umbrella organization of "law ands" rather than a particular school of jurisprudence. Nonetheless, a taxonomist willing to suffer some inaccuracy could describe the L & S movement as primarily a Law and Sociology or Law and Anthropology movement that attempts to study the development of law and legal systems as a social and cultural phenomenon. Compared to the other jurisprudential trends, L & S is more concerned with empirical measurement and case studies or field research. Not coincidentally, it is also the school with the most input by nonlawyers, which undoubtedly affects both its viewpoints and interests. L & S scholarship tends, for example, to focus more on people's attitudes toward or interaction with the courts than on specific legal doctrines. The patron saint of the L & S movement is Max Weber, the early 20th century German sociologist who wrote extensively and insightfully about the behavior of legal and bureaucratic systems. Roscoe Pound's influence is reflected as well.

In large part, the L & S movement and its association are simply shorthand ways of referring to a number of less pervasive "law ands." For example, during the 1960s, there was a sharp increase in issues of Law and Psychiatry. Most of the focus at the time concerned criminal culpability, particularly the insanity defense, which was revised substantially in case law and under a Model Penal Code drafted by leading experts. This submovement's goal was to utilize the learning of psychiatry and psychology to alter or shape legal rules or definitions regarding insanity and mental illness. A related development was the Law and Medicine submovement that became prominent in the 1960s and continues to be important within its more limited sphere. Law and Medicine scholars, now often referred to as "health law" experts, are concerned primarily with legal rules, doctrines and procedures that affect doctor-patient relations and the availability, delivery, and cost of health care.

A distinguishing feature of these core L & S movements is their relatively direct translation into actual litigation. For example, a lawyer representing a wife who shot her husband in his sleep to put an end to his constant beatings may readily use L & S insights by defending the case on a theory of self-defense related to the "battered women's syndrome," in which a woman who has been regularly abused may feel trapped and threatened even though she is not under direct physical attack at the time she kills her husband.[146] Two leading scholars have found social science used in litigation (a) to determine facts, (b) to make law, and (c) to provide a context for assessing the reasonableness of behavior, the veracity of claims, and the impact of proposed remedies. Social science has also been used to seek an advantage in litigation by various tactics such as the selection of favorable jurors through psychological profiles or by basing an attempt to obtain a transfer in venue on survey research that reveals prejudice against a party.[147]

Peripheral "Law ands." Although historical study has always been important to law, the invigoration of the "law ands" led to a more distinct Law and History component to legal scholarship, with new journals and greater specialization in this area. As with the L & S movement, legal history is frequently, perhaps even primarily, practiced outside of law schools as a specialty within university history departments.

Of more recent vintage, as evidenced by new legal periodicals devoted to the topic, is the Law and Religion school, which examines the interaction of law and religious institutions or theology. In addition, of course, scholars with an interest in law and religion are likely to devote considerable attention to the legal system's treatment of religious issues, such as separation of church and state, taxation of church property,

---

[146] *See, e.g.,* New Jersey v. Kelly, 478 A.2d 364 (N.J. 1984).

[147] *See* MONAHAN & WALKER, *supra* note 101.

regulation of abortion, and application of secular law to religious institutions (*e.g.*, whether an antidiscrimination statute prevents a church from firing a gay worker who is not part of that church's priesthood).

New "Law ands." Another relative newcomer is the Law and Literature (L & L) movement. One noted L & L scholar describes three strands of this movement:

> First, there is a growing body of scholarship from legal scholars regarding the legal and jurisprudential ideas contained *in* literature. Second, both legal and literary scholars are studying the relationship between literary criticism and legal criticism, and between literary theory and legal theory. Third, there is a growing awareness amongst legal scholars that both law and legal theory can profitably be read as *literature*."[148]

Strand One might, for example, argue that literary portrayals of humanity are sufficiently at odds with the implied conception of *homo legalus* as to undermine the accuracy of conclusions stemming from the lawyer's vision of human behavior.[149] Analysis of the relations between law and the portrayal of legal matters in literary works includes even popular writings and classics that do not expressly mention legal matters. As second cousin to L & S, L & L scholarship sometimes examines whether the literary treatment of the law reflects deeper social attitudes toward law or human behavior and thus sheds light upon modern cases or issues.

Strand Two, the relation of legal criticism and literary criticism, also has staked out a significant presence in the "Law as Interpretation" school of dialogue discussed below. This strand might also be termed "Law and Hermeneutics" (L & H), which explores the implications of the relationship between communication, word meaning, and interpretative issues in law. L & H is different than L & L, however, in that the literature movement tends to focus more on nonlegal writings about legal characters,

---

[148] Robin L. West, *Adjudication is Not Interpretation: Some Reservations About the Law-as-Literature Movement*, 54 TENN. L. REV. 203, 203-04 n. 1 (1987) (citations omitted).

[149] *See, e.g.*, Robin L. West, *Authority, Autonomy, and Choice: The Role at Consent in the Moral and Political Visions of Franz Kafka and Richard Posner*, 99 HARV. L. REV. 384 (1985); RICHARD A. POSNER, *Colloquy: The Ethical Significance of Free Choice: A Reply to Professor West*, 99 HARV. L. REV. 1431 (1986).

issues, and systems. By contrast, the hermeneutics movement focuses on the science/art/act of interpreting texts, particularly legal texts, in part by drawing on scholarship regarding the interpretation of nonlegal texts. Calling L & H its own movement is something of a misnomer since much L & H activity (perhaps most of it) takes place in the textual analysis performed by the Law as Interpretation movement, the deconstruction aspects of the Critical Legal Studies (CLS) movement, or the post-structural analysis of language that is generally considered part of the current trend toward postmodernism in legal scholarship (discussed below). For example, CLS scholarship frequently attempts to "deconstruct" legal texts to look for deeper meaning. The notion of deconstruction (the parsing of text and the subsequent reexamination of the component parts of the text from different perspectives, employing different assumptions) had its start in the writings of literary scholars such as Jacques Derrida and Paul de Man. A recent submovement in Law and Humanities blends a number of these "law ands" into a broader and more eclectic mix of studies concerning the relation of law and social, historical, and literary forces.

Clear boundaries are hard to find. Although the "law and" movements are bounded by clouds more than fences, they share a commitment to the idea that law is best studied in a broad and multi-disciplinary fashion. Rather than displaying a radical shift in jurisprudential perspective, the "law and" movements are probably better described as specific, restricted areas of interest related to law in which Legal Realist precepts are brought to bear.

Critical Legal Studies. Also arriving in the 1970s and becoming institutionalized during the 1980s was the Critical Legal Studies movement. Like the "law and" movements, CLS has a considerable beachhead in legal academia but has not ascended to the decisionmaking power of Legal Realism or L & E. For example, many L & E adherents are now judges or highly placed members of the executive and judicial branches. CLS has been regarded with suspicion not only in the outside world but also within the academy. During the 1980s, one prominent academician suggested that CLS adherents had no place on law school faculties since, in his view, CLS preached a form of nihilism too far at odds with the "rule of law."[150] Many legal scholars quickly counter-attacked, contending that the law school, despite its "job training" aspects for a system of social administration, must remain an open environment where all voices can be heard

---

[150] *See* Paul Carrington, *Of Law and the River*, 34 J. LEGAL EDUC. 222 (1984).

without risk of a purge.[151] CLS remains controversial. Many of the academics who defend the rights of CLS adherents are sharply critical of CLS,[152] essentially viewing it as an overstated critique without a discernible prescription for the ills it has identified in the legal system.

The system's shortcomings in the view of CLS scholars include: indeterminacy of legal doctrine; undue mystification of the law to exclude outsiders and enhance the power of lawyers; doctrine and procedure structured to obscure the political aspects of law; protection of the interests of the dominant under the guise of neutrality.[153] It has been stated that the slogan of CLS could be "law is politics." Unlike the Realists, however, CLS adherents often not only recognize the inevitably political aspects of law but also argue for a more self-consciously political approach to law, one which assesses legal outcomes not by application of formal rules or processes so much as by the distributional consequences of legal activity.

In addition to emphasizing politics, CLS scholarship is most famous for exploring in detail purported contradictions that result from widely accepted but overstated concepts, such as the objective/subjective dichotomy, the separation of individual and community, the public/private distinction, the false choice between order and anarchy, and other dualities. For example, a CLS article may seek to convince the reader that a supposedly objective legal rule really contains imbedded subjective value choices and that even though the rule appears neutral, it falls more heavily upon society's disempowered.

Because the focus of CLS, as the name implies, is criticism, it is often painted as a purely destructive movement. Others see in CLS criticism a basis for championing reforms directed toward making law less hierarchal, less protective of the current elite, and more capable of

---

[151] *See, e.g.*, Peter W. Martin, *"Of Law and the River," and of Nihilism and Academic Freedom*, 35 J. LEGAL EDUC. 1 (1985). For a summation of the controversy some years after the Carrington attack, *see* Minda, *Jurisprudential Movements, supra* note 145, at 601-03.

[152] *See* Daniel N.K. Chow, *Trashing Nihilism*, 65 TULANE L. REV. 221 (1990); Owen Fiss, *The Death of Law?*, 72 CORNELL L. REV. 1 (1986).

[153] *See* Minda, *Jurisprudence, supra* note 145. Minda further criticizes CLS detractors for misrepresenting the movement but also notes the evolution of CLS from primarily attacking law as indeterminant to assessing law's role in society's construction and vice versa.

promoting a progressive political agenda. For example, CLS writings suggest revising the current structure of representative government, supporting more activist judicial interpretation of statutes, and using law's status as authority to transform society by moving it away from the goal of wealth maximization and toward the achievement of greater rights for those with lower socioeconomic status.[154]

Perhaps because it is the jurisprudence of outsiders or anti-establishmentarians, CLS has not, to date, overtly reshaped the legal system or case outcomes. But it has enjoyed a high profile in the academic community, has been widely read and discussed by law teachers and students, and has certainly had at least an indirect effect on the thinking of the legal profession and, consequently, legal events.[155] The same can be said of many of the "law and" movements, such as Law & Society, Law & Literature, and the exploration of legal hermeneutics. None of these, however, appears to have made the substantial tangible inroads into legal education, practice, and decisionmaking of Legal Realism or Law & Economics.

Law as Interpretation. At the risk of pointing out the obvious, we note that much of the task of lawyers involves interpretation: of statutes, contracts, ambiguous behavior, letters, orders, earlier cases, treaties, or almost anything bearing on the resolution of a dispute or policy issue before courts or legislatures. To some extent, then, all law is interpretation. The word "interpretation" is so ubiquitous in law, however, that it can lead to confusion. For example, in discussing the "Law as Interpretation" school that distinctly emerged in the 1980s, we are not referring to "Interpretivism," which is a cousin of the conservative reaction to the Warren Court. Interpretivists argue for a constrained reading of the Constitution. They want judicially articulated rights to be quite directly traceable to the language of the document in order to avoid (a) constitutional holdings stemming from the personal preferences of the Justices and (b) the "counter-majoritarian difficulty" (discussed in Chapter Four) arising when an unelected Court invalidates statutes enacted by elected representatives.

---

[154] *See* ESKRIDGE & FRICKEY, *supra* note 111, at 329-30.

[155] *See, e.g.*, Kathleen Sullivan, *The Supreme Court 1991 Term -- Foreword: The Justices of Rules and Standards*, 106 HARV. L. REV. 22 (1992) (discussing differences in Supreme Court Justices' approach to cases by reference to CLS-developed scholarship on distinctions between more formalist "rule" approach to law and more discretionary "standards" approach that takes more account of case outcomes).

Interpretivists such as Justice Hugo Black, Judge Robert Bork, and the late Professor Alexander Bickel argue that both difficulties are ameliorated by this approach since the Constitution was enacted by a "supermajority" and, if strictly construed, may legitimately overturn majoritarian laws.[156] In addition to being a synonym for judicial restraint, "interpretation" can also connote a search for original intent in constitutional construction.

Interpretation has also been used as "referring to the activity that judges must do only in hard cases" or "as the name for the activity of applying a general legal predicate to the factual particulars of cases" or as "a general philosophical position proclaiming the senselessness and/or irrelevancy of metaphysics to the practice of some discipline, because the discipline's proper method has supposedly been discovered to be interpretation. 'Interpretation' in turn, shall name the activity one does to find the meaning of some text or text-analogue."[157] Our notion of interpretation does not focus on this broad vision of interpretation but instead focuses on the legal profession's understanding of key legal texts such as the Constitution, statutes, and important cases.

One view of legal interpretation relates to the observation that the meaning of legal text can become solidified through the ongoing examination by "interpretative communities" who subject the text to discussion, debate, and actual or theoretical application to various matters. This view is strongly associated with both Stanley Fish, an English and Law Professor who first gained prominence as a Milton scholar,[158] and the more recent writings of Ronald Dworkin, a noted legal philosopher who has described the evolution of legal rules and doctrine as something of a "chain novel" in which succeeding chapters are written by the next user of the legal doctrine.[159] This is seen as a shift in emphasis for Dworkin, whose writings during the 1960s and 1970s fit more comfortably within the "Fundamental Rights" school discussed above.

Several of the most prominent center-liberal legal academicians can be said to be members of a broadly, if perhaps ill-defined school of Law as

---

[156] *See* JOHN HART ELY, DEMOCRACY AND DISTRUST 3-10 (1980).

[157] Michael S. Moore, *The Interpretative Turn in Modern Theory: A Turn for the Worse?*, 41 STAN. L. REV. 871, 873 n. 5 (1989).

[158] *See* STANLEY FISH, IS THERE A TEXT IN THIS CLASS? (1980).

[159] *See* RONALD DWORKIN, LAW'S EMPIRE (1985).

Interpretation which holds that the legal system can maintain reasonable objectivity. They posit that through flexible, consistently updated interpretation of the law arrived at through fair decisionmaking structures, the legal system can render principled adjudication consistent with society's long-term values.[160] Note that many of these scholars also fit within the Fundamental Rights school, or at least did during its heyday. The popular reaction to even principled decisions may be quite negative -- but this does not make the decision illegitimate. For example, a court decision requiring desegregation of a high school may be immediately unpopular but justified as the principled application of equality principles to which society subscribes, at least in the abstract.

The Law as Interpretation movement also includes fairly direct descendants of the Harvard Legal Process school of the 1950s but differs in that it is more willing to depart from constrained interpretation due to a recognition of the imperfections of both government institutions and human rationality. For example, one author who generally objects to invoking the Constitution to strike down legislation absent a sufficiently clear textual basis would permit invalidation of the challenged law if it disproportionately applied against persons who were not adequately able to contest the law through the political processes.[161] Some have referred to modern interpretivists as a "new legal process" school.[162]

Feminist Jurisprudence. The emergence of a feminist jurisprudence also began in the 1970s and accelerated during the 1980s. Feminist legal scholarship is now well established in legal academia. It has undoubtedly influenced legal thought, having received substantial prominence in law reviews, casebooks, and class discussion. Particularly for women law students, who have comprised a large (approximately 40 percent) segment of the law school community during the past decade, feminist scholarship is well-known and influential. It stands to reason that the insights of this

---

[160] *See, e.g.*, BRUCE ACKERMAN, RECONSTRUCTING AMERICAN LAW (1983); SOCIAL JUSTICE AND THE LIBERAL STATE (1980); Thomas Grey, *The Constitution as Scripture*, 37 STAN. L. REV. 1 (1984) (*"We are all interpretivists*; the real arguments are not over whether judges should stick to interpreting, but over what they should interpret and what interpretive attitudes they should adopt"); Owen Fiss, *Objectivity and Interpretation*, 34 STAN. L. REV. 739 (1982).

[161] *See* ELY, *supra* note 156.

[162] *See* ESKRIDGE & FRICKEY, *supra* note 111, at 330-334.

area will affect legal outcomes, at least through indirection and penetration of the subconscious of the legal profession.

For example, in a case involving alleged sexual harassment, the U.S. Court of Appeals for the Ninth Circuit held that such claims -- particularly the issue of whether conduct claimed to be innocent by the defendant is in fact harmless or noninvidious -- must be judged according to the reaction they would create for a "reasonable woman" plaintiff rather than the traditional "reasonable man" or "reasonable person." In that case, a woman plaintiff had been ardently pursued by a co-worker and was unable to obtain protection (*e.g.*, his transfer to another office) from the employer against his unrequited advances. The spurned suitor argued that his intentions were honorable in questing after his "true love," while the employer saw the situation as one where intervention would place it at risk of legal action brought by the man (*e.g.*, filing a constructive discharge claim against the employer if he was transferred). As the Court memorably put it, the man may have seen himself as a latter-day Cyrano de Bergerac seeking his Roxanne, but the plaintiff might well regard herself as being forced against her will to star in a gender-flipped remake of "Fatal Attraction."[163]

Examples of the self-conscious judicial differentiation between the male and female perspectives is relatively rare but demonstrates the potential of feminist jurisprudence to obtain tangible results. In a nutshell, feminist jurisprudence proceeds by suggesting both that (1) women have been wrongfully denied equal treatment under the law and (2) traditional mainstream legal scholarship favors a type of reasoning more attuned to male-oriented values and ways of thinking, thus denying women a full measure of participation in the legal system as well as producing an excessively formalist, hierarchal legal system. One observer (male) has characterized the three themes of feminist jurisprudence as (a) the difference between men and women in life experience, (b) the different voice of women's reasoning, and (c) the dominance of the male legal and social hierarchy.[164]

A sex discrimination lawsuit provides a good example of the first deficiency seen by feminists. For instance, if an insurance company permits

---

[163]   *See* Ellison v. Brady, 924 F.2d 872 (9th Cir. 1991). The "reasonable woman" standard announced in *Ellison* has been both praised and condemned in the legal literature, by avowed feminists and others.

[164]   *See* Cass R. Sunstein, *Feminism and Legal Theory*, 101 HARV. L. REV. (1988) (reviewing CATHARINE A. MACKINNON, FEMINISM UNMODIFIED (1986)).

only men to be agents but has plenty of female "assistants" who do essentially the same work and are paid far less, this would be classic gender discrimination. Similarly, an employer who refused to hire a woman who otherwise met all criteria for employment (*e.g.*, education level, test scores, strength, speed, special training) would be guilty of discrimination. To the extent that the law permits this by accepting post hoc rationalizations for such discrimination or permits a "non-discriminatory" solution that falls more heavily upon women,[165] it wrongly supports a male-privileging society.

But feminist jurisprudence goes well beyond this basic "equal treatment" standard. A major part of the feminist project is to examine and criticize the impact of the law in view of the context and experiences of women. Feminists contend that the legal and political establishments have given short shrift to women's experiences, which have often been episodes of subjugation, frustration, and denial. The assumed neutral viewpoint of law is one that has generally privileged men and promoted a version of reality that simply is not accurate when applied to women, and often other "out groups" as well.[166]

Feminist scholars look at the world and the legal system differently and attempt to avoid or criticize the hierarchy of classic legal formalism, even as muted by the Legal Process and related schools. Feminists also contend that women often approach problems differently than men, with more of a focus on relationships and continuity and with less formalism. Key to this strand of feminism are the writings of psychologist Carol Gilligan, who in studying children observed differences in their approaches to problems (see Chapter One). She suggested that men see moral dilemmas as something of a "math problem with humans" in which logic is central to resolution, while women see such problems as a "narrative of

---

[165] *See, e.g.*, International Union v. Johnson Controls, Inc., 499 U.S. 187 (1991) (striking down employer's "fetal protection policy" of forbidding nonsterile women employees to work on tasks creating exposure to lead).

[166] *See* Judith Resnik, *On the Bias: Feminist Reconsideration of the Aspirations for Our Judges*, 61 S. Cal. L. Rev. 1877, 1906 (1988).

relationships" and address them through communication designed to provide mutually acceptable solutions.[167]

Feminist scholarship is quite varied but tends to fall into two generalized camps. "Cultural feminists" tend to agree with Gilligan and see women's subordination and difference as an outgrowth of women's social role, primarily the raising of children and the maintenance of families, including the mediation of intra-familial conflict. "Radical" feminists see women as relegated to second tier status because of biological chains (*e.g.*, bearing children) and sexual domination by men, a domination thought by some radical feminists to be inescapably inherent in the mechanics of traditional sexual intercourse.[168] To radical feminists, the imperfections and inequality of law flow more from gender hierarchy than gender role and almost certainly not from innate biological or psychological differences. Regardless of their disagreements, radical and cultural feminists argue for greater examination of context, reality, tradition, and hierarchy in the law, rather than swift resort to fixed rules or procedures.

Feminist jurisprudence, like CLS and L & E, has thus far enjoyed more success as a heuristic device or method of criticism than as a positive program for change. As developed to date, feminist scholars generally support such changes in the law as: more women on the bench, the legislature and other policymaking roles; less reliance on formalist rules for adjudication and greater judicial willingness to hear the stories of litigants; more emphasis in the law on the particular context of the litigants, their relations, and their dispute and less emphasis on broadly articulated rules; better education about, and attempts to dissolve, anti-women stereotypes.

Critical Race Theory. Related to, but diverging from Critical Legal Studies is Critical Race Theory, which examines legal and political issues from the point of view of persons of color, principally African Americans.[169] The point of the exercise is to illuminate the degree to which the current legal system reflects domination by a white majority,

---

[167] *See* CAROL GILLIGAN, IN A DIFFERENT VOICE 25-30 (1982). For a shorthand description of Gilligan's analysis in the context of other later feminist writings, *see* Minda, *Jurisprudential Movements*, *supra* note 145, at 626-628.

[168] *See* Robin West, *Jurisprudence and Gender*, 55 U. CHI. L. REV. 1, 13 (1988).

[169] *See* Kimberle Williams Crenshaw, *Race, Reform, and Retrenchment: Transformation and Legitimation in Antidiscrimination Law*, 101 HARV. L. REV. 1331 (1988).

prejudice against African Americans, or the historical fact of slavery. Much writing in Critical Race Theory is by scholars of color and often has an autobiographical dimension, using the author's own experiences at the receiving end of racism to illustrate and amplify the analytical points made by the author.[170]

Civic Republicanism. During the 1980s, many legal scholars associated with communitarianism (discussed in Chapter Three) wrote in favor of approaching law and policy issues from a perspective of "civic republicanism" in which decisions are consciously made through a reflective community-wide process of deliberation and agreement. The optimal outcome (*e.g.*, rule, interpretation, course of conduct) is sought by means of a self-conscious attempt to decide matters on the basis of "civic virtue" rather than the aggregation of individual personal preferences.[171] One justification of this approach is the claim that republican deliberation is a legitimate part of American political history that has been forgotten due to the popularity of a pluralist vision of policymaking in which individuals and interest groups compete to impose their policy preferences on society. The republican tradition dates back to ancient Greece and was held in part by the founders, although framers like James Madison also were strongly affected by a pluralist view of the political world.[172]

The term "republican" refers to a form of representative government rather than the modern partisan competition in the United States between Democrats and Republicans. Although, as with most movements, civic republicans differ in their prescriptions for the world's perceived ills, the general tendency of civic republicans is to place substantial faith in an active judiciary that functions as an ongoing deliberative community seeking wise and far-sighted legal construction and policymaking. The civic republican

---

[170] *See* Jerome McCristal Culp, Jr., *You Can Take Them to Water But You Can't Make Them Drink: Black Legal Scholarship and White Legal Scholars*, 1992 U. ILL. L. REV. 1021 (1992) (providing illustrations); *but see* Randall L. Kennedy, *Racial Critiques of Legal Academia*, 102 HARV. L. REV. 1745 (1989) (prominent black scholar criticizes autobiographical aspects of black scholarship as excessive and self-indulgent).

[171] *See generally Symposium: The Republican of Civic Tradition*, 97 YALE L.J. 1651 (1988).

[172] *See* Cass R. Sunstein, *Interest Groups in American Public Law*, 38 STAN. L. REV. 29 (1985); *see also* DAVID EPSTEIN, THE POLITICAL THEORY OF THE FEDERALIST (1981).

enterprise has been criticized as insufficiently sensitive to individual rights, particularly the rights of those unpersuaded by the community's conclusions as to what is "just" and "good."[173]   This criticism also suggests that the civic republicans are too insensitive to the need for constraints on decisionmaking through rules and institutions that restrict the power of the deliberative community, particularly where the community is composed to some extent of elite representatives such as judges, legislators, rulers, or key academicians.[174]

Postmodernism, Pragmatism, and Related Concepts.   Perhaps the most recent jurisprudential movement of note is a recognized postmodernism. In addition to being a movement of its own, postmodern thought is at the root of a number of the jurisprudential developments of the past generation, including CLS, feminism, critical race theory, and pragmatism.

To describe postmodernism, it is perhaps best to begin by defining modernism, the prevailing bedrock world view of the mid-20th century. According to one explanation, modernism has the central characteristics of "(1) Epistemological Foundationalism: the view that knowledge can only be justified to the extent it rests on indubitable foundations; (2) [A] Theory of Language: language has one of two functions -- it represents ideas or states of affairs, or it expresses the attitudes of the speaker; (3) Individual and Community: 'society' is best understood as an aggregation of 'social atoms.'"[175]

By contrast, and as its name might imply, the postmodern view rejects these central tenets of modernism:

> [Knowledge is] mediated by our social, cultural, linguistic,
> and historical circumstances, and it will thus vary as those
> circumstances change. The truth, consequently, can never
> be transparent to us; it is and must always be a social

---

[173] *See, e.g.*, Stephen Gey, *The Unfortunate Revival of Civic Republicanism*, 141 U. PA. L. REV. 801 (1993).

[174] A major Law & Literature scholar has made essentially the same point. *See* West, *supra* note 148 ("community" can be evil and racist rather than good and supportive of all members).

[175] Nancy Murphy & James W. McClendon, Jr., *Distinguishing Modern and Postmodern Theologies*, 5 MOD. THEOLOGY 199 (1989); *see also* PAUL JOHNSON, THE BIRTH OF THE MODERN (1992).

construction, one made even more opaque by the mediation of language, a system of communication inherently incapable of capturing reality. This includes the 'truth' about legal doctrines, legal principles, and legal interpretations: All are social constructions . . . . [K]nowledge of the world is filtered through the structures of the socially and culturally derived assumptions that each of us has accumulated as human beings, and because each of us is differently situated, there are different perspectives on objects and events and thus differing content to our knowledge of them. Knowledge is thus conceived by postmodernists as always contingent, always dependent on context and always 'local' rather than 'universal.'[176]

Postmodern thought has two branches: a post-structuralist branch and one of neopragmatism. The former "tends to emphasize the role of language and language's underlying structures in shaping our understandings of reality and texts."[177] It is familiar to the reader as the organizing principal behind literary deconstruction, which is embraced by many CLS adherents. By contrast, neopragmatism "emphasizes the social construction of knowledge and language,"[178] although it acknowledges the importance of language. For example, pragmatist philosopher and educator John Dewey once observed that "to name a thing is to know it."[179] Pragmatists and neopragmatists generally reject the notion that there exists logically certain, solid, objective knowledge. They see all knowledge as socially constructed. But neopragmatists also often reject or are at least highly

---

[176] Peter C. Schanck, *Understanding Postmodern Thought and Its Implications for Statutory Interpretation*, 65 S. CAL. L. REV. 2505, 2509-10 (1992).

[177] *Id.* at 2514.

[178] *Id.*

[179] As the names imply, American pragmatist philosophy is the precursor to neopragmatism. Some would in fact argue that the "neo" label is unnecessary and that today's pragmatist philosophers such as Richard Rorty are actually lineal descendants of Dewey. *See generally* JOHN P. MURPHY, PRAGMATISM: FROM PEIRCE TO DAVIDSON (1990); CORNEL WEST, THE AMERICAN EVASION OF PHILOSOPHY: A GENEALOGY OF PRAGMATISM (1989); *but see* Schanck, *supra* note 176, at 2539 n.126 ("Rorty and [Duke English and law professor Stanley] Fish differ enough from the Peirce/James/Dewey school to justify distinguishing them").

skeptical of empirical or scientific efforts to derive some pragmatic notion of truth.

What are the implications of pragmatism and postmodernism? And why are we talking about things anti-foundationalist in a book called *Foundations of the Law?* Well, we promised a comprehensive survey, not necessarily a consistent one. In fact, the rise of postmodern thought and the multiple jurisprudential schools of the past thirty years show that many commentators see law's underpinnings as less solid and imposing than they were once thought to be. Whether one agrees or disagrees with the post-modern perspective, it nonetheless remains a powerful influence upon recent and current jurisprudence, legal theory, and legal practice.[180] It has also been controversial, with many observers labeling postmodern influence as relativist and nihilist.[181] But a number of legal scholars have found pragmatism not to be so standardless, but instead to be a liberating methodology for deciding legal matters with situational flexibility. According to one self-avowed pragmatist, legal pragmatism in practice "essentially means solving legal problems using every tool that comes to hand, including precedent, tradition, legal text, and social policy." He "renounces the entire project of providing a theoretical foundation" for legal analysis.[182] This view of pragmatism is more like the Aristotelian concept of practical reason: one can reach a correct result in a given matter even if it is impossible to construct a theory or method that always produces correct results. So defined, pragmatism is hardly the nihilism feared by some. But getting anyone to agree on a particular vision of legal pragmatism has proven difficult in the postmodern world.

Does It Matter? An Illustration of the Impact of Different Jurisprudential Approaches.

Throughout this chapter, we have provided examples and illustrations, but mainly we have described major American jurisprudential movements and their key figures. Readers with even small doses of

---

[180] *See* Minda, *Jurisprudence, supra* note 145.

[181] *See* Schanck, *supra* note 176, at 2510-12 (collection of critical sources).

[182] *See* Daniel A. Farber, *Legal Pragmatism and the Constitution*, 72 MINN. L. REV. 1331 (1988); *see also* Symposium, *The Renaissance of Pragmatism in American Legal Thought*, 63 S. CAL. L. REV. 1569-1853 (1990); William N. Eskridge, Jr. & Philip P. Frickey, *Statutory Interpretation as Practical Reasoning*, 42 STAN. L. REV. 321 (1990).

skepticism may wonder whether jurisprudence, which is often excessively abstract, actually affects concrete case outcomes. We think it does and, to illustrate our point, close our sketch of the field by examining one case from several jurisprudential perspectives.

Suppose Wanda Worker was hired as a security guard at Acme Widget Company. As part of the selection process, she completed an application form which, among other things, asked whether she had ever been convicted of a crime. Despite her guilty plea to a DWI (driving while intoxicated) charge three years earlier, Wanda answered "no." Acme hired her after a minimal screening process (review of her application and resume, phone calls to two former employers) and an interview. She then worked as a guard for two years, receiving good reviews of her work (7.5 on Acme's 10-point evaluation scale). During her employment, she was hounded by her immediate supervisor, Sergeant Sam Security, who wanted to be sexually intimate with Wanda. Sam asked her out repeatedly, called her at home, contrived to have her work alone with him on isolated patrols, and was constantly pawing her. Wanda complained to the Security Unit's Chief, who told her to be firm with Sam because he was immature and going through post-divorce blues. But the Chief refused to reassign Sam, admonish him, punish him, or otherwise aid Wanda.

One day, Sam attacked Wanda with a ferocity that went beyond mere pawing. She fought him off but was too shaken to return to work. She quit and sued Acme for gender discrimination under the federal civil rights act (42 U.S.C. § 2000e *et seq.*) because of the hostile work environment at Acme. Acme admits mistreatment of Wanda occurred but is defending the lawsuit on the ground that Wanda's misrepresentation on her job application deprives her of the right to sue. Acme asserts that she would never have landed the job had she told the truth and that her blameworthy conduct estops her from relief.[183]

A Natural Law judge might verge sharply to either side in this contest. A traditional natural lawyer would be receptive to Acme's argument to the extent that it limits the statute's reach. A favorite

---

[183] The Supreme Court accepted a similar case for review in 1993 but the case settled before a decision was rendered. *See* Milligan-Jensen v. Michigan Technological University, 975 F.2d 302 (6th Cir. 1992); *see also* Ann C. McGinley, *Reinventing Reality: The Improper Use of After-Acquired Evidence in Discrimination Litigation*, 26 CONN. L. REV. 783 (1993) (criticizing *Milligan-Jensen* and other cases accepting similar defenses).

Blackstone canon of statutory construction was that statutes in derogation of the common law are to be strictly construed. The common law provided no right to damages for either race or gender discrimination. The civil rights law is a sharp break with the common law. Absent a clear text or other strong positive law statement in favor of allowing the "bad" employee to invoke the statute, the Natural Law judge would be receptive to restraint. In addition, the moralist/religious wing of Natural Law would generally condemn falsehoods, even those by persons desperate to earn a wage.

On the other hand, the neo-Natural Law view of persons friendly to the Fundamental Rights school would infer from the constitution and the web of various statutes (including Title VII) a principle of vindicating gender equality and human dignity. Since Wanda was denied these by Sam's lechery and Acme's refusal to provide meaningful help, the statute would likely apply and Wanda's "fib" to get the job would be considered far less important, legally or morally.

In contrast, a pure Positivist would strive to give full effect to the expression of the sovereign's authority in making statutes. But Positivists divide sharply over whether the statutory text alone constitutes this expression or whether indicia like legislative history, statutory purpose and the like deserve consideration. If the background of the civil rights act suggested a congressional desire to promote nondiscrimination policy even when it was in tension with other values, Wanda could prevail.

A Formalist judge would be perhaps the most likely to accept Acme's defense, reasoning that: the groundrules for getting the job required a clean record; Wanda lacked a clean record; therefore, she was never a legitimate employee and thus has no right (or "standing," *see* Chapter Four) to invoke the federal job discrimination law designed to protect bona fide employees. Of course, a Formalist starting with different axioms (*e.g.*, absent limiting language in the statute, both "honest" and "dishonest" employees are covered) could reach a different result. The importance and malleability of assumptions continues to be an Achilles Heel of Formalist analysis.

A judge practicing Pound's Sociological Jurisprudence would want to know more about the aggregate nature of the problem. Which is more prevalent and problematic: lying to get jobs or sex discrimination? In balancing the interests involved, does a finding for the employee jeopardize public safety by failing to deter falsehoods (what if Wanda's conviction had been for murder or grand larceny)? Is finding for Acme and other similar employers likely to deter future Wandas, or are similar inaccuracies on job applications likely to be unaffected by the decision? Does insulating the employer in the face of admitted discrimination imperil the public safety by giving an inadequate incentive to comply with the law (what if Sam had raped Wanda)? Express policy considerations of the greater good would likely determine the disposition of this case by judges who thought like Holmes, Pound, or Cardozo. Most likely, this sort of policy pragmatism would reject the employer's defense and find for Wanda.

A Legal Realist would take a similar interest balancing, semi-empirical, public policy approach to the problem but would more pointedly ask whether any acceptance of Acme's defense, whatever its virtues, would in essence strip society's least powerful workers of their important rights to nondiscriminatory treatment. The Realist and Sociological jurist would also work harder than the Formalist to ascertain any congressional intent on this point by consulting legislative history. In the main, however, a Realist is likely to invoke a bottom line of "common sense." No matter how Wanda got the job at Acme, she was an employee who was mistreated and should be protected by the statute.

A Legal Process judge would also consult the statute's background but would pay more attention than the Realist to the overall purpose of the statute, seeking the result most in harmony with the spirit of the law.[184] The Process judge would also be more concerned about the institutional competence of courts to deal with the matter but would likely find it permissible to fill the interstices of the statute with reasoned analysis akin to the Sociologist judge's interest balancing. A Process judge would be among the most torn by the case, reasoning (in a manner similar to the Natural Law judge) that since the common law provided no private right of action for gender discrimination, the judge should be leery of expanding the pathbreaking statute too much by implication. Unlike the Sociologist and the Realist, who would presumably invoke the maxim that remedial legislation should be liberally construed, the Process judge would worry more about whether a rational Congress, had it anticipated the issue, would prefer the statute to benefit a lying employee rather than permit a discriminating employer to avoid liability through happenstance. On balance, the Process judge is likely to rule for Wanda.

---

[184]   In real life, the courts depend substantially on counsel to flesh out these matters in their briefs and arguments to the court. *See* Chapter Five on the adversary system.

A Law and Social Science judge would conduct an inquiry similar to the Sociological Jurisprudence judge but utilize a greater variety of sources and more empirical rigor in making the policy choices and balancing necessary to decide the case. In addition, this judge might draw upon psychological, sociological and anthropological insights to empathize with the plight of Wanda and similar employees who are not really criminals but merely told a small lie to get work. Furthermore, the multidisciplinary judge, like the Realist and Sociologist, would note with scorn that the defendant had done nothing substantial to check out its supposedly vital criterion for hiring of "no criminal record."

A Law & Economics judge would focus on whether a decision for Wanda increases or decreases net social wealth both in the instant case and in the future. The judge might argue that finding for Wanda will unreasonably increase all employers' costs of checking applicant backgrounds. Instead, stripping the fibbing employee of certain legal rights creates strong incentives not to fib and provides a low-cost means of employer processing of applications. Wanda may suffer a sizeable loss but American commerce gains more, which makes a finding for Acme the more wealth-maximizing decision. This is a plausible approach for Chicago School L & E judges. A Yale School L & E judge might instead concentrate on productivity losses in the workplace from the underdeterrence of a sexually hostile work environment and find for Wanda.

A CLS judge would decide the case like an indignant Realist, seeing the civil rights act as progressive legislation that should take precedence over favoritism for the commercial power structure. The CLS judge would further view the civil rights law as cold comfort to workers who must continually work in harsh and underpaid circumstances with no job security. A Law as Interpretation judge would work to understand the statute as viewed by a relevant interpretative community drawing on standard sources of statutory meaning. She would probably conclude that the law was meant to protect imperfect employees as well as model workers.

A Civic Republican judge would engage in a decisionmaking akin to that of the Process judge, but with less concern over what the statute's legislative history might show as a result of the efforts of powerful employer interest groups. For example, this judge would be unimpressed with Senator Appartchik's floor statement that the law was intended only to benefit otherwise qualified employees. The Pragmatist, Postmodern judge would reach a similar result. The foundational, ultimate nature of the defense claim would sound tinny to her ear. Instead, she would want to advance the basic purpose of the law -- to protect workers -- despite syllogistic arguments to the contrary. The Feminist judge or Critical Race judge would have a similar but more vehement view in favor of Wanda, seeing the case as a classic example of law's potential to work in favor of the male, white, and conservative interests of society.

Even in this illustrative case, where the scorecard is overwhelmingly in favor of Wanda, we can see that different jurisprudential allegiances lead to pronounced differences in approaches to adjudication. In our schematic, only the Natural Law, Formalist, and Law & Economics judges are significantly likely to find for the employer. However, these schools enjoy substantial support. In fact, the majority of real courts facing issues of this type appear to have sided with employers rather than employees. This may illustrate the extent to which post-Realist jurisprudence, although dominant in the academy, has yet to dislodge more foundational schools from dominance in the real world. In addition, the potential changes in outcomes illustrate an imbedded conflict in jurisprudence: that between privileging rules of decision versus privileging the discretion of the decisionmaker. If, for example, Congress in passing the statute distrusts judges to apply it correctly, it could work to create the formalism it wants by prescribing precise rules that would be hard for even post-Realist judges to avoid. In doing this, it would limit judicial discretion to reach equitable results in unanticipated cases. This tension between rules and discretion is ever-present in the law.

Where Are We Now?

The wealth of jurisprudential debate makes for a more interesting academic environment. But law is more than an intellectual discipline or field of inquiry, it is a system of social administration. Too much division can create stalemate, partisanship, or even anarchy, hardly a type of law satisfactory to most persons. Despite the current diversity of jurisprudential viewpoints, there remains a sufficiently broad consensus in the profession to enable law to discharge its governing function while it engages in internal examination and debate.

The current environment certainly appears to have more friction and disagreement than earlier eras. Upon examination, however, the "good old days" sometimes invoked as a comparison with today were unusually quiet times of unity -- and not necessarily for positive reasons. For example, the legal formalism of the 19th century was possible in part because law was a closed profession of white males, usually with family background or money, although law school also served as a step up for many in the working or lower middle classes, including immigrants. When everyone is more or less the same, achieving agreement on rules, principles or values (and their application) becomes a relatively easier matter.[185] This was unity, but that alone does not make it worth reviving.

The unity of the post-War Legal Process school was possible in part because it occurred during the 1950s "end of ideology" period during which major political actors and scholars of America were in close agreement on most issues. This resulted in part from recent, united national purpose exhibited during World War II, which was remobilized in the Cold War because of fears of Soviet domination. As previously noted, the period of 1960-1990 saw a steady stream of scholarship that undermined many of the basic assumptions of the Process school. In the meantime, national political consensus was shattered by changing attitudes toward the Cold War, strong opposition to the Vietnam War, the civil rights revolution, the rising environmental movement, and increased economic competition from Western Europe and Japan (economic scarcity makes acceptable political solutions harder to find since some groups had to lose more often; the option of "building a bigger pie" is not as viable).

Thus, two of the celebrated jurisprudential movements of the modern era -- Formalism and Legal Process -- can be viewed as unusual in the degree of support they enjoyed during their periods of hegemony. Historically, law has reflected divergence as much as consensus: rational vs. mystical; religious vs. secular; patrician vs. plebeian; natural law vs. legal positivism; formalism vs. realism; Chicago School economics vs. Marxism. Against this backdrop, one can view today's clattering voices unleashed by the Realist movement as a time of relative normality in the law.

But much of the story remains to be written. Whether jurisprudential schools grow or decline depends to a large degree upon the views of the legal profession and the public. Although courts are unlikely to regularly talk of hermeneutics, postmodernism, or differences in reasoning based on gender, all of the jurisprudential movements will exert some influence. If a current or new movement obtains increased intellectual

---

[185] However, a formalist system can, of course, have a socially, racially, and ethnically diverse group of adherents who are united in their fidelity to the system.

dominance, law will change. As Holmes once wrote, the law "will become entirely consistent only when it ceases to grow.[186]

REFERENCES FOR FURTHER READING

Because of the many sources cited in the chapter itself, the following bibliography presents sources of more general application or those that supplement the works cited in the chapter footnotes. Interested readers are urged to review the chapter footnotes for additional sources of further reading.

JOHN L. AUSTIN, THE PROVINCE OF JURISPRUDENCE DETERMINED (1832).

DAVID BALDUS & JOHN COLE, STATISTICAL PROOF OF DISCRIMINATION (1980).

DAVID BARNES, STATISTICS AS PROOF: FUNDAMENTALS OF QUANTITATIVE EVIDENCE (1983).

DAVID BARNES & JOHN CONLEY, STATISTICAL EVIDENCE IN LITIGATION (1986).

DAVID BARNES & LYNN STOUT, LAW AND ECONOMICS (1992).

STEVEN BEST & DOUGLAS KELLNER, POSTMODERN THEORY: CRITICAL INTERPRETATIONS (1991).

JAMES BOYLE, CRITICAL LEGAL STUDIES (1992).

GUIDO CALABRESI, THE COST OF ACCIDENTS (1970).

BENJAMIN CARDOZO, THE NATURE OF THE JUDICIAL PROCESS (1922).

ROBERT COOTER & THOMAS ULEN, LAW AND ECONOMICS (1988).

RONALD DWORKIN, LAW'S EMPIRE (1986).

WILLIAM N. ESKRIDGE, JR. & PHILIP P. FRICKEY, CASES AND MATERIALS ON LEGISLATION: STATUTES AND THE CREATION OF PUBLIC POLICY (1988) (esp. pp. 240-247 and 322-334).

LAWRENCE M. FRIEDMAN, A HISTORY OF AMERICAN LAW (2d ed. 1985); LAW AND SOCIETY: AN INTRODUCTION (1974); *The Law and Society Movement*, 38 STAN. L. REV. (1986).

LAWRENCE M. FRIEDMAN & STEWART MACAULAY, LAW AND THE BEHAVIORAL SCIENCES (2d ed. 1977).

LON FULLER, THE MORALITY OF LAW (1958).

CAROL GILLIGAN, IN A DIFFERENT VOICE (1982).

---

[186] OLIVER WENDELL HOLMES, THE COMMON LAW 5 (1881).

GRANT GILMORE, THE AGES OF AMERICAN LAW (1977); THE DEATH
    OF CONTRACT (1974).
Todd Gitlin, *Postmodernism: Roots and Politics*, 36 DISSENT 100 (1989).
CHARLES GOETZ, LAW AND ECONOMICS (1983).
H.L.A. HART, THE CONCEPT OF LAW (1961); LAW, LIBERTY, AND
    MORALITY (1966).
OLIVER WENDELL HOLMES, THE COMMON LAW (1881); *The Path of
    Law*, 10 HARV. L. REV. 457 (1897).
MORTON HORWITZ, THE TRANSFORMATION OF AMERICAN LAW 1760-1850
    (1977); THE TRANSFORMATION OF AMERICAN LAW 1850-1960
    (1992).
IRWIN HOROWITZ & THOMAS WILLGING, THE PSYCHOLOGY OF LAW
    (1983).
LAURA KALMAN, LEGAL REALISM AT YALE 1927-1960 (1986).
MARK KELMAN, A GUIDE TO CRITICAL LEGAL STUDIES (1990).
HANS KELSEN, THE PURE THEORY OF LAW (rev. ed. 1967); GENERAL
    THEORY OF LAW AND STATE (1945).
Edward W. Kitch, *The Fire of Truth: A Remembrance of Law and
    Economics at Chicago 1932-1970*, 26 J.L. & ECON. 163 (1983).
ANTHONY T. KRONMAN, MAX WEBER (1983).
KARL LLEWELLYN, THE BRAMBLE BUSH (1933); *A Realistic Jurisprudence:
    The Next Step*, 30 COLUM. L. REV. 431 (1930).
CATHARINE A. MACKINNON, TOWARD A FEMINIST THEORY OF THE STATE
    (1989); FEMINISM UNMODIFIED (1986).
Gary Minda, *Jurisprudence at Century's End*, 43 J. LEGAL EDUC. (1993);
    The Jurisprudential Movements of the 1980s, 50 OHIO ST. L.J. 599
    (1988).
MARTHA MINOW, MAKING ALL THE DIFFERENCE (1991).
JOHN MONAHAN & LAURENS WALKER, SOCIAL SCIENCE IN LAW: CASES
    AND MATERIALS (2d ed. 1990) (esp. Ch. 1); *Social Science
    Research in Law: A New Paradigm*, 43 AM. PSYCH. 465 (1988).
Michael Moore, *The Interpretive Turn in Modern Theory: A Turn for the
    Worse?*, 41 STAN. L. REV. 871 (1989).
Note, *'Round and 'Round the Bramble Bush: From Legal Realism to
    Critical Legal Scholarship*, 95 HARV. L. REV. 1669 (1982).
Dennis Patterson, *Postmodernism/Feminism/Law*, 77 CORNELL L. REV. 254
    (1992).
RICHARD A. POSNER, THE PROBLEMS OF JURISPRUDENCE (1990);
    ECONOMIC ANALYSIS OF LAW (3d ed. 1985); *The Decline of Law
    as an Autonomous Discipline 1962-1987*, 100 HARV. L. REV. 761
    (1987).

Roscoe Pound, *The Scope and Purpose of Sociological Jurisprudence*, 25 HARV. L. REV. 489 (1912); *Law in Books and Law in Action*, 44 AM. L. REV. 12 (1910).

Margaret Jane Radin & Frank Michelman, *Pragmatist and Poststructuralist Critical Legal Practice*, 139 U. PA. L. REV. 1019 (1991).

DEBORAH RHODE, JUSTICE AND GENDER (1990).

RICHARD RORTY, CONSEQUENCES OF PRAGMATISM (1982).

W.E. RUMBLE, AMERICAN LEGAL REALISM (1968).

Peter C. Schanck, *Understanding Postmodern Thought and Its Implications for Statutory Interpretation*, 65 S. CAL. L. REV. 2505 (1992).

FREDERICK SCHAUER, PLAYING BY THE RULES: A PHILOSOPHICAL EXAMINATION OF RULE-BASED DECISION-MAKING IN LAW AND IN LIFE (1991).

John Henry Schlegel, *American Legal Realism and Empirical Social Science: From the Yale Experience*, 28 BUFF. L. REV. 459 (1979); *American Legal Realism and Empirical Social Science: The Singular Case of Underhill Moore*, 29 BUFF. L. REV. 195 (1980).

JULIAN L. SIMON & PAUL BURSTEIN, BASIC RESEARCH METHODS IN SOCIAL SCIENCE (3d ed. 1985).

ROBERT STEVENS, LAW SCHOOL: LEGAL EDUCATION IN AMERICA FROM THE 1850s TO THE 1980s (1983).

Symposium on the Renaissance of Pragmatism in American Legal Thought, 63 S. CAL. L. REV. 1569 (1990).

Mark Tushnet, *Critical Legal Studies: An Introduction to Its Origins and Underpinnings*, 36 J. LEGAL EDUC. 505 (1986).

WILLIAM TWINING, KARL LLEWELLYN AND THE REALIST MOVEMENT (1973).

Laurens Walker & John Monahan, *Social Facts: Scientific Methodology as Legal Precedent*, 76 CALIF. L. REV. 877 (1988); *Social Frameworks: A New Use of Social Science in Law*, 73 VA. L. REV. 559 (1987).

CORNEL WEST, THE AMERICAN EVASION OF PHILOSOPHY: A GENEALOGY OF PRAGMATISM (1989).

G. Edward White, *From Sociological Jurisprudence to Realism: Jurisprudence and Social Change in Early Twentieth Century America*, 58 VA. L. REV. 999 (1972).

MORTON WHITE, SOCIAL THOUGHT IN AMERICA: THE REVOLT AGAINST FORMALISM (1957).

GENERAL BIBLIOGRAPHY

In addition to the works cited in the text or chapter bibliographies, we also present the following bibliographic references for interested readers.

Law and Legal Education Generally

ALLEN, FRANCIS A., LAW, INTELLECT AND EDUCATION (1979).

CARTER, LIEF H., REASON IN LAW (1984).

CATALDO, BERNARD, INTRODUCTION TO LAW AND THE LEGAL PROCESS (3d ed. 1980).

COUGHLIN, GEORGE GORDON, YOUR INTRODUCTION TO LAW (3d ed. 1979).

DWORKIN, ELIZABETH, JACK HIMMELSTEIN & HOWARD LESNICK, BECOMING A LAWYER: A HUMANISTIC PERSPECTIVE ON LEGAL EDUCATION AND PROFESSIONALISM (1981).

EHRLICH, THOMAS & GEOFFREY C. HAZARD, JR. (eds.), GOING TO LAW SCHOOL? READINGS ON A LEGAL CAREER (1975).

FARNSWORTH, E. ALLAN, AN INTRODUCTION TO THE LEGAL SYSTEM OF THE UNITED STATES (1975).

GILLERS, STEPHEN (ed.), LOOKING AT LAW SCHOOL: A STUDENT GUIDE FROM THE SOCIETY OF AMERICAN LAW TEACHERS (1977).

GOLDFARB, SALLY F., INSIDE THE LAW SCHOOLS: A GUIDE BY STUDENTS, FOR STUDENTS (3d ed. 1984).

GRILLIOT, HAROLD J., INTRODUCTION TO LAW AND THE LEGAL SYSTEM (2d ed. 1979).

HARNO, ALBERT JAMES, LEGAL EDUCATION IN THE UNITED STATES (1980).

KELLY, MICHAEL J., LEGAL ETHICS AND LEGAL EDUCATION (1980).

LLEWELLYN, KARL N., THE BRAMBLE BUSH: ON OUR LAW AND ITS STUDY (1951).

MARKE, JULIUS J. (ed.), DEANS' LIST OF RECOMMENDED READING FOR PRELAW STUDENTS (1958).

MAYFIELD, CRAIG K., READING SKILLS FOR LAW STUDENTS (1980).

MCKAY, ROBERT B., LEGAL EDUCATION (1977).

MERMIN, SAMUEL, LAW AND THE LEGAL SYSTEM: AN INTRODUCTION (1973).

ROTH, GEORGE J., SLAYING THE LAW SCHOOL DRAGON (1980).

SCHAFFER, THOMAS L., ON BEING A CHRISTIAN AND A LAWYER: LAW FOR THE INNOCENT (1981).

SELIGMAN, JOEL & LYNNE BERNABEL, THE HIGH CITADEL: ON THE
        INFLUENCE OF HARVARD LAW SCHOOL (1978).
SHAPIRO, AMY & SANDRA W. WECKESSER, GETTING INTO LAW SCHOOL
        (1979).
SILVER, THEODORE & HOWARD R. SACKS, YOUR KEY TO SUCCESS IN
        LAW SCHOOL (1981).
STRICKLAND, RENNARD, HOW TO GET INTO LAW SCHOOL (1977).
SUTHERLAND, ARTHUR E., THE LAW AT HARVARD: A HISTORY OF IDEAS
        AND MEN, 1817-1967 (1967).
TUROW, SCOTT, ONE L: AN INSIDE ACCOUNT OF LIFE IN THE FIRST YEAR
        AT HARVARD LAW SCHOOL (1978).
VANDERBILT, ARTHUR T., II, INTRODUCTION TO THE STUDY OF LAW
        (1979).
_____, LAW SCHOOL: BRIEFING FOR A LEGAL EDUCATION (1981).
WARKOV, SEYMOUR & JOSEPH ZELAN, LAWYERS IN THE MAKING (1980).

The Legal Profession

AMERICAN BAR ASSOCIATION, HOW TO FIND THE COURTHOUSE (2d ed.
        1978).
_____, LAW PRACTICE IN A CORPORATE LAW DEPARTMENT (1971).
ASBELL, BERNARD, WHAT LAWYERS REALLY DO: SIX LAWYERS TALK
        ABOUT THEIR LIFE AND WORK (1970).
AUCHINCLOSS, LOUIS, THE PARTNERS (1975).
AUERBACH, JEROLD, UNEQUAL JUSTICE: LAWYERS AND SOCIAL CHANGE
        IN MODERN AMERICA (1976).
BLOOM, MURRAY T., THE TROUBLE WITH LAWYERS (1968).
CARLIN, JEROME, THE CHICAGO LAWYER (1962).
CLARK, CHRISTINE PHILPOT (ed.), MINORITY OPPORTUNITIES IN LAW FOR
        BLACKS, PUERTO RICANS AND CHICANOS (1974).
EPSTEIN, CYNTHIA FUCHS, WOMEN IN LAW (1981).
ERLANGER, HOWARD S., JOEL F. HANDLER & ELLEN JANE HOLLINGS-
        WORTH, LAWYERS AND THE PURSUIT OF LEGAL RIGHTS (1978).
FREEDMAN, LAWRENCE MEIR, A HISTORY OF AMERICAN LAW (1973).
GINGER, ANN FAGAN (ed.), THE RELEVANT LAWYERS: CONVERSATIONS
        OUT OF COURT ON THEIR CLIENTS, THEIR PRACTICE, THEIR
        POLITICS, THEIR LIFE STYLE (1972).
GOLDMAN, MARION S., A PORTRAIT OF THE BLACK ATTORNEY IN
        CHICAGO (1972).
HARRISON, GORDON & SANFORD M. JAFFE, THE PUBLIC INTEREST LAW
        FIRM: NEW VOICE FOR NEW CONSTITUENCIES (1973).

HOFFMAN, PAUL, LIONS IN THE STREET: THE INSIDE STORY OF THE GREAT WALL STREET LAW FIRMS (1973).

JOHNSTONE, QUINTIN & DAN HOPSON, JR., LAWYERS AND THEIR WORK: AN ANALYSIS OF THE LEGAL PROFESSION IN THE UNITED STATES AND ENGLAND (1967).

LEONARD, WALTER J., BLACK LAWYERS: TRAINING AND RESULTS, THEN AND NOW (1977).

MARKS, F. RAYMOND, KIRK LESWING & BARBARA A. FORTINSKY, THE LAWYER, THE PUBLIC, AND PROFESSIONAL RESPONSIBILITY (1972).

MAYER, MARTIN, THE LAWYERS (1980).

NADER, RALPH & MARK GREEN (eds.), VERDICTS ON LAWYERS (1976).

POWELL, RICHARD, THE PHILADELPHIAN (1956).

ROSENTHAL, DOUGLAS E., LAWYER AND CLIENT: WHO'S IN CHARGE? (1977).

SCHWARTZ, HELENE E., LAWYERING (1976).

SMIGEL, ERWIN ORSON, THE WALL STREET LAWYER: PROFESSIONAL ORGANIZATION MAN? (1969).

WHITE, JAMES B., THE LEGAL IMAGINATION: STUDIES IN THE NATURE OF LEGAL THOUGHT AND EXPRESSION (1973).

WILKINSON, J. HARVIE, III, SERVING JUSTICE: A SUPREME COURT CLERK'S VIEW (1974).

Biography

AUCHINCLOSS, LOUIS, LIFE, LAW AND LETTERS: ESSAYS AND SKETCHES (1979).

BAKER, LEONARD, JOHN MARSHALL: A LIFE IN LAW (1974).

BARTH, ALAN, PROPHETS WITH HONOR: GREAT DISSENTS AND GREAT DISSENTERS IN THE SUPREME COURT (1975).

DARROW, CLARENCE, THE STORY OF MY LIFE (1932).

DAVIS, LENWOOD G., I HAVE A DREAM: THE LIFE AND TIMES OF MARTIN LUTHER KING (1973).

DOUGLAS, WILLIAM O., GO EAST YOUNG MAN: THE EARLY YEARS (1974).

_____, THE COURT YEARS, 1939-1975: THE AUTOBIOGRAPHY OF WILLIAM O. DOUGLAS, (1980).

DUNNE, GERALD T., HUGO BLACK AND THE JUDICIAL REVOLUTION (1974).

FONER, PHILIP S. (ed.), PAUL ROBESON SPEAKS (1979).

GRIFFITH, KATHRYN, JUDGE LEARNED HAND AND THE ROLE OF THE FEDERAL JUDICIARY (1973).

HANDEL, SAMUEL, CHARLES EVANS HUGHES AND THE SUPREME COURT (1968).

HARBAUGH, WILLIAM H., LAWYERS' LAWYER: THE LIFE OF JOHN W. DAVIS (1978).

HIRSCH, H.N., ENIGMA OF FELIX FRANKFURTER (1981).

LYNN, CONRAD J., THERE IS A FOUNDATION: THE AUTOBIOGRAPHY OF A CIVIL RIGHTS LAWYER (1978).

MARKE, JULIUS J. (ed.), THE HOLMES READER (1964).

MASON, ALPHEUS THOMAS, WILLIAM HOWARD TAFT, CHIEF JUSTICE (1982).

MURPHY, BRUCE ALLEN, THE BRANDEIS/FRANKFURTER CONNECTION (1982).

NIZER, LOUIS, REFLECTIONS WITHOUT MIRRORS: AN AUTOBIOGRAPHY OF THE MIND (1978).

NOONAN, JOHN T., JR., PERSONS AND MASKS OF THE LAW: CARDOZO, HOLMES, JEFFERSON, AND WYTHE AS MAKERS OF THE MASKS (1976).

NOVICK, SHELDON, HONORABLE JUSTICE (1991).

REHNQUIST, WILLIAM H., THE SUPREME COURT: HOW IT WAS; HOW IT IS (1987).

REHNQUIST, WILLIAM H., GRAND INQUESTS: THE HISTORIC IMPEACHMENTS OF JUSTICE SAMUEL CHASE AND PRESIDENT ANDREW JOHNSON (1992).

ROSENBERG, J. MITCHELL, JEROME FRANK: JURIST AND PHILOSOPHER (1970).

SIMON, JAMES F., INDEPENDENT JOURNEY: THE LIFE OF WILLIAM O. DOUGLAS (1980).

STERN, GERALD, THE BUFFALO CREEK DISASTER (1976).

UROFSKY, MELVIN I., LOUIS D. BRANDEIS AND THE PROGRESSIVE TRADITION (1981).

WESTIN, ALAN F., AUTOBIOGRAPHY OF THE SUPREME COURT: OFF-THE-BENCH COMMENTARY BY THE JUSTICES (1978).

WHITE, G. EDWARD, THE AMERICAN JUDICIAL TRADITION: PROFILES OF LEADING AMERICAN JUDGES (1976).

_____, EARL WARREN: A PUBLIC LIFE (1982).

WIGDOR, DAVID, ROSCOE POUND: PHILOSOPHER OF LAW (1974).

WOOD, ARTHUR LEWIS, CRIMINAL LAWYER (1967).

Jurisprudence and Legal Issues

AYMAR, BRANDT & EDWARD SAGARIN, LAW AND TRIALS THAT CREATED HISTORY (1974).

BERGER, RAOUL, GOVERNMENT BY JUDICIARY: THE TRANSFORMATION OF THE FOURTEENTH AMENDMENT (1977).

BICKEL, ALEXANDER M., THE LEAST DANGEROUS BRANCH (1966).

_____, THE MORALITY OF CONSENT (1977).

CAHN, EDMOND, THE MORAL DECISION: RIGHT AND WRONG IN THE LIGHT OF AMERICAN LAW (1981).

CARDOZO, BENJAMIN N., THE NATURE OF THE JUDICIAL PROCESS (1921).

CARRINGTON, FRANK G., NEITHER CRUEL NOR UNUSUAL (1978).

CARRINGTON, PAUL D., DANIEL J. MEADOR & MAURICE ROSENBERG, JUSTICE ON APPEAL (1976).

COVER, ROBERT M., JUSTICE ACCUSED: ANTISLAVERY AND THE JUDICIAL PROCESS (1975).

DERSHOWITZ, ALAN M., THE BEST DEFENSE (1982).

DONALDSON, KENNETH, INSANITY INSIDE OUT (1976).

FLEMING, ALICE MULCAHEY, TRIALS THAT MADE HEADLINES (1974).

GRAGLIA, LINO A., DISASTER BY DECREE: THE SUPREME COURT DECISIONS ON RACE AND THE SCHOOLS (1976).

GREEN, MARK J., THE OTHER GOVERNMENT: THE UNSEEN POWER OF WASHINGTON LAWYERS (1975).

HOWARD, A.E. DICK, THE ROAD FROM RUNNYMEADE: MAGNA CARTA AND CONSTITUTIONALISM IN AMERICA (1968).

JACKSON, DONALD DALE, JUDGES: AN INSIDE VIEW OF THE AGONIES AND EXCESSES OF AN AMERICAN ELITE (1975).

KIRK, RUSSELL, THE ROOTS OF AMERICAN ORDER (1981).

KLUGER, RICHARD, SIMPLE JUSTICE: THE HISTORY OF BROWN VS. BOARD OF EDUCATION AND BLACK AMERICA'S STRUGGLE FOR EQUALITY (1976).

KONEFSKY, SAMUEL J., THE LEGACY OF HOLMES AND BRANDEIS: A STUDY IN THE INFLUENCE OF IDEAS (1974).

LEE, REX E., A LAWYER LOOKS AT THE CONSTITUTION (1981).

PECK, DAVID W., DECISION AT LAW (1977).

PFEFFER, LEO, GOD, CAESAR, AND THE CONSTITUTION: THE COURT AS REFEREE OF CHURCH-STATE CONFRONTATION (1975).

PHILLIPS, STEVEN, NO HEROES, NO VILLAINS: THE STORY OF A MURDER TRIAL (1977).

POUND, ROSCOE, LAW AND MORALS (1969).

REID, SUE TITUS, CRIME AND CRIMINOLOGY (1982).

ROSTOW, EUGENE V. (ed.), IS LAW DEAD? (1971).

RUBINSTEIN, RICHARD E., GREAT COURTROOM BATTLES (1973).

SEYMOUR, WHITNEY NORTH, JR., WHY JUSTICE FAILS (1973).

SHIRLEY, GLENN, LAW WEST OF FORT SMITH: AN AUTHENTIC HISTORY OF FRONTIER JUSTICE IN THE OLD INDIAN TERRITORY (1957).

SIMON, JAMES F., THE JUDGE (1976).

STRICKLAND, RENNARD, FIRE AND THE SPIRITS: CHEROKEE LAW FROM CLAN TO COURT (1975).

UNGER, ROBERTO M., KNOWLEDGE AND POLITICS (1975).

VAN DEN HAAG, ERNEST, PUNISHING CRIMINALS: CONCERNING A VERY OLD AND PAINFUL QUESTION (1975).

WASSERSTEIN, BRUCE & MARK J. GREEN (eds.), WITH JUSTICE FOR SOME: AN INDICTMENT OF THE LAW BY YOUNG ADVOCATES (1970).

WESTIN, ALAN F. & BARRY MAHONEY, THE TRAIL OF MARTIN LUTHER KING (1974).